A LIFETIME OF SEASONS

By Christopher Lloyd

The Well-Tempered Garden
The Well-Chosen Garden
The Adventurous Gardener
A Lifetime of Seasons

A LIFETIME OF SEASONS

CHRISTOPHER LLOYD

WEIDENFELD & NICOLSON

First published in Great Britain in 2021 by Weidenfeld & Nicolson
an imprint of The Orion Publishing Group Ltd
Carmelite House, 50 Victoria Embankment
London EC4Y 0DZ

An Hachette UK Company

1 3 5 7 9 10 8 6 4 2

Articles originally appeared in *Country Life* and the *Guardian*

A CIP catalogue record for this book is available from the British Library.

ISBN (Hardback) 978 1 4746 1985 1
ISBN (eBook) 978 1 4746 1986 8

Typeset by Input Data Services Ltd, Somerset

Printed in Great Britain by Clays Ltd, Elcograf S.p.A.

MIX
Paper from
responsible sources
FSC® C104740
FSC
www.fsc.org

www.orionbooks.co.uk
www.weidenfeldandnicolson.co.uk

FOREWORD
by Fergus Garrett

Christopher Lloyd (Christo to his nearest friends) left his mark on all who knew and loved him. His influence even stretched to those who never met him but read his words or visited his garden at Great Dixter. He was a prolific and terrific writer, conversational, acutely observant, descriptive, scholarly and witty, with words flowing from deep within him to his fingertips and then onto the page, as is clear from this wonderful collection. A fascinating man, he lived his life back to front, mixing with older generations alongside a dominant mother, and then feeling a sense of release when she was gone, living his life sharing Great Dixter with an eclectic mix of young and old. He was a great cook and entertainer, tirelessly interested in people, music, art, food, poetry and all that life brought. Christo surrounded himself with gardeners, writers, potters, film makers, artists and cooks from all walks of life. He cultivated people like he cultivated plants and Dixter was never dull under his occupancy, but a vibrant place where his immeasurable spirit and catalytic spark lit up the fire of life.

Christo was born at Great Dixter in 1921 and lived there all his life. He had an intimate relationship with the space that surrounded him. He was totally in tune with the sense of place and its unique atmosphere. His observations fuelled his words and, using the garden as a notebook alongside a fascinated mind and a masterful command of the English language, he wrote countless books and articles on a whole range of subjects. He wrote very naturally and, while scholarly, his literary style was easy and accessible, captivating a wide public. His witty sense of humour was ever present, making people laugh out loud with his prose. He wrote not just about gardening but about people, birds, bees, bugs and sometimes about art, music or food, but in almost every case with a link back to the place that he knew and understood so well. As I read this journey through Christo's life, I found picking up his words and his thoughts enthralling, enticing and stimulating. Hearing his voice through the page immediately transported me to his side, and into his mesmeric world.

Throughout his life Christo was gripped by, and never lost the zest for, plants and gardening. From an early age he gardened alongside his mother, Daisy, who was undoubtedly the major influence upon his life. After studying Modern Languages at Cambridge, and a spell in the army, he took formal training in Horticulture at Wye College. When Daisy died in 1979, Christo was already widely recognised as a writer and gardener, and in the years to come he became known as one of the greatest gardeners of all time – a truly dynamic and ingenious plantsman with a deep understanding of the science behind the art. Christo had more than just a stamp collector's attitude to plants; drawn to all aspects of his trade, he valued creativity and celebrated originality and expression. He was a wonderfully gifted, whimsical and free-spirited craftsman, experimenting and painting with plants within a rich framework of balustraded yew hedges, old farm buildings, York stone paths and a magnificent low-slung mediaeval timber framed house situated in the Weald of Sussex among rolling hills, ancient woodlands, meadows and pasture.

Christo's life was long and colourful. He lived it to the full, and throughout many turbulent years of ups and downs he became accustomed to the practical challenges entailed in running a garden like Great Dixter: juggling time and money, assessing and being reactive to the seasons, leading a team and constantly managing people's expectations. He was unlike any other person or gardener I know – a non-conforming, one-off maverick who constantly bucked the trends. Christo was never one to coast along doing the same thing year after year. I truly admired his ability to do the unexpected in the garden, to be adventurous and fashion the atypical. His formal training at Wye by no means clipped his wings, but instead gave him the confidence to take his experiments to deeper, more meaningful, places. And all done for the right reasons – not to shock or to make headlines but stimulated by an inquisitive mind, freedom of expression and untainted invention. First and foremost he pleased himself, evaluating, tweaking and improving, constantly on the move and dynamic. He also appreciated the value in uprooting and seeing different places and meeting new people. He loved visiting gardens where he would discover new plants and come across imaginative ideas. Notebook in hand, he was constantly observing, analysing and assessing, his mind brimming with ideas.

Christo was at his most inspired when amongst plants in the wild. To him this was the finest style of all and this observation and appreciation of Mother Nature's magic no doubt made Christo a better gardener. Although he loved colour, exuberant planting and big bold swashbuckling combinations, Christo had a deep appreciation for the finer things that a garden expresses: a crack in the lime mortar from which the wall rue grows, or a narrow sliver of soil between the lawn and paving making a home for a self-sown violet.

He was intelligent, caring, eccentric, quirky, tenacious, focused, at times difficult and undoubtedly one of the most creative and greatest gardeners of all time. His garden at Great Dixter remains as colourful, dynamic and experimental as ever, and, as you will discover in the following pages, his words are rich with timeless wisdom, intellect and joy.

PLANTS FOR A GRASS-LAND GARDEN

The words wild garden conjure up, in most people's minds, a spacious setting where trees and large shrubs predominate, intersected by winding paths and cunningly underplanted with ferns, primulas and bulbs, of all of which the crowning achievement will be the coarsely noble *Lilium giganteum*. Such gardens are more likely to be on one's visiting list than actual components of one's own plot. But any patch of rough grass, in a perfectly open, treeless setting, can provide us all with the opportunity for a most absorbing type of wild gardening, quite different from and much less exacting than the grander style.

The naturalisation of daffodils in grass land is, of course, already widely and effectively practiced, being, indeed, the most satisfactory way of growing them in the garden. I would like here, however, to discuss some of the smaller plants which do well in grass, and which will provide a mixed carpet of flowers, reminiscent of a Botticelli background or of the scenes in 16th-century French tapestries.

It is never satisfactory, in my experience, to attempt to grow spring bulbs in a lawn which will be mown in the normal way from May onwards. The turf thereby becomes compacted by the mower rollers to a firmness which only the normal grasses and weeds associated with lawns will tolerate. Other plants (the lady's tresses orchid excepted) gradually die out. Let the grass be unashamedly rough, then, and cut it just two or three times during the season. I find that the best times for doing this are, first, in early or mid-July, after the main flush of spring-flowering

1

plants has had time to set and scatter its seeds, next, at the end of August, just before the colchicums start to push through, and, last, at the end of October, when the autumn crocuses have faded. My garden soil being heavy and rather on the fat side, the natural turf consists of a high proportion of coarse grasses, such as cocksfoot and Yorkshire fog. This does not matter in itself, but it does make three annual cuts advisable, in order to prevent the grasses from becoming too rough and tussocky. On sandier soils, or on chalk, where fescues and bents predominate and the grasses do not in any case grow rankly, two cuts, or even one, would be quite enough.

No fertilisers of any kind, whether organic or inorganic, should ever be applied to the grass-land garden. Such treatment of it will inevitably result in a few grasses and weeds making tremendous growth at the expense of all else. The grass-land trials at Rothamsted Experimental Station in Hertfordshire, where various manure treatments have been applied over a period of many years to a large number of plots of natural turf, graphically demonstrate that the control plot, which has never received any fertiliser, is by far the richest in its natural flora.

Let us now take the seasons in order through the year and consider the suitability of the plants that may be grown in rough grass.

Snowdrops are by nature woodland plants; it is there they will really let themselves go and cover, in time, such acres that it would seem they must have grown there always. In grass they look delightful and will maintain themselves through the years, but always a little stunted and without ever increasing to any great extent. The spring-flowering crocus species do not, for the most part, compete successfully with grass, but the Dutch hybrids are admirable, and not a whit too gross for this setting. Indeed, it is by far the best place to have them, where their lank, persistent foliage remains unnoticed. The purples

2

and whites seed abundantly, and form great colonies in time. The yellow crocuses make clumps without seeding, and these should occasionally be split up, to make the most of them. Scented violets are often the natural occupants of turf as well as woodland. In my corner of Sussex we do not have them wild, but white violets, originally planted in other parts of the garden, have invaded the grass land and find themselves quite at home in it.

About the second week in March, the wild daffodils or Lent lilies begin to open. These should never be omitted from a grass-land garden, where they can be depended on to seed themselves and so increase. So, too, will the little Hoop Petticoat daffodil, *Narcissus bulbocodium*, but not on heavy soil or in coarse turf. For them the fine grasses of a sandy soil, with moisture near the surface, are ideal. I do not know of any other place in England where they can be seen so richly carpeted as on the Alpine Meadow at Wisley. They have a long flowering season, too.

April is the climax month for flowers in the wild grass garden, and queen of the whole company is our own native snake's-head, *Fritillaria meleagris*, its tremulous bells in graduated shades from the typical rich chequered purple to a chilly greenish-white. I have met a fruitless attempt to colonise this plant on chalkland, and I believe it to be equally unsuccessful on sand. Possessors of dour and ill-drained clay-land here at last come into their own, for this is where the snake's-head will really spread itself in most heart-warming fashion. It is worth giving a colony a good start, and this is most cheaply done by sowing fresh seed in boxes, thereafter planting the young bulbs out in their second autumn. Once established, they will naturalise to form incredibly dense patches. W. H. Hudson describes a river meadow where fritillaries grew 'so close that they darkened the earth over an area of about three acres', and when first approaching them from a distance he thought that he was looking at a dull, dark patch of recently ploughed land. What an illusion this would be with which to confound visitors to one's own garden!

The primrose tribe is excellent in grass. Though primroses themselves make the lushest plants when growing in shaded sites, yet the smaller plants they form when fully exposed will still flourish. Neither should the fragrant bunches of cowslips be forgotten. Cowslips are quite happy on soils other than their native chalk or limestone. From one plant which I originally dug up on the downs near Lewes more than 20 years ago I now have a colony ten yards or so across. Polyanthus, with their infinite variety of gay colours, make one of the most successful contributions to the grass-land garden. When grown in beds they are in need of splitting every other year or so, and then the surplus pieces can be quickly added to rough turf with the help of the bulb-planter. Once established in this medium, polyanthus plants will last indefinitely, never requiring further division, and providing, in course of time, an interesting record of the shades and strains which were once fashionable. They will, moreover, hybridise freely with cowslips and primroses, as also will these last two with each other, and the resultant self-sown seedlings are often most worth-while.

Windflowers of various kinds will make drifts in grass, including our own wood anemone and its varieties, and also *Anemone appenina*, in shades of pale pink and blue. Even De Caen anemones, not far removed from the species *A. coronaria* of the Mediterranean, will make themselves at home in fine turf. Other good April-flowering contributors to this kind of wild garden are grape hyacinths – again the stringy foliage of certain species is here well masked – the star of Bethlehem, which can become a rampant weed in cultivated ground, and leopard's bane, *Doronicum plantagineum*, happiest in a rather shady spot.

Then there are the native orchids. Field naturalists tend to see red when it is suggested that these should be dug up under any circumstances, even for transplanting to a place where they will grow equally well. When the species is as common in its own locality as the primrose, I cannot see that any harm is done, providing that the digger digs with discretion and is not greedy; the plants stand a good chance of becoming established in their new homes. Often they will naturalise as freely in the garden as in their native woods and fields. To transplant fragrant or pyramidal orchids from chalk to an acid soil would obviously be silly and wasteful, but transplanted to a chalk garden they can be as happy as beautiful.

The orchid season is a long one, starting in my garden with the early purples, *Orchis mascula*. Then come the green-winged orchids, followed by the marsh and spotted, taking the season right up to the last half of June. In late summer we used to have the little white lady's tresses orchid, whose charmingly descriptive botanical name is *Spiranthes spiralis*. But, as it came uninvited, though a welcome guest, so, too, it suddenly vanished. This is its way.

It is worth planting surplus tulip bulbs out into grass. They may not flower very often in such competitive conditions, but when flowers are produced they look prettier here, I think, in their green setting than in any other; the fact that their blooms are small makes them the more appropriate.

Late in May most of the grasses will be in full flower; and this is one of the greatest delights of the whole season to me, for I am not a victim to their pollen shedding. At the same time the close-textured pattern of yellow and white ox-eye daisies adds a dazzling touch to the now deep-piled carpet of the grass-land garden. Only in late June, when the grasses have seeded, does one long to cut the sward, yet one must wait awhile till the daffodils, fritillaries and orchids have shed their seeds. Meadow sweet and meadow cranesbill are flowering then; they have to be cut in their prime, but will often bloom again in August.

5

Then come the autumn bulbs, so welcome for being so fresh and spring-like. First the colchicums, wrongly called autumn crocus. The larger species do not really thrive in dense turf: in my garden I find that the small wild ones carry on year after year without ever increasing much. Doubtless they will, however, in certain soils, more nearly resembling their native meadowland.

Crocuses end the grass-land garden's year with a splendid flourish. *C. zonatus*, with pale lilac blooms, naturalises well and is one of the earliest autumn flowerers, but my favourite of all crocuses of every season is *C. speciosus*, and this does marvellously well in grass. Its flowers seldom begin to appear before September 20, but continue thereafter for more than a month. With their long perianth tubes that pass for stems, and the large chaliced blooms that never open too wide, they are exquisitely poised. Add to these graces the rich indigo veining of the petals, a brilliant orange stigma and a scent as of the sweetest early tulips; having once known this plant, one can never have enough of it.

– December 29, 1955 –

MAKING THE MOST OF ANNUALS

The charm of annuals lies mainly in the gaiety of their clean colouring; flower shapes come next in importance; the plant form, last and least. It is levelled against them that by their very transitoriness they lack interest both in their cultivation and in that beauty of line which a shrub can develop in the course of years. But in many ways the annual's short life is a great asset; most of all in that one can ring the changes on them. If one has grown rather tired of one kind after a year or two, it can be given a rest until, perhaps eight or ten years later, one suddenly thinks 'How nice it would be to grow balsam again; I've not seen any for ages.' And a few months later, there it is in one's own garden, an old friend that is most affectionately welcome. And then there are always new acquaintances to be made; annuals which one had never suspected to exist and which had hitherto been hiding their loveliness under a fearsome botanical name.

Most valuable to the gardener are those annuals which have a long flowering season. They can then, in large measure, be used instead of bedding plants like geraniums that are more trouble to grow, since they must be overwintered as struck cuttings in a frost-free place. Of almost equal value are those annuals, like China asters and zinnias, that flower late. They may not start blooming till the end of July or early August, but look fresh and full of promise in the early summer months. This is a far pleasanter order of things than with the early flowering ephemerals that blow in June and July, thereafter leaving us with brown and shrivelled skeletons.

One of the handsomest annuals with a long season of flowering is the spider plant, *Cleome spinosa*, the strain Pink Queen being the most generally recommended. The plant itself is, for an annual, statuesque and more like a perennial in appearance. Bold, five-fingered leaves are surmounted at a height of 3ft or more by a head of soft pink flowers with extraordinarily long stamens, which give the plant its name. Each plant will often have only the one central spike, but this is no matter, since it seems capable of producing an unending succession of buds. The seedpods, too, are decorative, being shaped like sausages, and held horizontally well clear of the plant's main stem. Although the spider plant thrives best in a hot summer, it should be grown in partial shade, since the flowers tend to wilt in full sunlight.

Of the great tribe of composites, the florists' zinnias must, given skilful cultivation, take pride of place. They are well known to us all, but I should like here to say a kind word for a dwarf zinnia with small double flowers of a rich golden colour. It is usually listed as *Zinnia haageana fl. Pl.* Superficially it might be mistaken for a dwarf *Tagetes* – a compact, neat plant, less than a foot tall, showy but not vulgarly so, as many strains of French marigold are. I believe that the only reason for its not being more popular is that it is a zinnia, but not what people consider a zinnia ought to be – in the same way as many people will not give marks to white gentian simply because it is not blue.

Rather similar to the zinnias is *Tithonia speciosa*. I shall never forget the remarkable sight of a carpet of tithonias naturalised beneath the trees in the public park at Nairobi. Torch is the best variety here, being only 4ft tall – quite a pigmy as tithonias go. The leaves are heart-shaped, rather coarse and hairy; but the single flower-heads are of the purest and most brilliant shade of orange – a really thrilling colour.

I think most of us get a bit bored with the normal run of white and pale pink *Cosmos*. But there is a rich, carmine purple cultivar available that I can most thoroughly recommend. The bold intensity of flower colouring here does much to counterbalance the cosmea's shapeless billowing habit. It is known as Crimson-scarlet and has an exceptionally long flowering season if sown under glass in March and planted out in May.

Another excellent daisy which can be had in bloom from late June till the frosts is *Venidium fastuosum*. Buds, stems and pinnate leaves are all most ornamental, being coated with silky grey down. The flower-heads have bright orange rays and a large central disc that is all shiny and black when it first appears, as though it had been burnished with boot polish. The new *Arctotis* hybrids are very lovely, too, with the same sort of leaves and flowers in a wide range of colours: cream, yellow, orange, bronze, pink and plum.

For August and September flowering, the annual Rudbeckias make fine, bold patches of colour where a fairly tall plant is required. They mostly grow 3 to 4ft high. My favourites are the pure yellow forms, of which Autumn Glow and Monplaisir are good selections. The black central cone is here most tellingly framed by uniformly golden yellow rays. In other strains mahogany creeps in, either as a central zone, in streaks, or overlaying the entire flower colouring. They all detract, in my opinion, from the cone flower's most individual feature, which is its black-eyed cone. It is well worth twigging these annual Rudbeckias before they grow too tall.

In the snapdragon family there are two long-lasting annuals that deserve special mention. *Diascia barberae* should be much more grown, not only on the rock garden, where its delicate, slender habit of growth is perfectly appropriate, but in all sorts of front-of-border positions. The flowers are quite like a nemesia's, but with two spurs at the back instead of one – a pretty shape, and also a very pretty warm shade of pink. They flower on and on and on in great abundance. Heavy rain will knock off the current crop of blooms, but more soon open. This is really a perennial, and odd plants will often survive the winter out of doors, but it is most efficiently treated as a half-hardy annual. *Alonsoa warscewiczii* is undoubtedly not more popular only because of the dauntingly hideous name that encumbers it. This species has a number of cultivated varieties of different habits and colouring, but the type plant is, I think, the best. Its slender, branching habit is much like that of diascia, but taller, being some 15ins in height. The flower stalks are twisted so that the outward-facing flower is always held upside-down. It is a clear, orange-scarlet throughout – an unusual shade which even the scarlet pimpernel does not quite match in purity. The plants will bloom continuously if the dead-heads are removed; in two flushes if they are not.

The pimpernels themselves bloom over a long period and their flowers open out on most days that are not too soppingly wet. *Anagallis linifolia* has large flowers, each ¾in across, and the cultivar *Phillipsii* is one of the best of all annuals. It is of a rich, unalloyed, Prussian shade of blue, quite startlingly intense. The base of each petal is (surprisingly) dull red. Best treated as a half-hardy annual, the plants never exceed 6ins in height and are a solid mass of bloom for months on end. The cultivar *Parksii*, generally described as bright red, is a disappointment in my opinion, being rather muddy-coloured.

A nice bushy little annual that forms a good solid clump 9ins. tall at the front of a border is *Cuphea miniata* Firefly. Its flowers do look rather like tropical insects; they are not brilliant, however, but a pleasant pinky purple. The disc-shaped seeds are green when ripe.

It is always a problem to know with what to follow biennials when their season has finished. Sweet Williams, Canterbury bells and foxgloves are all June flowerers. By early July one is wishing that one had not grown so many of them, lovely though they are. Certain annuals can take their place very well, providing the site is not too shady. A late sowing of China asters in boxes, for instance, still has time to develop and flower if planted out in mid-July. Portulacas are excellent for this purpose too. *Portulaca grandiflora* is a small succulent which grows only 6ins. tall and has the most brilliantly coloured flowers of any annual I know. Though it can be bought in single colour strains, I like the daring combinations to be had in a mixture best of all. The broad petals have a sheen on them which people unanimously agree to be like satin, and they may be orange, yellow, bronze, pink, or the most violent, unashamed magenta. If the plants are spaced reasonably far apart, say 9ins, they grow into characteristic and charming shapes that remind me of certain semi-prostrate junipers. They flower most freely in full sunshine and a hot summer. The seeds are fascinating in their resemblance to iron filings – a steely grey.

Some of the exceptionally quick-developing though short-lived annuals can also be used to follow biennials by making a direct sowing of them and watering well until they have germinated.

Limnanthes douglasii is one such; rather a liability in most positions, since it flowers itself to a standstill in a fortnight, but useful in this context.

One must grow certain ephemerals from time to time, since they are so heavenly while they last, and it is often possible to place them where their passing will not leave a void. Certain newly divided perennials can, for instance, be interplanted: irises in particular. Here one might place the prostrate *Mesembryanthemum criniflorium*, another succulent annual. Its flowers are like daisies, though they can claim no kinship. The narrow, glossy petals look brittle as spun glass and are most sensitive to light and damp. On a dry, sunny morning or early afternoon the plants are completely obliterated by their blossoms – pink, white, magenta and biscuit-coloured. The effect is even more dazzling than with portulacas, because the flowers are so much more numerous. On damp days the plants become so insignificant that they could easily be missed. Sometime in July the display will suddenly come to an end, and the irises can ripen their rhizomes unhindered. These fleeting annuals can also be used to great effect as a carpet to rose beds.

Another way to overcome their transitoriness is by combining two sorts in one patch, sown direct where they are to flower. A favourite team of mine is *Omphalodes linifolia* with *Asperula orientalis* (*A. azurea setosa* in catalogues). The ugly-sounding omphalodes is an upright-growing plant of 12 to 15ins in height, with decorative grey-green foliage and pure white flowers shaped like forget-me-nots, but larger. The asperula is an annual woodruff with clouds of powder-blue flowers; it comes out first, and just as it begins to run to seed, all signs of it are swamped by its grey-and-white companion. This omphalodes also combines excellently with the annual convolvulus, *Convolvulus tricolor*. The latter is richest in its deep purple blue form. Each flower lasts only a day, closing like a loosely-furled umbrella by four in the afternoon, but a great surge of new blooms appears on the following morning. Rather a weak-stemmed plant some 15ins tall, it normally needs twigging, but the omphalodes completely obviates this requirement. In this case the white flowers precede the blue.

Many other possible combinations will occur to lovers of annuals, and I shall mention just one more: eschscholtzias (of any colour strain) with *Phacelia viscida*. The phacelia grows quickly and soon makes a fine display with its pure, gentian-blue and white-centred flowers. Just as it becomes mummified and unsightly, the Californian poppies engulf every vestige and blossom untiringly for the next three or four months.

– March 28, 1957 –

BEDDING PLANTS TODAY – I
FOR SPRING AND AUTUMN

Ten years ago our thoughts were able, after a long period of abstention, to turn again to the pleasures of gardening. A new era was then heralded in which the labour-saving tree and shrub should reign supreme, but somehow things didn't work out quite that way. Flowering shrubs are, indeed, as popular now as ever before, and deservedly so, but other more exacting forms of gardening made an appeal that would not be denied. We find, in fact, that the cultivation of rock plants and alpines, herbaceous perennials, water and bog plants, annuals and bedding plants is in as great favour today as ever it was.

It is the bedding plants that I wish to consider here. Our approach to their uses has greatly changed – I would like to say progressed – since the hey-day of bedding out a century ago. At that time, ranges of heated greenhouses and conservatories, full of tender exotics, were yearly required to disgorge a large part of their contents into formal parterres in order that the household could admire them there for a few summer months. It was a most expensive luxury, and vulgar, too. The mantle of this style of bedding out has fallen, today, on our public parks and gardens. They can afford what private gardens (mercifully) no longer can. In the best of them, and especially in London and at some of our coastal resorts, some first-rate work of the most enterprising nature is carried out, but the fact that these public places must cater more for gapers than for gardeners ensures the survival of some of the worst abuses of bedding out. Even carpet bedding, where the system reaches its nadir, survives here and there in Britain. In France it is far more rife, and the bones of some of the most venerable Italian terraced gardens have been clothed with similar unlovely encrustations.

All this tends to give bedding plants a bad name among intelligent gardeners; in the less formal type of garden that is so often laid out today, they can see little scope for their use. Moreover, even when they like such plants, they may be put off growing them by the thought of special beds and of the large quantities of the same two or three species needed to fill them. But we are quickly discovering that the most satisfactory way to use bedding plants is without beds; that there is then the opportunity to grow an unexpectedly wide range of species in relatively small numbers, and that their place in the garden is almost everywhere – in ornamental pots and tubs, in the rock garden, above and in dry walls, in the partial shade of semi-woodland conditions and, supremely, in the mixed border with shrubs and hardy perennials.

Spring and summer bedding plants are the main types which one has to consider. Of the two, the latter are by far the more important, their principal requirement being a long season of interest, if possible from June to October. Four months is a very long time for any plant to go on flowering, and one should be most grateful to those which manage it. Spring bedding plants

13

have a much shorter season, seldom exceeding a month, so that, except when grown in special beds to be followed by summer bedding, they should not be allowed too much prominence in the smaller garden. They are all more or less hardy, and the perennials such as *Alyssum saxatile*, aubrietas and *Arabis albida* are most happily placed in permanence in dry walls and on rock banks. There are usually plenty of little-disturbed spots – among shrubs, for instance – where forget-me-nots can be allowed to seed themselves from year to year. Removal of old plants and a later drastic thinning of self-sown seedlings is the only attention they require.

Tulips are conveniently accommodated among groups of plants which will flower later; but since their display is not to be bolstered up by the traditional ground-work of spring bedding, they need to be planted thickly. The mixed or perennial border is not usually a happy site to choose; the tulips look lost in the vastness of as yet unclothed areas of bare soil. No, I have in mind for them those smaller, narrow borders in a garden; planted among groups of sweet Williams, for instance, the bulbs can be dug up for drying off in mid-July, when their partners have also to be cleared away. Where groups of bearded irises have been replanted in July, tulips can be set among them in the following autumn. This planting can be left undisturbed for three years, until the irises are again ready for splitting. The tulips can then be sorted out also. Or one can use them among perennials that will flower concurrently. An effective association that I have in mind is white May flowering tulips among the yellow-green spurge, *Euphorbia epithymoides* (*polychroma*), and, again, tulips of any colour but of late flowering, with the indigo-blue spikes of *Baptisia australis*.

Of all the spring bedding plants, wallflowers are the hardest to place satisfactorily except in special beds. The nicest spot for them, I think, is grouped at the top of a dry wall that has been devoted to not too precious things like alyssum, candituft, arabis, aubrieta and *Phlox subulata*. They will all flower at the same time, and if a few of the wallflowers are allowed to remain to seed, they, too will quickly colonise the wall face. Here, in their favourite and most natural site, the plants are very hardy and will often live to three or four years old. I am never without a few Siberian wallflowers in my garden, though they have had to look after themselves entirely for the past 20 years. If four or five plants are grouped originally in some sunny corner where they can be left to themselves, they will seed and maintain themselves indefinitely. Their colouring is clean, if rather crude, but they look quite well near forget-me-nots and, if for nothing else, are worth growing for their own special, warm brand of wallflower scent.

Before considering the main summer bedding plants that are to bloom for one-third of the year, there are two other minor categories that deserve mention. First, the midsummer flowering biennials – sweet Williams, foxgloves, Canterbury bells, certain mulleins, and the vivid blue *Cynoglossum amabile*. Their season is from early June to mid-July, and the only thing that deters us from growing them in great abundance is the thought 'What next?'. The foxgloves look their best in a wildish setting and will put up with a fair amount of shade. With such a position, the question of what is to follow may not be so urgent. If the position is not too shady, it is quite an idea to sow among them in spring some purple orach seed. This noble plant, *Atriplex hortensis*, is an annual, growing to 6 or 7ft, and has deep pinky-red foliage that is gloriously translucent in sunlight; it will take over where the foxgloves leave off, and continue in beauty till mid-September. Canterbury bells do well in the same sort of place, but the single types should be chosen. These have a grace of form entirely lacking in the grossly deformed-looking cup-and-saucers. The latter may give you more colour for your money, but that is all.

15

The giant mulleins such as *Verbascum olympicum* and *V. phlomoides* are excellently suited to a semi-wild setting, but like all the sun they can get. If a piece of rough turf can be cleared for an original planting, and thereafter merely kept free of the coarsest and most competitive weeds, the mulleins will re-sow themselves year after year. Their candelabra look especial-ly fine against a dark background. Sweet Williams also require sunshine, but they belong to the garden proper. They can be followed by my second minor category of bedding plants: those that belong essentially to autumn. These are mainly represented by the small bedding chrysanthemums – Koreans, Otely-Koreans, rubellums, pom-poms and the like – types that will not exceed a height a 2½ft and that are pretty well self-supporting. Too many Koreans are late flowering, not getting started until well into October. For a display in the garden, one must choose the early flowering types – the earlier the better. It doesn't seem to matter how early they start to bloom; indeed, they may be well away even at the time, in July, when one is moving them. They will still flower on into October, and chrysanthemums are most tolerant about being shifted when in full growth. The plants must be grown on in a spare row in the vegetable garden. If they are given a good soaking the day before the move, and then puddle in, with a gallon of water to each plant, when the actual move is made, they will scarcely flag at all.

Verbena rigida (*venosa*) is also a useful plant with which to follow sweet Williams. A spring sowing is made in a cold frame and these seeds germinate so slowly that the young plants are just right for putting out in July. They will flower abundantly in September and October, and it is worth leaving them *in situ* to give a display in the following summer; they will be blooming freely by early July.

BEDDING PLANTS TODAY – II
THE BIG RANGE FOR THE SUMMER

The range of good summer bedding plants that will flower over a three- or four-month period is really astonishing, and there should be no need to weary of any of them, as others are always pressing forward to be tried, and a change is so easily made – an advantage, this, over the hardy shrub. If one tires of the ample charms of a Pink Pearl rhododendron, say, or of a mop-headed hydrangea, the decision to be rid of it is hard, so many years having gone to making the shrub what it is.

The majority of annuals are too ephemeral to make the most satisfactory of bedding plants. There are many exceptions, of course, such as zinnias and tagetes, and these go especially well with herbaceous plants. The double border at Nymans in mid-Sussex demonstrates this blending as well as any other example I know. The background of trees and shrubs there is an ideal foil. Many bedding plants are technically perennials, but can be raised true to colour and so as to mature sufficiently quickly from an early spring sowing. It is interesting to reflect that before these colour strains were fixed, good forms of such plants as the dwarf blue bedding lobelias and of antirrhinums were raised annually from cuttings.

Antirrhinums particularly repay an informal treatment. Like wallflowers they should be planted near a sunny, dry retaining wall into which they can seed. Such self-sown plants are very precocious and develop enormous spikes by early June. The property of being able to sow themselves around is generally welcome in bedding plants. Some may be quite tender themselves and yet have seeds that are hardy and succeed in over-wintering. So it is with cosmeas (*Cosmos bipinnatus*). I am always glad to be able to lift a few of their later germinating self-sown seedlings to plant over my alstroemerias when they have died off in the third week of July. Alstroemerias are deep rooting; one can pull out their old flowering stems instead of cutting them down, and this leaves four inches of top soil in which to plant the cosmeas or anything else that will fill an awkward gap.

No matter whether his garden be large or small, there is nothing more shaming to the keen gardener than gaps where no gaps should be. To keep one's borders well furnished from spring to autumn is the greatest art in gardening, and it offers a most stimulating challenge to one's resourcefulness. Bedding plants are the most rewarding fillers of gaps, whether these are accidental or whether they have been left on purpose for later planting.

Much bedding comprises perennials that are on the borderline of hardiness. It may in many cases be worth leaving the plants out to stand the winter if they will – a procedure that is impossible where the routine of special beds is operating and summer bedding must inexorably be followed by spring, but perfectly feasible when bedding plants are growing side by side with hardy perennials in every part of the garden. Penstemons of the bedding type are hardy in many parts of Britain, but even if they look a bit untidy in autumn, their top-hamper must be left intact as a protection to the plants till spring. At that season it is of equal importance, for a good display, to cut the plants down to ground level. Flowering usually begins about mid-June. Some varieties, like the handsome red Southgate Gem, will go on blooming without letting up for a moment until October. Others, like Garnet, flower less profusely after a tremendous initial surge of blossom. The finer-leaved kinds with slenderly tapering flowers are a great deal prettier than the coarser-leaved, fat gloxinia-flowered hybrids. Penstemons may prove to be hardy, but they are relatively short-lived perennials and it is wise to replace one's clumps of them regularly every third or fourth year.

Many of the large-flowered fuchsia hybrids are surprisingly hardy. Those of traditionally fuchsia colouring with red sepals and purple petals are the most reliable – Mrs Popple, Avalanche and Scarcity, for example. But so, too, are many others. There is Mme Cornelissen, with red sepals and a white corolla marked with red pencilling; Display, with a pink calyx and a charmingly flared lilac skirt; Sunset, of similar shape, in flesh pink and salmon shading; Lena, a fat double fuchsia, flesh pink and violet purple; while the drooping habit of Marinka, whose globular red buds gleam like sealing-wax, fits it for a position at the top of a wall. But all the large-flowered fuchsias behave like herbaceous plants, not as shrubs, when grown wholly in the open, and this means that flowering gets under way rather later, in early August, than if they had been raised under glass and planted out.

When one feels reasonably confident of a bedding plant's ability to winter successfully in the open, it is still a necessary precaution to take a handful of cuttings each autumn, to keep by one in case of need. For the rest and where seed is not the answer, all the stock required for next year's planting must be raised from soft autumn cuttings. The young plants resulting will generally be freer flowering than old stock that one has attempted to over-winter by lifting and housing it. This practice is seldom successful and in any case requires too much space. The rooting of soft cuttings, taken in September, is very easy, and the young plants at the worst need to be kept at a temperature no higher than freezing point; many of them will cheerfully survive a few degrees of frost and for them, cold frame protection is enough. A dozen cuttings taken of each variety will allow bold groups to be made and a generous choice of sorts.

Verbenas, with their warm, summery scent, are a specially grateful tribe. Certain strains and mixtures can be raised from

19

seed, but cuttings must be taken of the best of the bunch, the deep, pinky-red Lawrence Johnston. Overwintered in 3½in pots, the plants can be put out in April and will flower from May to October – a good five months and a far longer period than could be had from spring-raised verbena seedlings. Lawrence Johnston has a vigorous, mat-forming habit, so the plants need be set not closer than 15ins apart. They are useful for breaking the hard line of a paved path edge. Firefly is pure red without a trace of pink, but it is scentless and exacts rather a lot of work for successful results. Here the habit is upright and plants need a close spacing of 9ins. They are very brittle at the collar, so that some twigging is advisable. Pure red, too, is a jewel for the rock garden, *Verbena peruviana (chamaedrifolia)*. It has a creeping habit and will cover a generous area in the course of one year. Plants will sometimes survive the winter in a really well-drained spot. Another not quite hardy bedding plant for the rock garden is the little convolvulus, *C. mauritanicus*. It has flowers the colour of dog violets, perhaps even a little bluer, and has none of its relatives' bad habits.

Gazanias are sometimes planted in rock gardens, being especially useful for extending this feature's season, but many of the gorgeous modern hybrids tend to be a little too flamboyant if they are to associate with precious alpines. Groups at the front of the mixed border look very well; best of all, if one can find it, is a place on top of a 4ft retaining wall, where they can be studied at eye level. For these South African daisies, when at last the weather is brilliant enough to coax them into unfurling, reveal a vivid ground colour that is overlaid near the daisy's centre with zones and spots of fantastic shading; most startling of these is a clear peacock green.

There are many good bedding plants among the South African daisies, and all want sun and free drainage before everything. One of my favourites is *Dimorphotheca ecklonis* with rays that are white above and blue beneath and with a bright blue central disc. Its flowers are radiant stars when fully expanded, but have a quite different appeal when half open or half closed, so that the dusky blue reverse is seen. The almost pure blue daisies of *Aster pappei* are sprinkled over its neat green bush like hat-pins in a cushion. The similar but rather coarser growing *Felicia amelloides* has a nice habit of flowering on so generously into the winter that old plants are well worth potting up in the autumn to pick from in the cool greenhouse.

Last, but not least, among the types of bedding plants, are those upon whose fleshy rhizomes or tubers we rely to bring them through the cold months: *Salvia patens*, cannas and, above all, the dahlias. I would plead strongly for the generous use of dahlias in mixed and herbaceous borders. They are valuable there for providing boldness of form at a season when purpose is most apt to run out at the border's heels leaving an amorphous mess behind it. There is a mistaken idea abroad that dahlias won't thrive among other plants, that they must be grown alone. Leaving their use for picking aside, I would say that the only sensible way to grow them is with other plants, with each group comprising one variety. Close planting also gives the best visual (though not the best cultural) results. The great essential in growing dahlias under these competitive conditions is to feed them really well. The small decorative and cactus types are the most satisfactory, and by merely starting the tubers in a closed cold frame, one can have them in flower from early July onwards.

– January 2, 1958 –

SIGNS OF SPRING IN WINTER SHRUBS

In the depths of winter our thoughts turn defensively to the spring that is to follow. Looking and planning ahead, we try to remain oblivious of immediate unpleasantnesses. It is inspiriting, during the short days, to scrutinise our flowering trees and shrubs for signs of spring. We need only to see those clusters of brown, scaly, insignificant little buds for the mind to work their consummation. The trick is done: spring is with us and winter, for the moment, banished.

Of some old faithful we can always feel sure – no point in examining the ornamental cherries, forsythias and wisteria. They will not fail us unless the birds later decide to strip them; and it must be admitted that in deep country the birds do seem to be getting more mischievous from year to year. That is the real snag about winter buds: like Thursday's child they have far to go, and it doesn't do to gloat overweeningly. They will have weather hazards to side-step too, and these are not just a simple matter of how much frost and for how long. Last winter's dismayingly heavy drop of camellia buds was a quite unexpected event in an exceptionally mild season. However, anxieties and premonitions mustn't be allowed to spoil the pleasures of bud-searching. The camellias' buds, which vary considerably in their numbers from year to year, are most satisfying to find, even to count, on a favourite bush. The encouraging help of surface dressings of old manure or of liquid feeds in July seems to give a great fillip to bud production, which is then in the balance and becomes apparent with most camellias in the following month.

A shrub that cheers us in the grimmest winter days, *Garrya elliptica,* reveals its intentions more than six months earlier, in the second half of June. From then on we can watch the progress of its lengthening green catkins. Garryas have a strong tendency to flower biennially. The catkins are produced along the previous year's young shoots; in a flowering season no young vegetative shoots appear, and hence no catkins the year after. As it is the male garrya which we all grow, it seems odd that the mere business of flowering should so exhaust our bushes, when there is never a question of seed production.

Piptanthus laburnifolius (*nepalensis*) always carries a huge crop of pea pods, yet never fails to flower with abundance. Its short racemes of substantial yellow blossoms open over a period of six to eight weeks, and this is probably the reason for our first intimations of its flowering being so tentative. 'Are those really going to be flowers?' we wonder, as we examine a few scattered, green cone-like growths, spikelets of overlapping bracts. They are indeed, but most of the inflorescences do not show themselves till months later. I have a specially soft spot for this shrub. I know it never makes a tremendous splash, but the large, evergreen trifoliate leaves are outstandingly handsome, while vigorous new shoots have a greenish purple sheen on them like the gloss of young bamboo canes. I believe the species to be hardier than is generally allowed – at least when young. In East Sussex, well inland, my bush came unscathed and unprotected through the bitter February of 1956, and it grows out in the open, far from any wall.

A wall seems necessary to *Sophora tetraptera*, for both shelter and support. This is a tantalising shrub, so beautiful and unusual that any true gardener, having once seen a specimen in flower, must yearn to own a plant. By relationship a pea, it is most unorthodox in that the petals all point forwards, so that the flowers are bell-shaped; they hang in small clusters and are buttercup yellow and about 1½ins long. The graceful pinnate leaves, when young, unroll like a fern's croziers. So far it is with the foliage of this shrub that I am most familiar. I have now watched and cared for my specimen for seven years; it is 15ft tall and has borne me four blooms.

The plant, which is very vigorous in its early years, clearly has to reach a certain degree of maturity before it can bloom. After that it is all up to the weather. That is where the tantalising part comes in. The little knots of brown buds – they took like apple pips – appear in August. Two years ago there were masses on my plant; come the February of 1956 and all were destroyed. That summer was wet and miserable: no buds (or rather, to be exact, two buds), and the next winter was one of the mildest on record. Now, at the beginning of 1958, I am apprehensively brooding over an enormous potential crop. If it blooms I shall, one balmy moonlit evening in spring, throw a special sophora party beneath its branches.

I find the spurges a fascinating group. Sympathisers will know the excitement of seeing a new hardy spurge for the first time. Best of the old favourites is *Euphorbia wulfenii* with its proud, lime-green columns so handsomely set off by further supporting columns of glaucous, evergreen foliage. This shrub varies a good bit from year to year in its freedom of flowering, so it is worth keeping a watch on it as early as the end of September, to see what may be expected. At about that time the tip of every branch that is going to flower starts to dip towards the horizontal. Soon it makes a considerable kink, pointing obliquely downwards. It is the oddest ritual, without any object that I could ever fathom, for eventually the shoots straighten up again; nothing could be more upright than their carriage at flowering.

Lilacs are enigmatic in their intentions as far as autumn looks go. A high proportion of buds may seem to look plumply promising, yet produce nothing but leafy shoots in the end. The only way to discover what they hold in store is by sacrificing a few representative-looking buds. If these are cut in halves one can soon see whether a truss of flower initials was present. When a lilac bush grows very large, drastic action may become necessary. It will respond very well to being chopped back to a stump, one or two feet high, in winter. But, of course, a year's blooming will thereby be lost. So this business of examining a few bud contents is especially worth doing before taking the big decision. If a mass of blossom is promised for the following spring, one will feel the more inclined to spare the axe for a twelve-month so as to do the job in the lilac's off-year.

Lilacs, in many of their varieties, are another example of shrubs with a tendency to flower biennially. Some authorities have given us to believe that this is due to our letting them set seed; we should go round our bushes cutting off all dead-heads the moment flowering is at an end. Where several 15ft tall specimens are to be dealt with at a particularly busy time of the year, this can be quite a task. But in my experience it doesn't work. I have tried it with a Mme Lemoine which flowers in alternate years so heavily that it manages to put on scarcely any leaves. I have snipped off its trusses the moment they seemed to be more brown than white. But the poor lady continues almost naked throughout the summer. None of the dormant leaf shoots breaks into growth following my kind action – and this in a heavily manured mixed border where there would seem to be every inducement to make fresh growth. So, with no new shoots made, there are no flowers the next year. Perhaps the plant physiologists could tell us something about this.

By early June, when lilac blossom is fading, leafy shoots for the season have all been made – have reached their full length and stopped growing. In fact, it seems that whatever we do to our bushes in June, we cannot induce them to react by making new shoots as though they were in early spring again.

– September 1, 1966 –

BYWAYS AMONG BULBS

If we are particular about what we want, no time should be lost in making our orders for spring-flowering bulbs. The mainstay

25

of the catalogues comprises hyacinths, tulips and narcissi, with crocuses and lilies as runners up, but I frequently find myself diving first of all for the section headed miscellaneous, to see what will tempt me among the oddities of the bulb kingdom.

Camassia, for instance, was called Quamash by the Native Americans, and the word was doubtless onomatopoeic, describing the noise of teeth scrunching into raw, edible bulbs. Some camassias carry spikes of pale, washed-out mauve flowers, but in the best strains of the best species the colour is richer than a bluebell's, the season slightly later and the bloom itself a wide-opening, though dished, star. The one I get from time to time at 11s. a hundred is listed (incorrectly, according to the botanists) as *C. esculenta*. It is an excellent shade and is able to cope with the rather rank turf flora carried by our clay soil. There, in rough grass, it always attracts attention, for blue at that season stands out among the yellows of hawksbeards and buttercups among white moon daisies and red clover.

Another bit of blue that you can introduce in the same way is that of the Dutch iris, in a good-natured, robust strain such as H.C. van Vliet. Indeed, we should grow these types of May-June-flowering, bulbous irises a great deal more than we do at present. Everyone knows that they are good for cutting, and the bunches of forced Wedgwood's (the best light blue cultivar for this purpose) seen in florists' shops in late winter have a depressingly stereotyped expression. But they are excellent garden flowers, and so cheap. Furthermore, the colour range is wide, and includes (as well as the obvious yellow and blue shades) lilac, pearl grey and warm brown. Groups of 25 or 50 can well be worked into borders where the growth of certain perennials – *Salvia superba* for instance – is late in developing. The decaying iris remains will be swamped shortly after they have passed out of flower. In a friend's garden I greatly admired the huge white sails of a Dutch iris – White Perfection very likely – behind a border edging of Tom Thumb and other low-growing fuchsias. The irises were making their contribution in June, before the fuchsias had got into their stride. Spanish irises are almost as versatile but, being more petite, would not cope with rough grass.

A Ring of Bells

Fritillaria imperialis, the Crown Imperial, is not cheap but it is an investment. Left undisturbed for a period of years on rich, reasonably slug-free, soil, it will increase and make the most splendid feature in your April garden.

I must move mine; they are in front of a lilac, whose roots are altogether too greedy and pervasive, so that the bulbs have been making only leaves for several years now. The inflorescence is so spectacular and unusual that one wonders how it ever came to be: a ring of bells surmounted by a bunch of greenery in pine-apple style. And one cannot resist lifting the bell-flowers so as to be able to look into the heart of them where the nectaries glisten like suspended tears. Of course the plant does smell appalling – a mixture of garlic and fox that is wafted afar on the wind. But then most people's sense of smell has atrophied anyway, and one can always hold one's nose.

I really must try the dog-tooth violet, *Erythronium dens-canis*, again, although this is not quite the ideal garden in which to site it happily. We have the moist soil they like, but not the open woodland conditions where they can be left to multiply undis-turbed. We used to have them on a shady bank, where they ex-isted for many years, but the rough-grass medium overpowered them in the long run. The flowers are shaped like a turkscap lily, with reflexed segments, and are usually pinkish mauve but with albino forms, while the foliage is beautifully marbled. They can be acquired at 39s 6d a hundred, if you know where to apply. Other species are apt to be expensive, but some are no less easy-going. *E. revolutum*, for instance is specially lovely in an albino cultivar such as White Beauty. These are 2s 9d each. Few erythroniums grow more than 6in to 1ft high, and the above two are of the lowest.

Beating the Cold

The bulb sold as *Ixiolirion pallasii* (actually a variety of *I. montanum*) makes a stringy 18in plant, but it carries in May wide-open flowers of the most heavenly and refreshing blue. It is not very hardy, but one can accommodate this sort of bulb – tigridias, zephyranthes, acidantheras, *Pancratium maritimum*, the less hardy nerines and amaryllis are others that come readily to mind – in a specially prepared, raised bed facing south, and the soil made up of a high proportion (say half) of horticultural grit. Good drainage and a thorough banking will enable them to put up with a considerable amount of cold.

– September 15, 1966 –

SLIDING INTO AUTUMN

It has not really been too bad a summer. Most people will look back with disappointment. That is their way; they start with such extraordinarily high expectations. Garden-wise it has, I reckon, been an excellent growing season. We have never gone for long without those highly desirable wet spells, and yet there has been quite a generous scattering, throughout, of anticyclonic weather with coolish northerly winds, but plenty of sunshine. Everyone's annuals seem to have flourished, while no early, mid-season nor late-cropping garden peas received a check to their growth at any stage. And there have been no gales, at least in this south-east corner of the country. The pelargoniums that I grow in tubs on our south-west-facing terrace are my yardstick for this judgement. Although I hedge them about with twigs from the start, and tie the ivy-leaved ones' main growths loosely to canes, there frequently comes a turbulent wind that sweeps half their top-hamper away before it. But not, so far, this year.

Now it is autumn, which should, I consider, be the gardener's pleasantest and most relaxed season. The weather is often beguiling and should be enjoyed to the full, in view of the rigours that lie ahead. There is plenty to be done, of course, but also, as growth slides to a standstill, plenty of time in which to do it. Better, while we may, to suspend activity and watch red admirals and comma butterflies guzzling on rotten pears.

Writing of rotting fruit reminds me of our mulberries. It never occurred to me, when I planted a variegated *Fatsia japonica* under the outermost branches of one mulberry, that the shrub would turn into a sort of mulberry trap. This fatsia has proved a most satisfactory evergreen. The white splashes on its lustrous green leaves are not very distinct while the foliage is yet young, but make a fine contrast as autumn wears on, and the bonus of globular white flower heads, so like an ivy's, are always welcome in November. But the leaves are cupped and fallen mulberries collect in the centre of each: one is constantly shaking them out, and even then the stains remain.

That is the worst of mulberries. They are shedding their fruit without intermission from the end of July until mid-October. The stains do not wash off the flagstones underneath until well into December. For three months, the trees are filled with squawking starlings; with blackbirds too, and with wasps and flies and bluebottles. Rarely are conditions just right for the maturing of ripe, undamaged fruit that is truly fit for a fastidious human's consumption. Now and again this does happen. The fruits hang on until they are almost black, and can then be transferred from tree to mouth in one smooth gliding movement, with the most satisfactory result. No better combination than sharp and sweet together, so that the palate contracts and tingles while the juice gushes separately from the bead-like fruitlets, of which the mulberry is made up.

Let me see now, where was I? Ah yes; well, the first thing about a mulberry tree, if you want to grow one, is to find a supplier. In any book on fruit growing, the author, who probably knows the last word on apples, pears, plums and all commercial fruits, but absolutely nothing about mulberries, will write on the subject of their propagation something like this: 'The mulberry is easily propagated by cuttings of considerable size which readily root if taken in September and October; shoots a foot or more in length, root with very little trouble in sandy soil in a cold frame.' Now, if the mulberry is so easily propagated, you would have thought that any nursery man having access to a mature tree from which to obtain cutting material, would be 'quids in'. And yet I do not know of a single nursery in this country that is offering home-grown stocks of the black mulberry.

We have, here, a trap for the unwary customer. It is not sufficient to order a mulberry; you must ask for *the* black mulberry, *Morus nigra.* Otherwise you are liable to receive a plant of the white mulberry, *Morus alba,* which is easily raised from imported seed. But, except as food for silk-worms, the tree has little to recommend it, and its anaemic white fruit is useless. I have never heard of viable seed being produced by the black mulberry. Most of its fruits, indeed, are seedless. The tree certainly can be increased from hardwood cuttings. I remember one of my form masters at school having succeeded in doing just this. I have not yet been successful myself! I think it must be one of those cussed plants that favours the amateur.

Having obtained a plant, everything is straightforward, for the mulberry has no troubles and grows fast on good soil. Usually, the tree has no trunk but develops from a series of branches near ground level. These get heavy in a matter of 60 or 70 years, and have to be propped, but even the propping, if well done, can be reasonably picturesque. The natural habit of the plant is weeping, and in many situations it will be necessary to remove a few low branches almost every year. The wounds never callus over, in this species, and it is very important to protect the scar from rotting, by painting it over with a bituminous substance – much more effective than the white lead paint we once used.

– June 8, 1967 –

A SUPREMACY OF FLORISTS' FLOWERS

Our house has lately been the scene of great activity. We were taken over by the flower-arranging society from a nearby coastal resort, for a display by its members in aid of charity. This, for me, was quite an experience. I know that similar jamborees are being held repeatedly up and down the country, but I had never myself been caught up in a floral tornado. One's happiest recollection, now that calm has returned, is of the organisers themselves; so considerate as well as efficient, and so exceptionally pleasant and good-humoured with each other as well as with us.

Naturally, I was especially interested in the flower material used, and here it was startling to discover what heavy reliance was placed on florists' flowers grown under glass. Out of a total of 31 arrangements, no fewer than 19 used carnations – enormous blooms whose stems had, in many cases, been reduced to a length of 6 or 9ins in order to accommodate them to small- or medium-scale arrangements. The flower of a well-grown, disbudded carnation is such a large, unyielding blob that only a very large arrangement can comfortably absorb it. But I was told, these splendid blooms had been available at a mere 6d, each.

If a flower is available to you the year round, you really need to impose upon yourself a certain restraint in its use, otherwise the joy of the changing seasons and of flowers in their season is lost. Chrysanthemums were represented in 11 arrangements, but all, mercifully, were grown as sprays. Forced gladioli occurred 14 times. Like the carnations they, again, had in many cases been reduced to very short stems, but in two instances the delightful little *Gladiolus nanus*, Nymph, gave us a change. And florists' roses were there in force (15 times); perfect yet soulless buds on long, thin stalks. Other forced flowers (each flower arranger had, I was told, spent on average some 26s. on materials for her arrangement) included alstroemerias, column stocks, hydrangeas, freesias, gerberas and sweet peas.

To appreciate that you were in England in late May, you had to search for the evidence. There were only four arrangements composed entirely of garden or hedgerow material. Rhododendrons or azaleas were used six times; euphorbias were there in strength but, of course, they do not make for big effects. *Euphorbia palustris*, exceptionally, does make a large head of its bright, lime-green bracts, and could be grown more extensively. Tulips occurred only three times. Most of the mid-season varieties were already over, but the parrot tulips, Orange Favourite and Texas Gold, were still at their best in my garden, while the slim lines of the soft orangy Dillenburg, used in one case, provided a welcome relief from glass-house roses, which might have found a place in the same context. The tulips' thicker stems were a distinct asset, as also their flexibility; they do not perform the mad contortions of a lupin spike or a red-hot-poker, when arranged sideways, but they do adapt themselves gracefully to this position. Incidentally, tulips can easily be held back and saved from the weather's vagaries if picked from the garden while still in almost green bud and kept in a cool room or cellar until required.

I do not want to seem unsympathetic to the flower arrangers' problems. Many of them have only small gardens to draw on; some have none. And, if they depend on garden flowers, they are so much at the mercy of weather, whereas buying from the florist they can depend on a standard product being available on any given date. One has to expect most enterprise in flower arranging to be shown in people's own homes, where risks can be taken in the use of unusual material. If it flops, nobody will mind. On a public occasion they tend to play safe. The results can be monotonous, and I would put in a plea for more experimenting in the home so that flower arrangers can build up in themselves the confidence to use a wider range of exciting material when the public occasions do come along.

There were some notable successes: for instance, a pedestal arrangement in the angle of two walls, all in green and white. There were arums and huge white Dutch irises, not all in full bloom but, in the upper part of the arrangement, in half bud – that was so clever; *Viburnum opulus* Sterile, with white snowballs, double white lilac (Mme Lemoine). *Hosta glauca* and *H. crispula* (in green and white), young hornbeam foliage, wonderfully well-conditioned and not a bit floppy, Solomon's seal and an inspired touch, the *young* pods of honesty, looking at first glance like eucalyptus leaves. A magenta and blue arrangement in an urn appealed to me. The former colour was provided by gladioli and stock, both single and double; the singles mix in very well. A blue pot hydrangea gave weight to the lower part of the composition. The soil had been washed off its roots and then enclosed in a plastic bag so that its owner could repot it after the display was over. And there were blue, almost wild, lupins that behaved themselves in exemplary manner; blue Dutch iris, mauve chrysanthemums, Pink Pearl rhododendrons and also a mauve variety; purple kale leaves and the foliage of forsythia, *Cotoneaster simonsii* and bergenias.

33

BULBS FOR EARLY PLANTING

Some gardeners find it rather depressing to be expected to think about bulbs for winter and spring flowering while we are still in summer. But we have to plan ahead by at least nine months or a year for best results, and we can't anyway do a Canute act on the progress of the seasons. Where we really must get a move on, without more than a few days' procrastination, is in the ordering of autumn-flowering crocuses and colchicums. Time and again we get caught out over these, admiring them in some garden during their September–October flowering season by which time, alas, we have already lost a year.

These, surely, are the answer to the most impatient gardener's dream, for they are no sooner planted than up push the flowers. Indeed, they sometimes start flowering in their packets, before they have been planted. Not unnaturally, then, the bulb firms put a date limit on when they will accept orders: the most famous of them sets it at August 15; another at September 1.

For general purposes, the easiest, cheapest and showiest crocus for autumn flowering is *Crocus speciosus*. It has large mauve flowers and a network of deeper-shaded veins that more nearly approach it to blue than any other crocus. This colouring is offset by the large, brilliant orange stigmata in the centre of each flower. And it is deliciously scented. The perianth tube (what the ordinary chap would call its stalk) is exceptionally long, with the result that the flowers habitually fall over on their sides on the second day of blooming. I can't see that this matters, myself; they still look very charming in a Mme Recamier pose, but it apparently upsets some gardeners. Undoubtedly this habit is less noticeable in rough grass, and *C. speciosus* can cope with the roughest turf, naturalising by means of bulbils and by seeding, until it makes quite a conspicuous sward of foliage, in early spring, before real grass has started growing much. In fact, this crocus should be kept out of the rock garden or any place where small and precious plants are grown, but it is excellent among shrubs. Its flowering season starts about September 10 and runs through most of October.

A Fascinating Crocus

One of the most fascinating of crocuses is *C. nudiflorus*, the only autumn-flowering species that finds a place in our *British Flora* (of Messrs Clapham, Tutin and Warburg). Although introduced, it has naturalised in grassland in various parts of the country. And yet the main snag for the gardener is in obtaining stock. The corms tend to be very small and, presumably, do not market well. A few years ago, it was being offered by a well-known Dutch bulb merchant and I bought a dozen. I think only two grew, and I imagine that complaints from customers may have been a reason for the species shortly afterwards being deleted from the firm's catalogue. However, my slight success was enough to give me a nucleus, and the bulbs have since increased, and flower well under our bay tree, among hardy cyclamen. The colour of the flowers is a particularly clear and lovely rosy lilac.

When staying in Ulster last March, my host showed me a coloured photograph of this crocus that he had taken in his own garden, and he had two or three enormous colonies of it that must have dated back many years, but in that part of the country it does not flower at all freely. Presumably it requires a summer baking. Peculiar to this species is its manner of spreading by underground stolons. In fact, if you dig up a clump in spring, as my host kindly did for me, you see more stolon than corm.

I cannot for the moment name a commercial source for

C. nudiflorus but recommend interested readers to apply direct to the newly set up Plant Finder service. It will be extremely useful to us all to be able, in future, to apply to this central pool for information on suppliers of less common seeds and plants.

Now, also, is the time to deal with the bulbs of the Madonna and Nankeen lilies (*Lilium candidum* and *L. testaceum*) and of the Crown Imperial, *Fritillaria imperialis*. These start making new roots before you would think they could or should want to. The Madonna lily even throws up tufts of overwintering leaves, in the autumn. So you want to catch them early, where it is either a question of buying new stock or of replanting them in your own garden. My Crown Imperials have been blind for several years now, and I know it's because they are at the foot of a lilac, whose masses of dense and greedy roots rob them of nearly all the heavy mulches I apply.

The bulbous irises – Dutch, Spanish, English and the smaller types – also make new roots surprisingly early if growing in the garden, and should be replanted, if they need it, as soon as possible.

– December 28, 1967 –

A HANDFUL OF HERBS

With rare exceptions, herb gardens are a mistake, an anachronism suggesting olde-worlde aspirations. They smack of the household where draughts whisk round every corner, the huge open hearth smokes remorselessly, the lady starts up from her spinning wheel as the cracked bell tolls midnight from the stable clock. 'I must gather my simples,' she wails, like a curlew that has newly lost its mate. She plunges through the open hall door, the door that has not moved on its aching hinges this many a weary

x

36

year; trips barefoot o'er the frosted mead (a pochette of lavender swinging wildly from her kirtle) and culls her bouquet garni of hemlock and belladonna; aconite, henbane, herb Christopher; night-shades deadly and black; seed of thorn apple, berry of bitter sweet and a soothful spring of feverfew. Back again, breathless but undaunted; back to her hearth and the old black pot, the faithful pot that never rests.

Into it she drops her simples one by one. Her lord and master sits slumped in the wan winged chair, his waxen face like parchment. 'We'll have you right in no time, ducks,' she whispers.

And when it comes to the practicalities of tending a herb garden, I can speak from bitter experience (funny, how experience is invariably bitter). For it should be understood that every honest herb is a weed at heart. The moment you turn your back on them – say for a week's holiday – the whole lot have ripened and scattered a billion seeds, and the next thing you know is that you're stuck on your hands and knees, winkling out each seedling, individually, from among those delightful herb paths that you use as a means of dividing the beds (instead of grass or paving), just like they did in Good Queen Bess's day.

In the herb garden that I am harking back to, some paths were of penny-royal (*Mentha pulegium*), others of creeping peppermint (*M. requienii*) and others again of double camomile. 'I can't think why we don't do this sort of thing more often.' Visitors would croon ecstatically, if they happened to see them on the right day of the right year. I will tell why. Gardeners have, nowadays, a wonderful range of selective weedkillers where-with to minimise the labour of keeping grass turf free of interloping broad-leaved weeds. But in a camomile or mint path, it is a killer working in exactly the opposite direction that is needed, and this does not exist. Camomile and the rest of them do not make a dense sward and the weed problem is demoniacal.

37

The Mint Problem

Furthermore, the mints either grow too strongly, invariably preferring the neighbouring beds, or else, on the paths themselves, they get tired and die out. The camomile rushes into flower, which is very pretty, but the moment of truth is revealed when it has to be cut. It then sulks and large patches disappear. Nowadays there is, admittedly, a non-flowering camomile available, but surely the main point of camomile is its flower.

As I see it, there are two kinds of herbs that are worth growing: those that look sufficiently attractive to take their place in the garden proper, with plants that are not herbs, and those that are constantly required in the preparation of food and should be grown unselfconsciously, near the kitchen. Unless you must have your little joke, forgo such whimsies as woad and tree onions.

The pot-herbs do not need to be assembled all together in one bed. After all, they have varying habits and requirements. Everyone should have a bay. It can be in a tub but, if space allows, looks handsomest when allowed to grow freely as a tree. Giant chives are exceedingly pretty in flower and just as good, leaf-wise, as the insignificant ordinary chives. The only savoury one need grow is the perennial, shrubby winter savoury, *Satureia montana.* It has a dwarf variant called caeruleam that carries bright lavender flowers in autumn and deserves a place among rock plants. Thyme has a similar, but more scented, flavour and is not so good, in my opinion. *Thymus vulgaris,* the garden thyme, is the most useful, growing about 1½ft tall. It will colonise dry walling very charmingly and has a mass of pale mauve flowers in May.

The flavour of sage is coarse and masterful, while the shrub is plain dull, seldom flowering in the culinary type. There are, however, a number of variants that have purple or variegated foliage and abundant purple flowers, and these are worthy garden plants. Tarragon (*Artemisia dracunculoides*) is preferable in the

French rather than the Russian type. It is less hardy than most herbs, should be frequently divided, in spring, and never have its old growth cut away until the spring. Purple fennel is so pretty in the mole colouring of its young foliage that one might grow this, rather than the green.

Mints are for the most part terrible rampers, and while many of them have interesting aromas, they are scarcely worth their nuisance value. Concentrate on spearmint (*Mentha spicata*) and apple mint (*M. rotundifolia*).

The variegated form of the latter is a must for its looks alone, and is only a foot tall. The golden form of marjoram is one of the best foliage plants of its kind, a foot tall and retaining its colour throughout the growing season. It makes good flavouring, too.

Lovage (*Ligusticum scoticum*) is a 7ft-tall herbaceous perennial akin in flavour (and related) to celery. I love to snatch and nibble a leaf, as I pass it. It contributes well to a green salad.

– February 8, 1968 –

FLOWERS FROM SEED

There are some gardeners who cannot be bothered with the business of seed sowing in pots and boxes but who will, nevertheless, take the trouble to make a few direct sowings of annuals in the garden. On my heavy, easily panning soil, I find the latter procedure most unsatisfactory and far from labour-saving. Except for a very few items like love-in-a-mist and opium poppies, I would rather do all my sowings in pots and boxes. In this way you can always retain control.

Mignonette is a case in point. It is a heady annual generally recommended for sowing where it is to flower. But all too often,

39

the seeds fail to germinate. If, on the other hand, you sow a few seeds in each of, say, half a dozen 3½in pots, they will germinate without any trouble. You can reduce them to two per pot before the seedlings start competing with each other and then plant them in their flowering positions without disturbing the ball of roots. Mignonette, *Reseda odorata*, flowers non-stop for several months and the unimproved, wild kind has the best scent.

I like the practice of associating plants that are alike in colour but of contrasting leaf and flower form. This year I intend to try the bedding plant, *Melianthus major* (frequently mentioned in this column), which has wonderful sea-green, pinnate foliage, with the green form of love-lies-bleeding – *Amaranthus caudatus* Viridis (alias Albiflorus). To be worth growing at all, amaranth needs to be grown well. It is a hardy annual (but, again, I shall start it in a pot, in April) and is capable of making a large and handsome plant, 3ft across, if allowed the necessary space and not starved. Other possible associates for this are the green-flowered zinnia Envy, and the nicotiana called Lime Green. But I am considering making up my trio with *Kochia childsii*, the burning bush. This turns a somewhat disconcerting shade of magenta in the autumn, but is a vivid and attractive cone of green throughout the summer.

I am mad on stocks, but have always found them tricky. Those who garden on light soils are well away with the biennial kinds, East Lothian and Brompton, sown in early August, but on clay one must get what satisfaction one may from summer-flowering stocks grown as annuals, last year I discovered the secret of success. No short cuts, I'm afraid. It's a question of taking a bit more trouble. I used the Beauty of Nice or Mammoth stock, which makes quite a large, well-branched plant, and I used it in the Hansen 100 per cent double strain. The seed was sown in a cold frame on May 1. After germination, the seedlings need to be submitted to lowish temperatures, in the 40s, in order to reveal the colour difference between pale-leaved seedlings. Which will carry double flowers, and dark-leaved seedlings that will be single and can be weeded out forthwith. May last year was not unusual, it will be remembered, in producing some very chilly weather, so I had no difficulties there. Next I potted the double seedlings off individually. This individual treatment for annual stocks is, I'm sure, the only way to produce a really fat, juicy plant that does not flower prematurely. They were planted out in the third week of June and flowered from mid-July onwards.

This year I plan to sow them about May 7 and plant them out at the turn of June and July to follow Messenger sweet Williams (interplanted with tulips) that went in last autumn. The stocks will be followed by winter-flowering pansies, which I shall sow at the end of May, and line out until their final positions are ready for them. They don't make much of a show in winter here, any flowers at that season being rapidly devoured by slugs, but they are excellent in the following spring, when slugs are easier to control.

What do you plan to follow your wallflowers with this year? If you prefer excitement to a quiet life, I suggest the Livingstone daisy, *Mesembryanthemum criniflorum*, in its galaxy of glorious, striking colours. Rumour has it that, to quote one catalogue, 'the hotter the position and the poorer the soil the better this plant seems to grow'. Rumour, as is its way, has got it only half right, however. A hot position, yes, but a well-nourished soil, too. No annual looks more miserable when badly grown, each plant consisting of a few writhing, lopsided shoots of hectic colouring. Try it this way. Sow in a pot or box in the first week of April. Prick out 40 seedlings to a box (preferably 3ins deep) and plant out 9ins apart in fat soil in the fourth week of May. The plants will grow fast into great pools of colour. Of course it's wasted if you're not at home in the middle of the day, this being a high noon flower – and it will run to seed at the end of July, dead-heading not being practicable, so you need a follow-on such as China asters, sown late May.

Of all the numerous strains of asters available, I've come to the conclusion that the Princess type are the most satisfactory. The plants are well branched, the flower heads beautifully formed with quilled florets filling the centre, and the colour range is excellent.

— March 21, 1968 —

NOT AN UNKIND WINTER

We are now in a position to issue a post-mortem on winter. As usual, it was not nearly as bad as we had feared. The fact is that, just as we always approach summer with quite unwarranted optimism (as though our shores were Mediterranean rather than North Atlantic), so also we enter the dark days in a spirit of contagious foreboding. No one, except furriers, fuel merchants and others commercially dependent thereon, will look back on last winter with grief at the parting but it was, from a plant's-eye view, the best that we could hope for, much colder than 1966–67; indeed, in the analysis, it was probably a colder than average winter, but there were only two severe spells. Both were short and neither was vicious.

For most of the time from December to March, plants were kept in that state of suspended animation that suits them best. They were not lured into premature activity as last year, and so, if we do again have late spring frosts, these will not be nearly as damaging as in 1967. For us as individuals there is nothing more beguiling than an early spring, with its effect of shortening the winter. But from the garden's point of view one has to admit that a forward season is disastrous in the long term.

What has anyone lost in their gardens this last winter? It's too early to tell, for sure, but nothing, I think, that we did not more than half expect to lose. The weather pundits tell us that we entered a colder climatic cycle round about 1940 and so, 28 years later, we are well placed for deciding how it has affected our gardening. Surprisingly little, I should say. Temperatures persisting in the low thirties over long periods would give us a much colder than average winter, but the gardener very sensibly reckons that nothing is cold where the thermometer does not sink below the thirties. The only winter that is going to worry him seriously and his charges is the kind where there are long hard spells, of which 1962–63 was the last example and the worst we are ever likely to experience.

My first article in this series was written, nearly five years ago, on the outcome of that ordeal, and it is interesting to note the subsequent behaviour of certain shrubs I was discussing then.

Gigantic Ceanothus

Although many people lost their evergreen ceanothus, many did not. My own *Ceanothus rigidus,* now 18 years old, has gone from strength to strength and is gigantic. Those ceanothus that were planted soon after the bad winter have also grown enormously. The problem in this genus is to find an evergreen that does not grow too large, for wall space is often limited. Even the delightful *C. impressus*, with the neatest little deep-grooved leaves of any, is a hearty grower.

Our myrtle (*Myrtus communis*), had to be cut to the ground in 1963 – for about the third time in its long life. It had been 15ft tall and had stood out 15ft from its wall. Now, after five years, it is already 7½ft tall again. A young myrtle would never grow as fast as that in our part of the world, but an old one has a terrific root system wherewith to boost a new crop of shoots.

I had a young plant of *M. luma* (a Chilean species) that came through that deep freeze winter unscathed. Just as well it should, for this is a long-term shrub whose beauty is revealed only at maturity, when it has reached tree-like proportions. Visitors to Irish and Cornish gardens will know what I mean, but this is obviously one of those shrubs that is considerably hardier than it is given credit for being, and would probably do well in many parts of the country. The stems or trunks of the tree are a remarkable and vivid shade of cinnamon. My plant is now about 7ft tall but has no stems to speak of yet.

Buddleia auriculata is reckoned to be pretty tender and I expected to have lost it in '63, but it came up from ground level again and was soon its customary height of 12ft or more. I have it against a wall, of course. It has been flowering ever since September and is still carrying a few trusses. Admittedly the flowers are modest but they are so fragrant, and the glossy, evergreen foliage is a decided asset.

Wallflowers were virtually wiped out in '63. This year there is not a single death. Their worst hazard was from the heavy, wet snow we had in January and that made such a mess of conifers and other evergreens. We plant our wallflowers very thickly, with the result that, in the main, they held each other up. Only here and there where the planting had not been as close as it should, had they been knocked sideways. From every point of view it is worth being lavish with your wallflowers if they are to be grown at all. A small group planted thickly is twice as effective as a sparse grouping with the same number of plants. By the same token it is preferable not to interplant your wallflowers with bulbs, but to group the latter to one side or behind.

THE BEST VEGETABLES TO GROW

Those of us who grow vegetables at all must always be holding family debates on what can be cut from the list and what, on the contrary, is essential. Even if the nearest greengrocer is a few miles distant, we don't want to grow things that he can supply, of as good or better quality, just to save ourselves the trouble of dealing with him.

When my brother comes to stay, he does a good slice of the cooking and never loses an opportunity for pointing out that it's a waste of time, space and energy to grow your own vegetables. 'The difference between this cabbage and what I should buy at Bristol', he was saying at Christmas, 'is that there is twice as much waste on what you have grown'. I couldn't argue; it was only too obviously true. The slugs had made deep inroads. In fact our cabbages get picked with the slugs inside them and, if not dealt with for a few days (and one is apt to leave a cabbage lying around) the slugs emerge and are found at night crawling around the kitchen draining board. I have a special slug skewer.

However, when he saw our leeks, my brother did exclaim that they looked delicious. He made no comparisons this time, but I knew that he had in mind the market article, more than half of which consists of green leaves with only a very short, blanched stump. In a garden you can do the job properly, taking out a trench wide enough to plant a double row and then earthing them up to get a really nice long white stem. But our leeks are never large enough round for my satisfaction. They always seem to take ages to get moving in the early stages. This year I plan to space-sow them in large pots (instead of sowing in the open

45

ground) in April and shall thereby hope to give them the benefit of something like a month's start.

Writing in this column four years ago on the subject of vegetables and what could well be left out of the seed order, I said that the frozen peas you buy can be very good indeed. I am inclined to revise that opinion. The brand I particularly liked has disappeared and whatever I try nowadays seems either to have very little flavour or to have had an inordinate amount of sugar added. And it tastes like added sugar. A good pea correctly harvested and swiftly eaten or processed has a tremendous store of natural sugar, and doesn't need it as an additive.

Frozen food has got a bad name for itself. You ask your friends about a restaurant they have visited. 'All the vegetables frozen', they tell you, and this is obviously intended as adverse criticism. The trouble from an intelligent consumer's point of view is that there are too few brands; there is too much standardisation, in fact, and he meets the same brand of the same vegetable over and over again, wherever he goes. Again, what brands there are, are the best available from the processing point of view and perhaps for looks, but not for flavour.

Deep-frozen produce has got itself a bad name but it is not the fact of it having been in the freezer that is really at fault, as anyone who has done the job in his own home will readily testify. Deep-freeze your own peas and they will give you the greatest joy out of season, retaining almost their full flavour for a year at least. It's just a question of growing a sensible variety like Onwards; picking it young, when it will already be quite large yet none the worse for that; then shucking, blanching and freezing the peas as quickly as possible within a few hours of picking.

If you can deep-freeze your own peas then you can save yourself the considerable trouble of making successive sowings: early, mid-season, late. Just grow one large mid-season batch; mid-season, because that is when peas will grow fastest and best.

Ours come on about the end of July, usually. The great thing then is to be sure that you have all the help you need on the day you need it.

Calabrese is the kind of green-sprouting broccoli that is widely used for deep-freezing. Unfortunately this is a vegetable that really does seem inevitably to lose most, if not all, of its flavour in the freezing process whether it's done by the factory or by you and whatever the variety chosen. It's just a 'for looks' frozen vegetable. But picked fresh it is unrecognisably good.

I wonder, though, how most people do actually pick their various sprouting broccolis (whether green, white or purple). There was a photograph of a trugful of calabrese in *Amateur Gardening,* the other day, showing a dozen or so pieces that had been picked with 6 or 9ins of stalk, off the bottom half of which the foliage had been plucked, leaving it intact on the upper half. This is a gastronomically disgusting way to treat the vegetable. You should pluck the tight flower heads only, with not a leaf among them, and they can be picked straight into a colander requiring no further preparation.

— July 31, 1969 —

ANNUALS IN A HOT SUMMER

A pattern of weather has become established, as I write in mid-July, which seems to suggest that we shall, for 1969, be able to record one of those summers that everyone longs for and even expects, but that rarely actually occur, in England. This brings its own gardening problems, but it is always far easier to make a success of a hot dry summer than to have to battle against an endless chain of depressions, with the wet and the wind and overall mouldiness that attend them.

This year we shall congratulate ourselves where our choice of annuals required decent weather to do themselves justice, but shall regret having decided to leave out, for instance, petunias, salpiglossis and schizanthus, as happens to be my own case.

But I am particularly pleased with a large L-shaped bed I have in full bloom now of the Livingstone daisy, *Mesembryanthemum criniflorum*. I hadn't grown it for 6 or 7 years, and one always returns to an annual that has been rested in this way, with renewed enthusiasm. It is on the best and richest soil in the garden and has made plants averaging 9ins across in the usual range of brilliant colours. On a sunny day, the flowers expand around 9.30 or 10 a.m. and they remain open till about 5 o'clock in the afternoon, which is pretty generous, as these light-sensitive flowers go. Even on dull days they will open if the weather is warm and dry. Mesembryanthemums have only a limited season and I plan to follow them with China asters, but if you hadn't a follow-on they would be worth dead-heading. Both hands need to be used, holding the plant or a branch of the plant with one and pulling the heads off with the others. But it's a job that has to be started as soon as dead-heads first appear and kept up with regularly. It's no good waiting till the display is already on the wane and then having one grand beheading session. The plants will already be senile beyond retrieve by then.

The annual dimorphothecas have a similar brilliancy and freshness, are similarly light-sensitive and of a limited flowering season. Neatest and dwarfest is *Dimorphotheca pluvialis* Ringens: white with a large purple zone at the centre of each daisy. Glistening White is well named: a larger plant in all its parts and really dazzling. The orange, lemon, biscuit and apricot-flowered types derive mainly from *D. sinuata* and make rather sprawling plants, but knit together well enough in the mass and are all very beautiful without any crudity in their colouring. As young plants,

48

they should never be allowed to become leggy through over-crowding or insufficient light and they want planting out while still quite young and small. As the seeds germinate extremely quickly, there is a general tendency to sow them too early and to have the plants ready for planting out before their sites are ready for them. For late May planting, a mid-April sowing will be early enough.

What a fetish gardeners make about sowing sweet peas early. The longer you have them on your hands in the early stages before planting out, the more trouble they are. Thanks to their popularity for exhibition work, sweet peas are among those plants that have suffered most from the breeders, who have de-veloped for our benefit a race of muscular monsters, with great thick, obtrusive flower stalks and enormous, frilly blooms that are practically without scent except when massed.

This year I have grown a hedge of the old-fashioned sweet-scented kind that were the only kind known to our grandparents before the advent of the modern Spencer varieties. These old ones are reminiscent, in their way, of the old roses; their col-ours are soft and warm, but devoid of the hot orange shades so prevalent today. The flowers are not frilly and are quite small, only 2 or 3 to a stem, but wonderful for cutting, being gay but unpretentious. The scent is something you had forgotten was possible in a sweet pea.

I sowed mine in a box in a cold frame, and not till April 13. The seedlings were then potted individually and planted out in early June. I picked my first good-sized bunch from them on July 12, by which time the plants were about 3½ft high. I see little point in striving to get flowers earlier than this. Two-and-a-half to three months of blossoming is about as much as most of us expect from sweet peas, whenever their season may start, and I shall get that if I keep my plants in good order.

Sweet peas, on good soil, are marvellous value in a hot summer, as they never suffer from drought. But in a wet year on heavy soil it's a sad little story.

Nemesias, on the other hand, are particularly long lasting in a wet season, but apt to run quickly to seed in a hot year, so perhaps I have chosen unwisely in growing them this season for the first time since the war. But they are large plants in fat soil and, if I keep them watered, should do me proud. Anyway, I have interplanted them with the hardy large-flowered fuchsia, Lena, and this can take over in the autumn.

— November 13, 1969 —

BIRD BEHAVIOUR IN THE GARDEN

When showing friends round the garden, recently, we passed within 4 or 5 feet of a cock blackbird who was eyeing us with a zany expression that implied he would get on with what he was doing when we had gone. We paused and looked at him while he continued to look at us. I was admiring his new plumage, actually, for Cassius (it happened to be) had been a sorry sight till recently. 'Poor thing,' murmured one of my companions. I was indignant and asked whether we must take it that any wild creature that fails to flee at man's approach is sick or wounded. That was, indeed, the inference.

Most birds, on the contrary, will become tame if you go about your business and let them go about theirs without interference. When really used to you, it becomes no embarrassment to them to be stared at, spoken to or even sworn at, on occasion. Blackbirds can swear back.

We have a long, narrow apple shed with the door at one end and the apples at the other. There is a bench near the door at which several people will congregate, but this does not deter Blackie (a hen blackbird) from going in and out and helping herself as she pleases. But she swears at us and quite startles those who don't know her if we don't allow her much of a gap to fly out by.

In fact, she knows she's not allowed to help herself to apples in this way (there's no question of finishing one before starting on the next) and the bargain is that if we'll throw her an apple to eat outside the shed, she'll finish that completely except for the core and skin, before attempting to help herself from the racks again.

This year she nested successfully in the potting shed. We have no cats to make this impossible. Earlier broods in the garden had been robbed by magpies, but she was safe from them in the shed. The cock was very shy and I wondered whether Blackie would have to do all the work of feeding the young, and whether she would be able to cope with that as well as with brooding them (though it was so hot that little brooding was, in fact, necessary). However, the cock plucked up sufficient courage, though his visits were accompanied by the maximum of protesting noises and I had to keep my head down attending resolutely to my business and not look up at him.

A Shy Song Thrush

On the outside of the potting shed grows a large specimen of the evergreen *Ceanothus impressus* and this has one branch lying against the wall and a strong side-branch coming off it at right angles. The T-formation is particularly popular with birds. Blackie has used it in former years, but it has always been plundered by magpies. This year a song thrush took over. She was so dreadfully shy at first that I thought she could never succeed where people are continually passing and the crowds were worst of all when she was already brooding her eggs and the ceanothus came into flower – such a display that everyone was stopping and staring. However, I was much surprised and greatly pleased to notice that she became increasingly unconcerned and successfully brought off her young. I forthwith removed the nest, as I always do, and she was soon back making another. The second brood was successfully launched in August. But the thrushes are far less apt to be tame than the blackbirds.

Roy Hay sometimes writes that he wouldn't mind sharing his fruit with the blackbirds if they would take only 20 per cent and leave him the rest. This is a difficult sort of bargain to strike and I think one should either make up one's mind to protect the fruit properly, or to let the birds eat as much as they want or, if this arrangement upsets you, not to grow fruit. To plant and then to have to prowl apoplectically with a pop-gun is bad for one's character.

I can think of at least four gardening friends who are also peacock fanciers. Peacocks, of course, have a bad name as destructive vegetarians but, as is so often the way when you come to examine a subject at close range, they're not nearly as black as they're painted. It is quite untrue to say that you must choose between peacocks and a garden. They are perfectly compatible for most of the time but you will have to protect your green vegetables, for instance. They can be netted at some expense but little trouble. Indeed, even without peacocks, I am beginning to think seriously of netting my lettuces and young brassicas, because the moorhens keep taking gashes from their leaves when the foliage is not yet sufficiently abundant to be able to cope. Peacocks will also tend to peck at anything new, but they soon lose interest.

Another fallacy about peacocks is that their voices are unbearably harsh. They are no more cacophonous than the pheasant's. The one disappointment in their respect is that they seldom take up just that position in your garden where, scenically, you feel that a peacock should be standing.

PROBLEMS FOR THE PANEL

At a gardening brains trust panel held recently in the next village to mine, the first question was on rose diseases. The questioner's roses had contracted less black spot than usual last year but more mildew, although he had sprayed them three times against mildew. The agreed verdict was that he should have sprayed them far oftener to achieve protection: at least once a fortnight from spring to autumn, in fact. A member of the panel of experts made him a point blank offer of a membership form for the National Rose Society, for which he would obtain the best advice, but it turned out that he was already a member.

I wonder whether this amateur rosarian has, in consequence, resolved to spray this year as he has never sprayed before, or whether on the contrary to give up spraying altogether. Nothing in between serves much purpose. My own feeling is that rose varieties which become unsightly from one disease or the other are not worth persisting with; let them give way to roses that are disease resistant. If there are not enough of these, let the pampered rose give way to trouble-free shrubs, of which there are still plenty.

The same gentleman also bewailed seeing so few ladybirds in his garden nowadays, for ladybirds give him pleasure. He was, I hasten to add, perfectly aware of cause and effect, and that his anti-greenfly sprays were also dealing death to the greenflies natural predators, of which the ladybird is one.

The only spray my roses ever receive is a tar oil wash in January, after I have pruned them. This gets rid of overwintering greenfly eggs and adults. Come the spring, aphids appear sooner or later, flying or blown in from elsewhere. Their numbers build up rapidly in May and June; you must either develop strong nerves or look the other way. Then, low and behold, they vanish. Their parasites and predators have got the better of them, glory be. Inactivity has been rewarded.

I was amused to read of a method for catching greenfly on the hop, recommended in *The Floral Cabinet*, July 1838. 'The destructive effect of the aphids, which too frequently attacks rose bushes, more particularly in ungenial seasons, may to a great extent be prevented by allowing the bushes to remain unpruned until the middle of May, by which time they will be pushing out their young shoots from the extremities of the plant, and if sudden changes have taken place in the weather from heat to cold etc. the aphids will appear in numbers. Then is the time to prune back the shoots to where the buds are not burst. The leaves on which the aphids are feeding being thus destroyed and none left upon the bushes to feed the insects, they consequently perish, while the plants soon push afresh with a more genial season, although sometimes a little later.' More ammunition for the late-pruning brigade.

Moles in Lawns

Next the worry of moles in lawns was aired. If we got rid of the earthworms in our lawns, would the moles (which feed on them) keep away on a voluntary basis, perhaps? This was an ingenious thought. The panel, however, was of the opinion that worms were not so easily to be got rid of; apply a chlordane wormkiller and many worms would just go deeper; so would the moles and their heaves would be the larger. 'Don't breathe the word strychnine' (against moles), one panel member murmured to another. It was not breathed.

I don't know quite why it should be, but worm casts on old lawns, such as ours, are not nearly as conspicuous or unsightly

54

as on newer ones. I let them be, and enjoy watching the thrushes and blackbirds going after the worms.

How to get rid of moss in lawns was another query and some proprietary remedy was advocated. I didn't dare stand up and confess that my lawns would be nothing without their mosses and that these make them a wonderfully vivid golden green at this season and like a deep-piled carpet to tread upon. Soon the mosses will turn brown and I shall regret them, but every lawn has its season.

Then pigeons. Pigeons on the vegetables. The only good pigeon is a dead one, was firmly pronounced. But nobody could suggest a deterrent whose effect would last for more than a few weeks – days, more often. Neither was it suggested that pigeons were ever likely to be dead in large enough quantities to save our vegetables. It was the result of the recent snows that had put the subject in everybody's mind. When the fields are covered, the wood pigeon, which prefers grain when it can get any, moves perforce to greens. My own greens are skeletons but it is my general experience that with the return of warm weather the sprouting broccolis will stage a worthwhile recovery and the sprouting sprouts will provide useful spring greens.

Lloyd's Law for Relaxation suggests that if you don't care too badly about the pigeons, you will find them interesting birds to have around the garden. They nest in ours and are frequently to be observed doing no harm whatsoever. I was entertained the other day by one, sitting in an ivy clad tree at the bottom of our garden and craning its neck to reach out for the ripe berries.

JUMPING TO CONCLUSIONS

The current celebration of World Pollution Year has given us all a deep sense of involvement. Our eyes have been opened to examples of pollution on our very doorsteps that would previously have passed unnoticed.

The ladies residing in an area of urban sprawl that fringes an expanding industrial town 20 miles from where I live, have been alarmed to discover that many trees and shrubs in their gardens are sick and dying. Putting their heads together over coffee, of a morning, they came to the conclusion that this area, measuring some 100yd wide by half a mile long, was being polluted on one side by traffic fumes from a busy bypass; on the other by no less toxic fumes from a perfumery.

One of them asked a horticultural expert, who is my friend and from whom I have this case, to examine the evidence. His diagnoses are instructive.

Part of the 'estate' is built on the site of an old orchard. This nearly always has dire consequences for the gardener. Old orchards habitually harbour the dread honey fungus, *Armillaria mellea*, and from an old, infected stump my friend found that this killer had wiped out a considerable area of rose bushes.

Thoughtless earth moving is one of the building contractor's cardinal sins and leaves the unfortunate gardener with the thankless task of trying to make plants grow on sub-soil. In this case, earth had been piled around the base of some 80ft tall ashes. This had impaired the land's natural drainage and the trees had died apparently from asphyxiation or from collar rot or from both together. Collar rot, incidentally, is a frequent cause of death in young trees and shrubs that have been planted too deeply, as a misguided method of making them firm in the ground.

A line of pollarded limes had succumbed to premature defoliation at one end: the end nearer the by-pass. However, it transpired that a late infestation by red spider was here the instrument. The creatures were still clearly visible, in their millions, on the leaves under surfaces. They are very small and almost colourless (not red) so it helps to use a hand lens if your eyesight is not perfect. Red spider is always troublesome under dry conditions, whether in the garden or the greenhouse and on a wide variety of plants from plums to polyanthus. They are sap suckers, and cause complete desiccation of the leaves on which they batten.

Next an ornamental cherry: probably the ubiquitous double pink Kanzan, from its stiff, upright habit. This proved to be dying from bacterial canker, which is a terrifyingly common disease in cherries. Before it actually starts killing a specimen the fact of the bacterium's presence can often be detected by a shot-hole condition of the leaves; they are full of small holes as though peppered from a shotgun. If a plum or cherry is dying back or one or more branches are gumming (exuding a resinous, amber-coloured substance), bacterial canker is often (but not always) the cause.

But a dying ornamental plum, *Prunus cerasifera* Atropurpurea (previously known as *P. cerasifera* Pissardii) proved, from the bracket-like, bluish fungus growing on its dead branches, to be dying of silver leaf, caused by the fungus *Stereum purpureum*.

An elm had been killed by oil from a central heating supply tank. Careless fuelling of a tank all too frequently causes this trouble, as I know to my cost. If our tanks are filled too rapidly and the valves are not open, there is a blow back of oil through the air intake vent, and it gushes into the garden. You can claim from the oil supplier, but that won't restore a valuable plant nor guarantee that the same thing won't happen again.

Last, in this tale of disaster, some lilacs had prematurely lost their leaves, but then the common lilac is subject to several bacterial and fungal defoliators. You can apply protective sprays against a fungus; there is little you can do against a bacterium, but you can always get rid of the lilac, which is one of the dullest features in a garden for eleven months of the year.

So there was no build-up, no story after all. Life was simply taking its natural course. Bacteria and fungi have got to make a living, like the rest of us.

If you deal with living material, animal or vegetable, you must expect a quota of troubles. There are compensations enough, and the gardener is really in a strong position. If a plant dies, there are umpteen others with which he can replace it.

– October 9, 1975 –

ORKNEY PERSPECTIVE

The fact that I am on born territory for 49 weeks in the year probably means that I am more receptive to impressions when I go away. At any rate I hope so, otherwise one's outlook would become dangerously limited and introspective. My last sally took me to Mainland, the largest island of the Orkney group. Not much scope for a horticulturist here, you might think, but you would be wrong.

Because they are potentially so fertile, the Orkneys have been continuously inhabited for a very long time – 5,000 years at least, and man denuded them of their natural scrub covering at a pretty early stage. They are bare and windswept, except where efforts have been made to restore some shelter. I was recommended to visit one such oasis, a quarter acre lying in a slight dip on a cruelly exposed moorland slope. Its owner, a retired Orcadian, has always lived in Orkney and Shetland. He loves plants, but not the flowers that most of us go in for. Dahlias and floribunda roses would look wholly out of keeping with the surroundings anyway.

Edwin Harold (I'm afraid I never gave him my name) was walking back to his low cottage, scythe in hand, across a brilliant green lawn, when I approached. I explained that I was a gardener (I hope I didn't say horticulturist – it is so easy to turn pompous under stress) and had been told of his garden and might I look round? 'Yes, you can go round', he said, with a wave of the hand. We then got talking. Had his lawn once been heath like the rest of the surroundings, I asked? 'When I came here it was all dock-ens', he told me, but before that, yes, it would have been heath. All the scrub surrounding us, now some 8 or 10ft high, had been planted by him, and so the oasis had developed. 'I'll just go in; I might have left the kettle on – and then I'll go round with you.'

I suspect, in fact, that he went in to switch on his waterworks because at the bottom of his garden was a stream, and this he had diverted most cunningly and efficiently to drive a dynamo which had originally supplied him with electricity. Now he was on the mains and the dynamo only did occasional battery charging for a radio. (It always amazes me how the Scots seem able as a natural part of their heritage to turn their hand to any sort of works, including the building or extension of their own homes.)

Bird Talk

Mr Harold put to me several wistful enquiries on what it must be like to garden in Sussex, and I agreed that there was far more scope, but on the other hand the north had its own attraction, which was why I was there. 'I suppose you can grow all sorts of lovely fruits in Sussex', he mused. There was an irony in this which struck home. Not a fruit have we gathered this year from apples, pears, plums, cherries, peaches, apricots or blackcurrants. The bullfinches stripped the flower and growth buds off the lot of them last winter and spring. Only where we had netted was there a harvest. So wasn't he really better off for not even having made the attempt?

I don't believe he'd ever seen a bullfinch in his life. But then that again, I further reflected, was a deprivation in its way. Even the most hardened trappers must be struck by the beauty of this bird from time to time. I pointed to an old nest in his elder scrub and asked him who had tenanted it. A hooded crow. It was my turn to be envious; we never see them at Dixter, and they are such fine birds. For two years Mr Harold had robbed the nest and not allowed a family to be raised, but this year, clearly, he had relented. They had brought off three young. His satisfaction was evident. We agreed that the crow family were an intelligent lot, but mention of the magpie drew another blank. He didn't think he'd ever seen one in Orkney.

Edwin Harold is considered naughty by serious botanists because he tries to establish aliens such as London Pride in the wilds of Orkney. I don't think they need worry. His current protégé in this line is the pinky-mauve-flowered balsam, *Impatiens glandulifera*, whose seeds are carried by water. It has, I told him, taken over the banks of many Sussex streams and rivers. I think he was aware of this potential, but I don't think he realised that in Orkney, where it was only coming into full flower in mid-September, it would never ripen its seeds. His plants were 2ft tall at most and had been given his special care. In Sussex the naturalised plants grow to 6ft without encouragement.

He was most successful with plants that keep their heads down and that can cope with rough grass: the common montbretia, for instance, and *Lilium pyrenaicum*. I have again and again noticed in the north how this lily builds into prosperous clumps under apparently wild conditions. 'But it doesn't flower for very long.' Summer is short in Orkney. The wild screaming of departing terns was a reminder that autumn was well advanced.

60

Perhaps for soft southerners like myself Orkney is only for visiting in its short season, but the vigour of its year-round inhabitants suggests that we are a poor lot, however lush our gardens.

AFTER THE ELMS

All my confrères in the gardening press have been leaping into the breach created by dead elms. Dog don't eat dog, of course, and no names no pack drill, but it naturally strikes me, when reading them, that they should have said this or should not have said that. So now I shall give them the opportunity of murmuring *tu quoque* by airing my own views on large trees suitable for planting (not necessarily within our gardens) in the place of elms that have succumbed.

The subject is large and juicy, and I have no intention of rushing it, but I don't want to cause mental indigestion either in myself or in readers, so shall write on trees when I feel like it over a period. The planting season is, after all, a long one.

The question of expense is of primary importance. If large numbers of a particular tree are required we shall need to resort to a supplier who offers comparatively little choice but at very reasonable price – say up to £1 per tree for specimens 5 to 6ft tall. If a tree is required for a key position, however (and there are many such positions within the boundaries of many gardens), then we shall be prepared to pay a lot more for something rather special. For the more patient of us the possibility of raising our own stocks from seed should not be discounted. This can be much quicker than is generally supposed, and I shall mention some of the possibilities as I go along.

61

One genus to avoid planting at this time is *Zelkova*. It is so closely related to *Ulmus* as to be susceptible to the same dread elm disease. I only mention it because one garden pundit particularly recommended it as an elm replacer, but we must wait until the disease has fully run its course and all our elms are gone – wretched thought. I do so love them.

Obviously one should start with oaks and ash, our basic forest fare. On the whole I should steer off oaks except for special purposes. After all, there are a tremendous number of them around already. However, having written that it occurs to me that most of the oaks we see are already past their prime, so we should really be planting young ones to take their place.

Fall of Honeydew

They are always recommended as the ideal providers of overhead shade in woodland gardens where rhododendrons predominate. The oak's roots (I write of our two native species and their hybrids) are deep and do not much compete for nutrients with the shrubs beneath them. Furthermore their fallen leaves are not large and obtrusive, and they rot down to mould in a reasonable space of time. The great snag is that the honeydew that falls from their leaves in early summer, when aphids are feeding on them, coats the rhododendron and other leaves beneath them, and this sticky-sweet substance is then colonised with black sooty moulds which make the young rhododendron leaves hideous and prevent them from functioning properly.

I have asked a few rhododendron specialists if they have any suggestions of alternatives to the common oaks which combine their virtues without including this fault (some leaves, after all, are distasteful to aphids, as we shall see when we come to the limes) but so far none have been forthcoming. Another essential in this kind of overhead shade is that it should not be too heavy.

An oak that is cheaply available in quantity is the North American *Quercus rubra* (syn. *Q. borealis*), a great favourite of mine; 6 to 8ft specimens are quoted by a nursery in my neighbourhood, at £1.80 each for ten or more plants, and cheaper still for 50 or more. It is easily raised from seed, and Messrs Barilli and Biagi of Bologna, whose seed list I once devoted an article to, offer acorns at 25p per lb.

This is a large-leaved oak of singularly fresh yellow-green colouring in spring, and a marvel at that season when partnered with a purple beech. It is really fast growing on decent soil; too fast for its strength sometimes. The red oak is handsome in autumn too, but takes on nothing like the fiery tints of *Q. coccinea* Splendens. *Q. coccinea* is the North American scarlet oak, but it is generally raised from seed, and seedlings vary greatly throughout their lives in the amount of colouring they take on in autumn. *Q. c.* Splendens is a clone whose flamboyance can be relied upon, but it has to be grafted and you have to pay for it. Tree for tree I prefer *Q. rubra*.

If it is only one specimen you are seeking then be a little adventurous. After all, Hillier's of Winchester list scores of oaks, and we should take advantage of this unique quarry, for who knows how long it will last? One I long for when I have the space is the pin oak, *Q. palustris*, another North American with graceful semi-weeping branches and a distinctive cut to its leaves, which are not as large and coarse as in the last two species.

By all means avoid the Turkey oak, *Q. cerris*, which was greatly overplanted by our fathers and grandfathers, and we are now paying the price. In appearance it is without distinction: it is thoroughly unsound in wind and limb and its wood is useless.

So much for the ash!

ROLE OF THE GREENHOUSE

A beautiful plant needs to be seen in a beautiful setting. The setting should not compete with the plant for our attention but it should, as a frame to a picture, help us to appreciate and enjoy the plant.

This truism is never so likely to be forgotten as in the realm of greenhouse plants, and the subject swam to the front of my mind in reading Allen Paterson's 'On the Edge of the Bench' in *Country Life* last month. There he wrote of 'an amateur's greenhouse with its invariable mixture of species, from food plants to ornamentals in every stage of development'. This hotch-potch is an inevitable fact, for the most part. The only exception will be when you can afford two greenhouses, the one as a work place and growing-on area servicing the other, which can then be treated entirely as a conservatory, wherein the contents can largely be changed with the seasons. Every plant can then be required to pull its weight. Even *Plumbago capensis* and *Bougainvillea* Mrs Butt can be grown in large boxes and removed from the scene during their winter's disarray, although it may alternatively be possible to cut them hard enough back to mask them with luxuriant pot plants placed in front of their skeletons.

If I had the sort of house where it was possible to attach even quite a small conservatory to the living room so that it formed an extension of the living accommodation; if I could also site my servicing greenhouse near by so that it was not too great a chore moving the contents of the one into the other and back, always remembering that a greenhouse can be seen from the outside as well as from within and that its style and siting must be such as not to ruin the appearance of your garden; if these conditions could be met together with the cost of keeping the plants comfortably warm, then the two-house arrangement is undoubtedly what I should opt for.

But in the commoner eventuality of only one greenhouse being feasible then I should (and indeed do) use it purely for bringing plants on or sheltering them, to display elsewhere, either in the house or in the garden in summer. It is not fair on a beautiful streptocarpus, let us say, or a pan of pleiones, to expect to enjoy their flowering on a greenhouse bench where they are surrounded by endemic clutter.

My greenhouse is working hardest in winter. Under the benches are stored dormant or shade-tolerant plants that might not be quite safe left out: *Salvia patens*, zantedeschias, *Cyclamen libanoticum*, pleiones, *Galtonia viridiflora*, and others. Old fuchsias go into the cellar but would otherwise be here as also is the case with cannas and dahlias.

Light-demanding Refugees

On the benches are other, more light-demanding refugees from cold, but even more important are the many cuttings that were taken in the autumn, 7 to 15 to a 3½in pot. They will now be potted individually and transferred to cold frames until ready for planting out or into tubs and ornamental pots. In the latter category there are the shrubby apricot-flowered *Mimulus glutinosus* and its copper-toned variety Puniceus; trailing *Helichrysum petiolatum* (together with its variegated and lime-green cultivars) and *H. microphyllum*; pelargoniums, notably ivy-leaved types and Crimson Unique; the prostrate *Verbena peruviana*, with scarlet flowers; *Cuphea cyanea*, of an upright habit but much more intensely orange-coloured when its roots are restricted by tub competition; *Convolvulus mauritanicus*, as good a trailer in an ornamental pot or front-of-border plant, flowering non-stop for five months. This long-flowering propensity is, of course, a primary virtue in all half-hardy or hardy-on-sufferance bedding perennials.

Then there are gazanias, of which you can retain the most strikingly coloured and marked only by rooting them from cuttings each autumn. They are not entirely frost tender, and the young plants that I am potting individually now can be safely planted out any time in May. It is the same with the blue daisy bushes *Aster pappei* and *Felicia amelloides*. Best of the bushy, white-flowered chrysanthemums that do not look like chrysanthemums and that include the Paris daisy of London window boxes is the glaucous, filigree-leaved *Chrysanthemum foeniculaceum*. And there are dimorphothecas, trailing or bushy, and a tender lavender for which I have a soft spot, *Lavandula dentata*. Its leaves are deckle-edged and have a different aroma from lavender hedges, and its flowers are borne continuously.

Other greys besides the helichrysums include *Artemisia arborescens*, which can make a huge perennial shrub against a warm wall but is also useful for bedding at a modest 2ft level. Also *Senecio leucostachys*, to which the same comments apply although it is more rambling in its activities. *Centaurea gymnocarpa* is more compactly bushy, and its long, lacy leaves are quite the most distinguished of all the greys, never looking confused.

If for every square foot of greenhouse bench you allow yourself three of cold-frame space, you will have no regrets. Cold frames are invaluable, especially those with solid walls that retain heat at the end of the day.

– April 7, 1977 –

POSITIVE MOANING

Those connected with the land who make a profession of moaning about the difficult conditions under which they labour, are a very great bore. I try not to fall into the same easy, negative ways, but there are times when conditions in the garden strike me as spitefully awkward. There have been so few days without rain for so long – and even now that the wind has shifted north the rain continues – that water lies at or near the surface of our clay-based ground even on quite steep slopes. Though we have laid emergency drains in a number of places, drainage remains a dominant problem and many fleshy-rooted plants like platycodon, the balloon flower, and incarvillea, which cannot bear to sit in water, have rotted.

There are gaps in more than half our globe artichoke plants (three longish rows of them), not because of any cold we have sustained – it has not been a hard winter at all in the south east – but because of rotting, and as for the lawns, I have never seen such a mess. They will look better when they are mown; even the moss will look better then, but we have not been able to get on to them with a mower for six months. Always, hitherto, we have mown right through the winter, with 6- to 8-week gaps.

As for weeding, one's attempts are ludicrous. You cannot get any leverage on the soil. Even a broad-tined fork goes straight through without resistance. A trugful of weeds culled with the tip of a trowel is a trugful of very heavy, wet mud. Undoubtedly, wherever the practice is feasible and you are digging a fairly uncluttered piece of ground, it pays to turn the weeds in, which obviates carting away loads of mud – soil, in normal weather – from where it is wanted to where it is not. In farming terms, the practice would be called green manuring.

As though we had not difficulties enough, we are now hamstrung even on our rubbish dump, where a blackbird is nesting and already has fledglings among the tree and shrub prunings. No bonfire till that is all over.

There are some prunings of evergreens which it is well worth saving. They make an excellent adjunct to arrangements in

67

which daffodils predominate. I never enjoy arranging daffodils; they will only look in one direction, invariably the one in which I do not want them to look. Furthermore their foliage is hopelessly inappropriate as a setting for their flowers. Gertrude Jekyll recommended wild arum leaves for this purpose, and they certainly are very good if you have first taken the trouble to condition them against wilting.

Birds Seeing Red

Of the evergreen shrubs, I particularly like mature branches of ivy with rich yellow daffodils or jonquils, especially if the ivy is laden with ripe berries, as it now should be, but the birds (birds again) have been at them. If red berries are supposed to be red so as to attract the birds, surely birds should be unable to recognise a berry that is black. But they do. There is neither justice nor logic in nature. Meantime the red berries on my female skimmias are as gleaming and fresh minted as they appeared six months ago, and are looking particularly fetching if incongruous, just now, interspersed with bunches of white, scented blossom.

But I was saying about evergreen foliage for the daffodils. *Bupleurum fruticosum* is first rate. This is a shrubby evergreen member of the cow parsley family and it makes 2 to 3ft young shoots of glossy, round-ended leaves that are best cut back now to keep your plants reasonably shaped. In cutting, a pleasingly sharp and astringent odour will be conveyed to your nostrils. Hebes that have got out of hand may need drastic treatment now, and the whipcord types look well with flowers. All leafy sprays from *Danaë racemosa* can be removed now, as its young asparagus-shoots push up. It is a splendid foliage plant in damp shade, with shining foliage of a warm green colouring.

Then, pittosporums. *Pittosporum tenuifolium* is the one you are most likely to have, and it is notably useful in floral art (what a nauseating phrase). I am training my specimen as a tree and have removed some lower branches, which came in apropos, but it also makes a first-rate clipped bush. You can clip it now or you can wait for a few weeks until their chocolate-coloured flowers are opening, and then enjoy their scent indoors. If you do enjoy their scent, that is; I find it coarse and rank, like stewed cocoa.

Bamboos are useless as cut material, yet this is the time for sorting through your bamboo clumps, a task that is far too seldom performed. Left unattended to, bamboos become clogged with an unsightly, tarnished clutter of old canes that do not actually die but limp along. With dwarf kinds like *Arundinaria auricoma* and *A. variegata*, the best policy is to cut the entire stand right to the ground. With bigger, clump-forming types you can remove all canes that are older than two years. Indeed, with my *A. falconeri* I have just removed all but three of its 1975 canes, leaving a healthy colony of 9ft long almost unleafed, as yet, canes from last summer.

— June 16, 1977 —

LINGERING LEGACIES OF LAST SUMMER

My garden is still far from reaching its best in early June, and that probably holds good for most gardens. It is better to look forward, with new plants coming on all the while, than to have to look wistfully back.

Legacies from the extraordinary heat and drought of 1976 are still with us. Everyone wondered, as our *Choisya ternata* all flowered themselves silly last autumn, for the second time in one year, whether they would have any flower buds left in store for May–June 1977. Half a crop seems to be the general experience. My bush has blank patches but is free on others. If we get another

69

hot summer, however, we shall doubtless have a second innings this coming autumn.

Daffodils were not the only bulbs to flower with exceptional freedom. Tulips did also, but what with much cold in April and May, accompanied by a little rain on most days, tulip fire, caused by the fungus *Botrytis tulipae*, has been very bad, shortening the display in many cases almost before it began. It would be wise (but how many of us are wise?) to lift the bulbs now, dry them off in a shed, cleaning them when they are dry. Then to plant them in a new site in the autumn (if the mice have not eaten them in the meantime), first rolling them in a large bag with a fungicide powder.

Another bulb that has given exceptional value is *Camassia esculenta*, which grows and is coloured like a bluebell but has star flowers. It colonises splendidly in rough grass and has suffered from none of the blindness to which it is sometimes prone.

The blossom on whitebeams is less spectacular than some because its whiteness is not pure but tinged with cream. At close quarters, however, you can appreciate the harmony of blossom and young foliage, so wonderfully silver on its undersurface. I strongly recommend *Sorbus mitchellii*, if you are wanting to plant a whitebeam. It has great vigour and carries enormous orbicular leaves, and these retain the silver on their undersides right up to leaf fall. Actually the size of the leaf does diminish when first youth is past but remains impressive, and the tree will grow to 60ft in time. Mine set some fruit last year, each of which contains one seed. Romke sowed a few forthwith and they germinated promptly this spring.

Corokias have made a special effort this Jubilee year. They all have star-shaped yellow flowers of no great size but telling when massed, and anyway the shrub itself has character. This is most intriguing in the best-known species, *Corokia cotoneaster*, called the wire-netting bush, for its thin branches are all twisted and turned like scrumped-up wire. Ours has grown in the darkest, draughtiest spot in the garden since the 1930s, so I rate it as out-and-out hardy, although a New Zealander.

Chocolate Scent

As a shrub, *Corokia* × *virgata* is more beautiful and stately, upright of growth to 8 or 9ft and always pleasing with its small evergreen leaves, grey underneath. It carries orange berries in autumn but just now is seething with blossom, and I had never noticed before what Romke and I have both been made strongly aware of this year, to wit its delicious chocolate scent, most notable at breakfast time, disappearing in the heat of the day. At first I thought I was smelling our *Pittosporum tenuifolium*, which flowers at the same time and is about 20 yards distant, but that has a much ranker scent.

Then I have *Corokia macrocarpa*, from the Chatham Islands, and this has the largest flowers of the three, so densely set this year that they make a thoroughly effective display. Whether it will be hardy in a really cold winter, I cannot yet say, as I have only had it ten years or so and there has been no winter to cry over since '63.

I do think that shrub roses and camellias combine well in large plantings. Camellias provide substance and evergreenery, and the roses take over for a summer display. There has been some overlap this year and *Camellia japonica* Mercury, with large red flowers, is competing with its neighbour *Rosa rugosa* Scabrosa, which is brilliant magenta. The effect is so excruciating as to be quite funny. Surely camellias have no right to be flowering in June?

The large-flowered clematis are starting their main season, and as usual after a cold spring the first flowers on many cultivars have a strong green tinge and little colour. This is disconcerting if

71

you are not expecting it, but successive flowers will come nearer and nearer to the colours you were expecting. There is not really too much to get worked up about. It is sometimes recommended that a dose of potash will put things right. If you feel better for having made some active contribution, go ahead and put on the potash, but there is no evidence that it makes any difference.

Last year, after my double-flowered Vyvyan Pennell, which I grow on a pole in the Long Border, had finished flowering, it looked rather scruffy, so I cut the whole plant back to within a foot of the ground. That was in early July. It had the rest of the summer in which to make good with new growth. Despite the drought but helped with some watering, it refurnished reasonably well and is about to make a good display.

— April 27, 1978 —

MOSS AND MAGNOLIA

In the second week of this month, when the weather was being particularly vile even for fickle April, I visited The Savill Garden in Windsor Great Park. I had left home in heavy sleet and there were showers all day, although they mercifully turned to rain, but the light in between was dramatic and the gardens scintillated.

In pale grey-green, the undulating carpet of white forked moss under the beeches at the entrance was just in prime condition, for even mosses have their seasons. This is a wonderfully satisfying colony; it has perhaps half an acre of ground entirely to its uninterrupted self. All intruders are removed and you could not wish for anything more. Someone had told me, a day or two before, that the moss area had been cruelly encroached upon in order to make room for a new plant sales centre, so I was greatly relieved to find that this was just one of those mischievous untruths which some people rather enjoy telling (I wish I could remember who it was). The moss has neither been molested, nor will it be, as the sales area develops.

Looking down across the valley, to your left as you enter the gardens, is a huge meandering drift of the little pale yellow hoop-petticoat daffodil, *Narcissus bulbocodium* var. *citrinus*. It is one of the greatest sights that you could see anywhere in England at this time. Florists' daffodils in the same open woodland setting would look gross, obtrusive, wholly inappropriate, and yet they are what the majority of gardeners would have planted, given the chance. The hoop-petticoats are natives of Iberia but so natural do they look in The Savill Garden, that it is only with a wrench that you force yourself to realise that they cannot be wild but have been naturalised. In other words they have been given a jolly good start and then allowed to seed themselves and do the rest, which they have, with a will, conditions evidently being much to their liking.

The ground in much of their colony is very wet, as the growth of rushes testifies, and I thought at once how much at home snakeshead fritillaries could also be. But that just showed my ignorance. John Bond (Keeper of the Garden) explained that the soil is far too acid for them. Even snowdrops will not do. Any ordinary sort of lime dressings that you might apply would be a mere fleabite in their effect and as ephemeral. So he is in the process of making a new scree area, in which great chunks of old builders' rubble is being applied as a thick dressing. This really will have staying power.

Exciting Effects

There were two other specially exciting scenic effects at the time of my visit (which followed a frost that had marred or destroyed a great deal of early rhododendron and magnolia blossom). There was a ditch planted with the yellow American aroid, *Lysichiton*

73

americanus, and its substantial vertical spathes contrasted with the globular knobheads of *Primula denticulata* on the banks: especially satisfying because the greater proportion of the latter were the pure white form. The mauves were there, too, in a patch of their own, and worked in well, but yellow and white is a particularly agreeable blending of flower colours. I love doing large flower arrangements in early summer with yellow flag and Dutch irises, branches of *Piptanthus laburnifolius* with yellow pea flowers and white water dropwort (*Oenanthe crocata*), a substantial member of the parsley tribe, yellow Spanish broom (*Spartium junceum*) looks good in early July with white *Philadelphus* stripped of its leaves. Why have I never seen a yellow-and-white border (or borders) in anyone's garden? Someone must surely have one; it would be great fun to do.

Of course, it was the form as well as colour of arums and primulas that set each other off, the more so as neither was diluted with foliage, which develops after flowering.

The other stunning 'effect' (in quotes this time) was a weeping willow, on which every raining wand is now picked out in yellow with only a touch of green, side by side with an Asiatic tree *Magnolia, campbellii* subsp. *mollicomata*, covered on naked branches with pale pink, waterlily blossoms that had largely escaped the frost.

It would be a challenge, come to think of it (and I tend to reduce my scale to border terms when I start thinking), to do a border in yellows and pinks. You'd have to be terribly careful in your choice of plants because no two colours can quarrel more violently if you get them strong and wrong. But pale, really pure pinks without mauve in them (and one might even get away with a bit of mauve, now and again) next to pale sulphurous or greeny yellows, could work out a treat. Perhaps I may return to this theme in more detail, sometime.

Visiting a good garden always sets a whole series of trains of thought in agitated motion. You find yourself really living, instead of ambling along in a routine existence. The right companion is also an enormous stimulus.

HARSH AND NASTY OR NICE AND BRIGHT

The endlessly fascinating subject of colour in the garden reared its head at me again, recently, in a letter from an American correspondent. It was a warm and generous letter, following a reading of my book, *The Well-Tempered Garden*, but I had hurt her a little in this one matter: 'In your discussion of flower colors in the garden, I thought I detected a tinge of disdain in your attitude towards oranges and reds, particularly those of marigolds and salvias. You referred to them as coarse, vulgar, harsh, etc. We all have personal preferences in color but that seemed rather a strong indictment. Here in northern Ohio on Lake Erie, our winters are long and dismal with snow that lingers forever to become dirty gray patches, so we welcome these bright colors when spring finally arrives.'

Very understandable and, I believe, a fairly general reaction. In Finland, for instance, where the scope of gardening is anyway much restricted by the climate, a bedding-out blaze is the general rule, during their short growing season. We are particularly lucky in Britain to be able to choose between so many styles of gardening and from so wide a range of plants that adapt easily to our climate.

I have no hang-up, no block in respect of any flower colour, be it orange, red, yellow, pink, white, blue or green. Not to mention my beloved mauves and magentas. If the plants and flowers that wear them are good of their kind. I love all these colours.

75

The disdain, which I cannot altogether deny, is towards their presentation. The plants producing them have been asked, by the breeders, to please us with the maximum possible brilliance to the square inch; slabs and chunks of colour on a plant that is much reduced in size. This in itself has a condensing effect so that flowers are more closely set. The plants are easily managed without support. Uniformity has become a criterion of excellence. If each plant can look exactly like its neighbour the eye is not distracted. We can then make patterns with our flowers, as is found in the most highly organised displays of bedding out, where geometrical expertise is more important than a love and understanding of plants.

This is where I rebel although, unlike many plantsmen, I do greatly enjoy bedding out of the most original and imaginative kind as I was describing it, for instance, at Kew last summer. The theme in front of the Palm House was orange (with yellow) and blue (with purple). It was exciting because all kinds and shapes of bedding material had been roped in, not only dwarf marigolds but also the tall blue *Salvia coerulea* (*S. ambigens*) which has a completely free, uncorsetted habit. The breeders have never set about improving it.

Plants with Personality

I do not like depersonalised plants. Some of the modern marigolds carry very large flowers on very dwarf units. Useful and showy, their admirers will say, but wholly lacking in balance and proportion. When an African marigold makes a 3ft by 3ft plant, strongly branched with quantities of feathery leaves, then it is perfectly geared to a generous spangling of large double orange or yellow blooms. It is a noble plant of its kind and, when thoughtfully used, will gain my wholehearted applause. For smaller settings there are plenty of smaller-flowered annuals and bedders including marigolds. They can still be bright but every plant needs more than mere brightness to lend it personality.

What, then, of the scarlet salvia encountered in such seedsmen's strains as Scarlet Flash, Blaze of Fire, Hot Shot, Flarepath, Hell Fire, Scarlet Pygmy, Flashing Light, Scarlet Fire, Tetra Scarlet, Tom Thumb Scarlet, Red Hussar, Royal Mountie and Fireball? Brilliance combined with dwarfness is the image these names invoke. All salvias have prettily shaped flowers but here they are too closely set in the spike for the flower to be individually enjoyed. Furthermore the calyx is the same colour as the corolla so that the one is not set off by the other. They just merge. The leaves are unexceptionally large and coarse, as is so often the way. Flower 'improvement' takes little note of what is happening to the foliage.

I should very much like to see *Salvia splendens* in the wild. I should be surprised if it were not an agreeable plant. It is agreeable no longer except as a provider of visual warmth in drab surroundings. If we have a genuine love of flowers we can do better than this and no need to subdue our taste for red. I shall discuss red-flowered garden plants next week. Meantime, who hasn't revelled, during the early summer, in the sheets of field poppies that we still see, even in these days of weedkillers, and especially on new road verges and embankments? Surely the gardener can learn something from them.

— September 7, 1978 —

LOOKING FORWARD TO AUTUMN

After a late spring, summer itself was so cool and cloudy that the season never caught up with itself. This has the advantage, when we reach the autumn, that many flowers are still with us that would normally have faded. To be able to walk round the garden in early September and think with happiness about all the flowers that there will yet be to enjoy is reassuring. I love autumn anyway, with the feeling of quiet and relaxation that it brings, the softness and warmth of its light and colours.

There is spring-like freshness about some of autumn's flowers, notably the colchicums and crocuses. I'm sure we should be growing as many of them as we do their spring counterparts if their prices were as low. *Crocus speciosus*, the easiest as well as the best of its kind at this season, is reasonably cheap, but is never offered at cut prices by the 100 or 1,000. However, its corms do multiply incredibly fast, so you can soon work up your own stocks (mice permitting) and spread it around. Its colouring is more nearly blue than in any other crocus and this offsets a brilliant orange stigma. The scent is of early tulips.

Colchicums have a rosier tinge to their mauve colouring. Having no leaves of their own, they show up best in a background of rough turf, but if you want to work up stock quickly, grow them in quite rich, cultivated ground.

Sternbergia lutea would not cope with turf, and anyway its own leaves appear at the same time as its brilliant yellow, crocus-like flowers. This is no relative of crocuses, however, but of daffodils. If you sniff a broken sternbergia stem you'll find it smells exactly like the daffodils you picked in spring.

Nerines belong to the same family (the plant smells acrid) and there is perhaps no less autumnal colour than that of the hardy *Nerine × bowdenni*: vivid pink with a touch in it of mauve. The lank foliage of these nerines is a bit dreary, by now. That won't matter if they are being grown behind other plants but if fully exposed to your critical gaze, then I can recommend cutting all their foliage away now, before flowering begins. From experience I find that this will not weaken the bulbs.

I have a patch of this nerine behind my autumn-flowering

Cyclamen hederifolium (syn. *C. neapolitanum*), which are pinky-mauve or white, but in practice most of the cyclamen have finished flowering before the nerines have got going. I think a better foreground for the latter might be a Michaelmas daisy of which I am especially fond, *Aster ericoides* Esther. Without in any way creating a dwarf or dumpy impression it grows a mere 15 or 18in tall. Its leaves are tiny and a fresh, invigorating shade of green all through the summer. Then, late in September, the display starts of small rosy mauve daisies on feathery branching stems.

One can, of course, make a great autumn feature of Michaelmas daisies, but I am exceedingly critical and selective in their respect, nowadays. The popular novae-belgiae types suffer from such dire pests and diseases and anyway their season is short and they make dull, heavy-looking plants through the summer months. *Aster amellus* and its cultivars are trouble-free, and I have recently acquired one of particularly sumptuous colouring called Violet Queen. The similar *A.* × *frikartii* has a tremendously long flowering season from early August onwards and is a beautiful lavender shade contrasting well with the yellow daisies that so richly endow the autumn scene – rudbeckias and heliopsis, heleniums and golden rod.

Another aster of which I have a big patch in the same company is *A. sedifolius*, better known as *A. acris* a European species whose spidery mauve flowers are nothing individually but gathered into huge pouffes or sumptuous featherbeds. It grows to 3½ft and is a collapsible plant that requires early staking. It is in full flower now.

Michaelmas daisies and kniphofias look well together, too. The stateliest red hot poker for autumn borders goes by a variety of names, I had always known it as *Kniphofia uvaria* Nobilis but Beth Chatto has the same thing by the better sounding title Prince Igor. It grows 6ft tall and carries substantial orange-scarlet spikes. The delectable *K. caulescens* is September flowering, of softer orange and citrus colouring. The great thing about this plant is its tufts of glaucous foliage on woody stems, but it must have excellent drainage and is not for a clay soil like mine. Beth Chatto's Little Maid is doing splendidly for me, however. It has creamy white spikes, is only 2ft tall and exceedingly prolific over a long, long season.

Of the many other border plants that are still sustaining us, *Crocosmia* Citronella is a robust and hardy montbretia with fresh green foliage and spikes of bright yellow flowers. Solfatare has greater distinction but is weaker growing. It needs good soil; also a sunny position to bring out the coppery colouring of its leaves. These offset flowers of a soft apricot shading. Last year, by chance, a gate-crashing plant of *Codonopsis convolvulacea*, which is a twining herbaceous climber with fleshy tubers, wound its way up some solfatares and was entrancing in their company, with its light blue, saucer shaped flowers.

I find this late-flowering codonopsis a most useful and easy-going plant (so quickly raised from seed to flower). I also have it in large pots outside my porch, growing up a framework. It is perennial and hardy.

Blue is a rare and precious colour in the autumn. *Aconitum × fischeri* is the most useful late-flowering monkshood. Three foot tall and an efficient ground-coverer. The fact that some of its foliage has changed to yellow by the time its short blue spikes open is surprisingly effective.

There are blue salvias, for now, notably the 6ft *Salvia uliginosa*, a coerulean shade, but its name is deceptive as it thrives in light soil (not on my clay) and even then it is wise to lift and over-winter some of it in a frame. *S. coerulea* (syn. *S. ambigens*) is a more intense shade of pure blue. A 3- to 4-footer, self-supporting, it makes large tubers like a dahlia's and can usually be trusted to overwinter outside. *S. patens* is tuberous again and only as hardy as a dahlia. But if you treat it as an annual sowing its seeds afresh each April, its main display will come in now, whereas plants from overwintered tubers will already be looking weedy and straggling.

The hardy, deep blue plumbago, *Ceratostigma willmottianum*, carries heads of disc-shaped flowers on 3ft bushes and contrasts especially well with red-flowered fuchsias. *Caryopteris* are 4ft blue-flowered shrubs and there is little to choose for intensity of colouring between Ferndown, Heavenly Blue and Kew Blue. Good drainage is again essential to hardiness.

Quite a number of wall shrubs reach their peak now. The common myrtle, *Myrtus communis*, with its delicious aromatic scent and clouds of white, bee-attended blossom is my favourite, perhaps because we have such a gigantic specimen. It must be given a warm wall. And so must *Abutilon megapotamicum*, with slender red and yellow lanterns, dark brown stamens protruding.

The twining climber *Solanum jasminoides* Album carries swags of pure white, yellow-centred blossom that is really a great deal more telling than jasmine itself but without the scent. Talking of which, the most generous honeysuckle for autumn flowering is *Lonicera japonica* Halliana, with cream and white flowers but it is a rank grower, and I also prefer the scent of the late Dutch honeysuckle, *L. periclymenum* Serotina, red outside, cream within. By pruning it hard each winter its main blossoming is delayed till about now.

Perhaps, as a postscript, I might add that, as much as any of its flowers, I look forward to the figs of autumn. There is mouthwatering promise of the large Brunswick fig, to come, and this will be the third successive season in which it has done me proud. Yet why in 1978? It's been a funny year. So many gardeners, after ritual moans on its horrors have added, 'and yet my garden has never looked better'. A fine autumn would suit us all, flowers, fruit and fractious humans alike.

MURDER IN THE SHRUBBERY

How much should, or can (if the space available is restricted) a forsythia be pruned? 'Should forsythia be pruned every year?' is the way my nephew puts the question in a letter, and continues: 'Those which I pruned last year have barely flowered and ones I did not prune have flowered exceptionally! It is possible that I might have pruned a little late and severely, but I wonder whether pruning of this particular shrub is really necessary each year?'

Certainly any pruning undertaken should not now be delayed. As soon as the flowers are fading and the shrub is greening up, get into it, if you mean to do anything at all. Then it has the whole growing season in which to make and mature new wood for next year's flowering. 'Mature' is the key word in that sentence. Making new wood requires plentiful supplies of nitrogen, promoting growth in the early part of the season. But as autumn approaches growth needs to come to a stand-still and the wood must harden, ripen and build up its store of carbohydrates: for a high ratio of sugars and starch in relation to nitrogen is a prerequisite to flowerbud initiation.

If you prune too late, the ripening process never has time to take place. By the same token, if the summer and autumn are cool and wet, the young wood won't ripen either, growth continuing far too late in the season. But if the summer was exceptionally hot, you can get away with murder.

The hedge (or hedgehog) treatment of forsythias is uncertain too. Determined that the hedges shall not outgrow their meagre allowance of space and ignorant of any better way to prune them, thousands of gardeners simply set to, about now, with shears or hedge trimmers. The young shoots subsequently produced often flower very poorly but after the baking summer of 1976, the hedgehog treatment paid off as well as it ever can and every rod of young growth was densely set with blossom in 1977.

Forsythias are as sensitive to climate as to weather. Those of us who garden in the south-east can flower any forsythia reasonably well, if bullfinches are not around to thwart us. But because the climate is so much cooler in Scotland and the north, forsythias often need coaxing to make them flower in any worthwhile degree. The best place for them is against a south wall.

On North-Facing Walls

But in the south, the lax-habited *Forsythia suspensa* is particularly suitable to train against an exposed north-facing wall. The ambient temperature in summer will still be high enough to ripen its wood.

Another factor that makes this subject more opaque, is varietal. Some species and varieties of forsythia respond more obligingly to hard pruning than others. Thus Bean, in the earlier editions of his great work on trees and shrubs, told us that *F. suspensa* var. *fortunei*, which is one of the stiffer varieties of the species, can be pruned hard back each spring as soon as the flowers are over. The whole shrub is taken back to a low stump. 'Treated in this way, healthy plants will make shoots 6 to 8ft long in a season, furnished the following spring from end to end with golden blossom.' This interesting detail has been deleted from the lately revised 8th edition of Bean's work.

Given a run-of-the-mill forsythia like Spectabilis or Lynwood in an average sample of British climatic conditions, the best pruning will be to remove some of the oldest branches every year; perhaps one quarter of the bush. These older branches will, in the main, be on the outside of the shrub or congesting its lower centre, while the young stuff that we shall leave has shot up strongly, making the plant's greatest height. We shall, in fact, be thinning out rather than cutting back.

The cutting-back treatment will, however, be dead right for some early spring-flowering shrubs that unequivocally flower for all they are worth on young shoots made last year. Hard pruning of this kind must go hand in hand with generous feeding to make good the brutal removal of so much wood.

The double form of the pink-flowered shrubby *Prunus triloba* is a delight when well grown (against a sunny wall or in the open) and so pruned. No less charming is the double white form of *Prunus glandulosa*, which grows only 3ft tall. The suckering dwarf almond, *P. tenella*, makes a comelier, freer-flowering thicket if taken back annually to 6in or so. Two early spiraeas can have all their flowered wood shortened back as soon as their confetti of fallen petals has showered. *Spiraea thunbergii* is the shorter of them and the earlier; *S.* × *arguta,* called Bridal Wreath, is the showier.

Never believe the often repeated falsehood that *Clematis armandii* should not be pruned. This is the moment and you can be severe. Indeed you'll be only too glad of my permission, for most *C. armandii* took a beating in the winter and are looking horribly dishevelled. You can remove most of last year's growth.

— May 17, 1979 —

BRIDGING THE JUNE GAP

What is this June gap, so often cited in gardening literature, some may wonder. 'Tradescant', writing in last November's issue of the Royal Horticultural Society's *Journal,* doubted if it could really refer to the flower garden at all. But it can and does; the June gap is a failing, or threat of failure, that has to be reckoned with in certain styles of gardening, including my own. It is the gap in flower power that occurs in late May and early June when spring bedding plants have been discarded and the summer replacements have not yet made their mark. Roses are contributing little as yet. Herbaceous and mixed borders are generally planned to contribute the longest possible season at high pressure, which will be from July till September. They will be showing little colour during 'the gap'.

It has traditionally been bridged by four flamboyant hardy perennials – peony, iris, lupin and oriental poppy – backed by lesser lights such as columbines and pyrethrums. Yet it is incautious to lean heavily on these flowers as they themselves leave a complete blank from late June onwards.

The shrub enthusiast may smirk at our problem but his will mature later. Few gardens are duller in summer than those which specialise in azaleas and rhododendrons.

To consider the bedding out aspect of the June gap first. There is no need to adopt the parks and public gardens regime of two set periods, spring and summer. June-gap-bedding displays are easily obtained from summer and early autumn sowings in the previous year. Pansies sown in early August can be bedded out from their seed boxes in March and will be at their peak through our difficult period. The same with Brompton stocks treated as biennials.

I always find it instructive, when seeking hints on procedure, to turn to the RHS reports on trials conducted at Wisley. There they sowed Brompton stocks under glass on August 6, potted the seedlings first into 3in pots on August 19, then into 5in pots on October 27. They were plunged into ashes in cold frames for the winter, planted out where they were to flower on March 31 and inspected in flower on May 5 and 19 and June 1.

The foxglove is a biennial that can be sown in spring or early summer, lined out till the autumn, then planted where it is to flower throughout the following June. I use foxgloves as an early feature in my mixed border and after they have finished, replace with a tall, fast growing annual like cosmos, lavatera, malope, nicotiana or the orange, zinnia-like *Tithonia rotundiflora* Torch.

Biennial anchusas (*Anchusa italica*) can be grown from seed, like foxgloves, or you can propagate them from root cuttings. They are most free-flowering as year-old plants, coming into bloom during mid-May. Each plant should be supported with a cane, for safety. I had them once with the daisy bush *Olearia* × *scilloniensis* (which I shall have to replace, after the last hard winter). Dazzling blue anchusas next to bushes of dazzling white daisies are quite impressive. As the anchusas begin to get stemmy and tired-looking throw them out and replace with annuals.

Sweet Williams tend to flower too late for our purpose except for the early Messenger strain. To pep this up you can interplant with tulips. As there will be a follow-on (say bedding dahlias or zinnias, sown in May), when the sweet Williams have finished in July, you will take three crops in a season from the one piece of ground, harvesting the tulip bulbs at the same time as discarding the sweet Williams.

Sown in early September, hardy annuals such as cornflowers, larkspurs and the delicate flax-like viscaria, in shades of carmine, pink and blue, will be in full flower during the gap. So will *Cynoglossum amabile* Firmament from an autumn sowing. This is related to anchusa but is a lighter, more brilliant blue on 2ft plants. It would look powerful grouped behind the perennial *Lychnis flos-jovis*, which is a foot-tall campion with pure pink flowers above grey foliage, but you would want to move the latter out of the way into a spare plot when making your change-over in late June, as it turns dull in summer.

What can we do about the four flamboyant perennials that I mentioned earlier and which flower during our May–June period? I should use peonies in a spare plot for cutting. If you have room for a peony border that can be sited so as not to distress you later on, well and good. You can interplant the peonies with early spring bulbs like hyacinths, scillas and chionodoxas to provide a March–April display when the peonies' own, fat carmine shoots will add a succulent contribution.

Bearded irises need a border or enclosed area to themselves. Their dreadful appearance after flowering can in no way be mitigated since they need baking by summer sunshine, so nothing of a masking nature can be planted close to them. You could include them in a mixed border of May–June flowers that it is possible to turn your back on in summer and autumn. Perennials like the mauve powder-puff-flowered *Thalictrum aquilegifolium* look well with irises. So do the white-starred spikes of *Anthericum liliago*, which is a kind of asphodel. Aquilegias are in delightful harmony with irises.

There would be scope for a few shrubs such as the rich yellow rose Canary Birds or the paler, softer yellow *Rosa × cantabrigiensis*. The bridal veil-type *Spiraea × vanhouttei* I have seen as a strikingly appropriate background to the white-trumpeted St Bruno's lily, *Paradisea liliastrum*.

But these suggestions presuppose a large garden with scope for an early summer feature whose dereliction later on will bear stomaching. If you must have lupins treat them just as biennials as I suggested for anchusas. Oriental poppies, on the other hand, can be absorbed into a setting where late summer flowers will dominate. This is because they are tolerant – unlike lupins, irises and peonies – of being cut to the ground immediately after flowering. You can site them next to late-developing perennials like Michaelmas daisies or Japanese anemones that will fill the gap, or you can actually interplant the poppy clumps, after they have been cut down, with cannas, dahlias or any other reserve stock.

Indeed, the most valuable June gap-bridgers are those that can either be treated in this way or that start a very protracted flowering season in May. I must mention the vegetable seakale in a border context. It was a favourite of Miss Jekyll's. Following white clouds of honey-scented blossom in late May you cut the plant down and it quickly refurnishes with glaucous, wavy-margined foliage for the rest of the growing season.

Clumps of Dutch irises and also the elegant, magenta spikes of *Gladiolus byzantinus* fit into a later-flowering mixed border on the oriental poppy principle – that they can be cut down as soon as flowered.

Hardy cranesbills are among the most valuable of the stayers, *Geranium sanguineum*, the bloody cranesbill, is excelled in this respect by the even more persistent Russell Prichard, whose season of magenta flowers (magenta again; how I do harp on it) lasts from mid-May till November.

– August 2, 1979 –

WIND, WEEDS AND WATER

We've been watering in earnest for the past 10 days or more. Six thousand gallons a week seems to be the approximate rate. When I warned a friend who gardens on chalk – and chalk dries out twice as fast as my clay – that she, too, needed to be giving her plants water, she remarked resentfully that it seemed to have done nothing but rain so far this year. It did rain early on and everything grew like fury. That growth now needs sustaining. When the weather becomes settled in early July, as it did this year, it generally stays that way for the rest of the summer. Watering is quite hard work even with spray lines and sprinklers, but it's better to have to do it and be able to enjoy some sunshine than to be enduring the misery of wet, wind and weeds.

My weeds are doing very nicely, as it happens, and much of my time is spent chasing them up. The lesser willowherbs are the ones I'm mainly concerned to extract before they self-sow, as they seed by the billion and every one germinates. Unless their stems are kinked near the bottom, they pull out very easily just now, even if the ground is hard and dry. As autumn approaches, however, they make basal, over-wintering leafy rosettes and then become tenacious, so that a levering trowel becomes a necessity if they're not to break off.

Incidentally, I do wish the visiting public wouldn't try and help me by pulling the tops off my sow thistles and then dropping them on the ground. Not only is the pulled-off flower head quite capable of running to seed where it has been left lying, but the stump of the decapitated plant becomes much harder to locate; yet located it has to be and dug out properly, if it is not, hydra-like, to start into growth all over again with numbers of side shoots instead of a single central one. I don't think the aforesaid visitors are really trying to be helpful at all; probably just showing off to friends. 'I know sow thistles when I see them', their gesture implies, 'and it is an insult to my sensibilities to find them in a garden that I have paid to see.'

Weeding in a methodical way is most enjoyable, but if I have it in mind to tackle a certain area, I have to approach it with three-quarters-closed eyes (just wide enough not to walk into a pond or anything silly), otherwise I shall be distracted by other weeds or tidying jobs en route and shall never reach my destination. It's the same when my trug is full and needs taking to the rubbish heap or wherever it's to be emptied. Distractions on the way there or back may prevent me from ever returning. So I'm most reluctant to empty the trug at all. I take the largest one I have and fill it to overflowing till it's so heavy I can hardly move it. I know I should do better to bring a barrow to the scene of operations, but then there are manifold distractions en route to fetching that.

89

Radical Treatment

Of course weeding is much more than just that. As I come to them I'm cutting all my early-summer-flowering cranesbills to the ground, even if the clumps have fresh shoots at the centre. Within a week they'll have refurnished, and some, like *Geranium sylvaticum* Album and *G. grandiflorum* Flore Pleno, will carry a small but worthwhile second crop of blossom.

Foxgloves become derelict before they've finished flowering. A rope of seedpods crowned by a short spike of still-opening flowers looks unbalanced and gawky. In any case a large proportion of your self-sown plants turn out to be the wrong colour for where they are. All such need radical treatment.

Border phloxes can be mischievous. The trouble here is that every root you break makes a new plant. Many such will be outside the margins of your official group, and unless dealt with can easily outgrow and smother the neighbours through which they're shooting.

My pink and grey Versicolor fuchsia are being an awful nuisance. I decided last year that the old clumps had become tired and woody after 20 or more undistributed years, so the Dutch girls who were helping me at the time lifted them all – quite a task as they're very woody and deep rooted – threw away most and just replanted a few. What has happened is that some roots, the deepest, were inevitably left behind. Fuchsias grow from root cuttings but the variegated kinds revert to plain green; in this case to straight *Fuchsia magellanica*, a very dull plant. I've now lots of it coming up all round the struggling, weaker variegated bits. I could move the variegated to another site but I want them where they are. Very vexing.

More intriguing is what's happened, just behind the fuchsias, in the spot where I dug out a plant, on its own roots, of the Bourbon rose Variegata di Bologna, three or four years ago. It used to get mildew badly, and I wearied of this. In its place, a new rose appeared last year, grew strongly to 4ft and flowered for the first time this summer. Instead of being variegated pale pink and carmine, it was pure crimson throughout. Again a self-struck root cutting of the old plant has developed, and again it has reverted to the type-plant from which Variegata di Bologna originally sported.

– November 1, 1979 –

DISAPPOINTMENTS IN SHADE

Recently I was reading an article in *Popular Gardening* (to which I contribute) on 'Plants For Shady Places' and found myself disagreeing with some of the recommendations. Granted that it is always more fun to disagree than to tag meekly along, there is still a point on this subject that is repeatedly overlooked and that needs repeatedly re-establishing. There are plants that will exist indefinitely in shade but, in fact, they are waiting for better times and until those times arrive they are but a shadow of their true selves.

You have only to walk into deciduous woodland and observe the brambles to convince yourself of this. Brambles under a dense canopy of trees are much reduced in vigour, they carry large, often evergreen, leaves but not flowers or fruit. As soon as some of the trees are felled or coppiced, the extra light enables them to grow with renewed luxuriance. They flower again and are visited by the White Admirals, described by Hugh Newman in his recent article in *Country Life* on woodland butterflies.

In the *PG* article referred to above, a glamorous picture of *Symphoricarpos doorenbosii* Mother of Pearl, carrying thick clusters of white berries, gave the impression, in its context, that this is how the snowberry will behave under shady conditions.

91

Whereas in fact it will make a dowdy thicket of suckering shoots that looks worse in its position than would a complete void. An empty house is better than a bad tenant. Only in light conditions will the snowberry flower and fruit to any extent.

Another plant recommended for shade was *Cotinus coggygria* (*Rhus cotinus*) in a purple-leaved form Notcutt's Variety. Cotinus will certainly grow in shade. I saw masses of it in low suckering colonies under oaks in Hungary last summer, but it neither flowered not fruited in such a situation. Where suffusion of the leaf with red pigment is required, as is the case with all purple foliage, the colouring in fact is reduced to a dim and dirty green as in the foliage of a purple beech when you stand underneath it and your main view is of its lowest, shaded foliage.

Variegations can likewise be obliterated in deep shade, as you find with the many cultivated forms of ivy. A sunless position against a north wall will still allow these variegated ivies to show their colour contrasts, provided the sky above is clear of obstacles, but if this, too, is obscured, as under trees, then their foliage becomes uniformly green. I hasten to add, however, that that paragon of spotted laurels, *Aucuba japonica* Crotonifolia, is capable of maintaining a scorbutic complexion under far darker conditions than most variegateds.

Roses and Honeysuckle

Roses are thin and spindly in shade. The rugosa Frau Dagmar Hastrup was recommended in the *PG* article. But the author might have gone to town on climbing honeysuckles. Our woodbine, *Lonicera periclymenum*, flowers freely in woodland twilight. Its flowers are very pale off-white and this wanness has its own appeal. But if it was colour as much as scent that you were seeking, as in the Dutch and Belgian clones, they'd need the light again.

Mind you, honeysuckles are pretty well able to look after themselves and will spiral into a sufficiently light position if their host gives them half a chance. I constantly get self-sown honeysuckles turning up in unlooked-for spots. Mostly they have to be weeded out, but sometimes their choice is brilliant. For instance, one has climbed to the top of my 30ft *Eucryphia* × *nymansensis* Nymansay. The eucryphia only starts performing in August and the honeysuckle provides interest, without occupying extra space, in June and July. Even its red berries are numerous enough to make a worthwhile contribution.

Skimmias are often relegated to shade. They put up with it good-naturedly and become drawn into much larger, looser shrubs than normal. Their leaves are dark green, but their berrying is far from spectacular. Get *Skimmia japonica* into the sun and its growth will be dense and comparatively slow, though attaining 6ft in the long run. Its foliage often wears an unhealthy bleached tone, but this in no way inhibits its flowering and (in the females) fruiting, which will be prodigious in most years.

This is one of the garden's stalwarts. You can fault it – the leaves are an uninteresting shape – but those berries! And especially in low autumn or winter sunshine. What a wonderful, gleaming, energising red, and they sustain us right through till spring, with birds rarely claiming a share.

A true shade plant for which I feel warm affection is *Euphorbia robbiae*, with its dark green rosettes of evergreen foliage that uncoil into pillars of lime-green blossom each spring. But it is a strange plant that resents being taken for granted and neglected. If you just leave established colonies untended, they not only become cluttered with the unsightly remains of old dead flowering shoots; they will actively show their displeasure by dying out in large patches. But if you clear away the old remains and leave space for new shoots to develop, they will repay the attention and give quiet and sustaining pleasure.

ANOTHER WINTER

Winter is the season that nearly all of us look forward to with dread, but when it's actually with us we take it philosophically, getting through each day as it arrives, until there comes one of them when a brilliant shaft appears from the end of the tunnel and we live fully once again. Of course it is the discomforts, even hardships, in human terms that are our main concern. Plants, after all, have no nervous systems; if they die we're the only ones that will suffer, more or less, according to temperament.

After a hard winter like the last, everyone is extra cautious and precautious. Cautious in not having replaced those hebes that we lost in such bulky abundance. It'll take a few years before some gardeners' shattered nerves not to say egos (for those deaths were a personal affront, were they not?) are sufficiently restored, to plant such treacherous material again. By that time, years of potential enjoyment will have been lost.

Those who did replace will be the precautious ones. Elaborate protective scaffoldings and tents will be erected over their charges. If these survive the festival of fungi induced by darkness and stale air, there will be great rejoicings and the operation will be repeated in advance of successive winters until the operator, weary of the effort, begins to ask himself if it was really necessary. He'll read, somewhere, the encouraging information that such-and-such is not nearly as tender as is generally supposed; delightedly he'll have off the wraps. The triumph of bringing a tender plant through the winter with elaborate protection is nothing to the triumph of bringing it through with no protection at all.

How often has one not heard a gardener boasting that he never lifts his dahlias and they always survive? Granted that 'always' is a bit of poetic licence and that slugs will have done for quite a percentage of his tubers, it's perfectly true that many dahlias do survive like any hardy perennial. They may, indeed, benefit from not having to go through the hazards which storage itself so often initiates; drying out and shrivelling, for instance. Many survived in gardens even last winter.

And there were other even more flattering survivals. *Cosmos atrosanguineus* for instance, which, with its tuberous roots, always strikes me as being nearer to a dahlia than to a cosmos. Like the very dark-flowered hellebores that most plantsmen get so excited about, it is one of those thoroughly ineffective garden plants that yet (for some) has irresistible charisma.

Cocoa-scented Cosmos

The flowers are dark maroon and they smell of cocoa, thus recreating cosy overtones of nursery elevenses with digestive biscuits. An old-established colony of this plant at Boughton House, in cold Northamptonshire, only returned to life in June, but return it did.

And in that same garden, as also at Burford House in the Teme valley of south Shropshire (a frost trap of outstanding malignity), *Melianthus major*, that paragon of glaucous, soap-smooth pinnate-leaved foliage plants, came through. In both cases they were deeply entrenched, securely established colonies, and this does make all the difference.

Melianthus is naturally shrubby, but you can forget that as it really makes a comelier and more effective feature if allowed to break from the base or from below ground level each year. However, you should protect its crowns against frost (as also those of the cosmos and of *Erythrina crista-galli* and of any slightly tender bulb like *Eucomis*) with a thick frost-insulating layer of bracken.

If bracken encourages a dank matrix wherein slugs cavort,

substitute with grit: the sort stored for use on icy roads in bright yellow bins that have proliferated all over the Kent countryside.

I regret to record that we forgot to protect both the erythrina and the melianthus in my garden last winter and they were little the worse for it, which proves what we have long uneasily suspected, that negligence often pays.

Let's say that it wasn't negligence but that we were taking calculated risks. If the calculated risk pays off, we can boast, or else shrug it off, if not. But if a plant just dies like that, without our having thought of the possibility, it makes us look foolish. I'm so used to looking foolish (any kind of mechanical device laughs when it sees me coming) that I've given up caring. Even so, I shall protect (when I get around to it) one or two newly established treasures, or take precautionary cuttings where appropriate.

Cleyera fortunei, admired on Hillier's stand at many shows and fallen for at last, has evergreen leaves marbled in green and grey-green, cream margins and, in certain weathers, red rims to these margins. It looks destined for death, but I'd held it in a pot for long enough. I planted it out last spring and it promptly shed nearly all its leaves but it's looking reasonably settled now.

In May I was given a *Mutisia oligodon*, which is an evergreen South American climber with pink daisy flowers – most distinguished and unexpected. That'll deserve a bit of padding in its first winter. And there's a young mimosa and a fremontodendron. But if they should die notwithstanding, the gaps will come in handy.

– February 14, 1980 –

TIDYING WINTER OFF

Spring first poked its nose around the corner on January 29 and 30. Two *Crocus tommasinianus* opened wide and a bright orange

C. aureus, beating *C. chrysanthus* Snow Bunting to it, this year. Even more spring-like was the tame hen blackbird collecting bits of grass from the compost heap we were turning. She's started a nest in the yew hedge close by, silly girl, and the cocks not even singing yet.

It came cold again soon afterwards, but clearly there's not much of the relaxed season left and one makes a list of jobs that have yet to be completed before the spring rush. We've still got bits of ground to dig. Today we're grubbing two lengths of old box hedging. It was planted around 1912 and had become bulbous and unshapely, for box is a soft, spongy sort of shrub. So two Aprils ago we cut it all back almost to the ground, to see if it would break and rejuvenate from old wood. It did up to a point but unevenly.

Box hedging suits this place, but it is an undoubted nuisance, not because of the clipping entailed, which is by no means arduous, but on account of the perennial weeds and fruit tree suckers (from an old pear) that keep coming up in and through it. I am inclined to let the shrubs planted behind the box spread forwards and fill the gap informally.

Then there are a lot of young trees planted in our orchard and other areas of rough grass that need mulching with compost and have to be weeded before they can be mulched. Grass is so very competitive and I'm a great believer in giving any tree or shrub that's planted into turf a good start, in this way. Also their stakes need renewing and an expedition to cut chestnut will have to go forth into the woods.

There's still hedge clipping to be completed and then the yew hedges must all be weeded, where they adjoin rough grass, prior to feeding them with meat, blood and bone compound. We completed the tar oil washes in good time, including some of our mossy, north-facing roofs and also some of the yews whose shoots have become encrusted with lichens. Really the lichens

97

are a symptom of the yews' slow-down of growth in these instances, and that's because of poor drainage, but drainage works are a major operation which we really cannot contemplate at the moment whatever the weather does.

The roses had a tar oiling too quickly done because I'd already pruned them so that's one big job behind me (the Rose Garden alone took me 20 hours). This is just as well as the Long Border and several others have yet to be overhauled. I've sorted through most of the hardy shrubs in them, but the clearing of debris, re-organising of herbaceous plants and manuring can wait till March.

Manure and Weedkiller

I don't use garden compost or farmyard manure, here, because of the weeds they bring in. But the chicken manure rotted into and with sawdust from our deep litter hen-house is ideal for the purpose; light, dry and weed-free. That doesn't mean we shan't be bothered with weeds, alas, and to keep our heads above water in the growing season we are using pre-emergence weedkillers in some borders; simazine among the roses and other shrubs, the less powerful lenacil (which we buy wholesale as Venzar) among mixed collections of shrubs and plants. Some, which are sensitive, we've learned to steer clear of, especially ferns and foxgloves.

Meantime a mild day enabled me to spend a happy session in the potting shed, mainly sorting through and repotting lily bulbs. We were pretty successful last autumn in preventing them from getting over-wet, and so they have mostly come through with a lovely lot of perennial basal roots. The annual stem roots, which are much more fibrous, are dead and can be discarded.

Some lilies have a greater tendency than others to lose their basal roots if wet. Such are the auratums, speciosums and trumpet lilies of which I have African Queen. So I set each bulb, when repotting, on a handful of grit. Otherwise the compost used is John Innes No.3 – the strongest, in fact, but not too strong, Bulbs can be planted a mere ½in or 1in deep, stem roots require no special encouragement. They develop and grow downwards without being told how.

I am becoming increasingly tired of lilies with very weak stems that demand early, thorough and skilfully applied support. I do wish more breeders would consider this point when raising new varieties. Particular culprits with me are Lemon Tiger, Hagoromo, Citronella and Stardust (very like Bright Star). I shall gradually reduce their numbers and give preference to Dr Christopher North's Scottish hybrids, bred near Dundee with special reference to their weather worthiness.

These are sturdy as ramrods and I've added another four to my collection for this season. I would not choose Adonis, which is the only weak variety I've had. The others, started in 1977, are increasing nicely and some, like Minos, carry stem bulbils, enabling you to work up stock very fast indeed.

– April 3, 1980 –

BEATING THE WEATHER

It is hopelessly wet, chilly and depressing again in the garden as I write. Nothing unusual about that, in spring, which invariably disappoints and infuriates because there are so many jobs we long to press forward with. Some of the more fundamental and constructive of these will simply be put off for another year, if we cannot seize a chance quickly now, and that is frustrating.

However, I did get one piece of replanting done on a heavy bit of ground before it sogged up again. To feel that he has beaten the weather is one of the gardener's compensating satisfactions.

I have here a fair-sized group (five plants, to be exact) of the dwarf hortensia Westfalen. In front of it, viewed largely and prominently from descending steps above, I planted two years ago a large apron of *Rodgersia podophylla*. You can never securely predict how a plant will behave in a given position until you've tried it out, and this idea did not work.

The hydrangea, on my soil, flowers a beautiful rich shade of red with very little blue in it (on acid soils it can be violet, which is exciting in a different way). *Rodgersia podophylla* has leaflets about a central axis that are shaped, as its name implies, like a webbed foot. They are reddish on unfolding in spring but, more to the point, they frequently take on a reddish flush in summer if their position is reasonably sunny and this, I thought, would harmonise well with the hydrangeas.

The rodgersias, which make woody rhizomes near the soil's surface, have grown strongly, but even wet soil can dry out at times and one may not be there to apply water at the necessary moment (or one may be thinking about something different). Its leaves scorched in quite early summer and remained in this unsightly state throughout the hydrangea's flowering. In retrospect I realise I should have cut all this browned foliage back to the ground as soon as it became evident that it would otherwise remain an eyesore. A second crop of leaves would have been produced and the plants were quite strong enough to sustain this taxing effort.

Still, I don't want to be forced into repeated salvaging efforts and I asked a friend whose taste I respect what he would plant in lieu. He suggested the water forget-me-not that I was describing in this column a few weeks ago, the pale blue *Myosotis scorpioides* Mermaid. I think that might look rather good so I've planted some pieces but couldn't resist including other oddments.

A finely dissected variety of the common male fern forms a

divide between hydrangea and myosotis. This is *Dryopteris filix-mas* Linearis which I acquired from Fibrex Nurseries (Evesham, Worcestershire) two years ago. The main crown had divided into three, which were easily pulled apart.

A Suckering Peony

I have also made room for a May-flowering, peony seedling that had been hanging around in a pot for too long, the vivid scarlet (not crimson) *Paeonia peregrina*, which you may find listed by nurserymen as Fire King or Sunbeam. The epithet *Peregrina* correctly suggests that this is a traveller.

It has a mildly suckering habit when suited, but I must admit to no great optimism in respect of the peony tribe in my garden, as so many of them are seriously weakened by botrytis, the fungus disease which attacks them in leaf, bud or stem and sooner or later wrecks their constitution.

Hard by, where the fern was growing before I divided it, now appears to leave a blank spot, but it will not long remain so. The border here abuts at right angles on a low retaining wall between flights of steps, and into this wall has self-seeded the goat's beard, *Aruncus sylvester*. It seems just the right position for this voluminously space-consuming plant.

It has fine, boldly dissected leaves and its multiple plumes of creamy blossom are indeed a crowning glory, but only for a week. After that they ignobly turn brown and I remove them. This is really the ideal weed-suppressor if you have a large, rough area near water that would otherwise be colonised by docks and nettles. You must get rid of these perennial weeds first – easiest with chemical weed killers – and then establish your aruncus.

My self-sown specimen is, by good fortune, a male; males have the showier panicles and will not themselves bother you with unwanted seedlings, but the developing seed beads on the females are attractive in their way.

Close to this, but not so close as to be overshadowed, I have *Bergenia ciliata,* whose foliage is in complete antithesis. This is a deciduous species and is, as I write, showing only a series of thick rhizomes, which rise to 9in above soil level. Very soon and unexpectedly they will carry heads of pure, pale pink blossom, the young leaves developing shortly afterwards. These are susceptible to late frosts, but a replacement crop is held in reserve.

The orbicular leaves are enormous, the largest of any bergenia I know, and yet they are soft and furry of texture and not in the least coarse. If you can get it on to a *moist* ledge, this species shows to greatest advantage, but ledges are apt to be dry and in that case the leaves do not develop as they should.

– October 23, 1980 –

CHICKEN-COUNTING

There is no pleasanter gardening diversion than counting your chickens before they're hatched, alias (if you're not of the grizzly locks-shaking, you'll-pay-for-it-later school) pleasurable anticipation. For it is surely a happier frame of mind that looks forward to something that may never materialise than feels that there's nothing, except death, to look forward to at all.

So when I see the next season's or next year's flower buds developing on my shrubs. I think Aha! and my mouth slobbers like the Walrus's and Carpenter's before their feast, and they weren't denied, were they?

This happens to be rather a good year for chicken counting, at any rate in the south. The poor wights up north have had a thin time of it, by all accounts, with early drought followed by rain, rain, rain for the past three months and precious little sunshine to warm their bones or ripen their shrubs' new growth, so perhaps their carbohydrate levels are too low for much flower bud initiation.

I don't know: I am guessing, but certainly down here in Sussex we've had some pretty decent weather since late July, while the rain earlier that month and in June ensured phenomenal growth. At least that's what I put it down to, but some ascribe it to high sun-spot activity. I haven't been sun-spot counting lately, so cannot confirm this.

Anyway, here I am with my dogs, basking in October sunshine on a stone seat in our sunk garden, and the year seems distinctly mellow, yet with that kind of forward thrust that takes little account of 1980 ending, 1981 starting up. The plant world is always on the move.

Perhaps one's first anticipatory thoughts are for magnolias and rhododendrons. Some of these will never fail, and one is grateful to them in a cursory way, while rather taking them for granted. Who could ever expect *Magnolia stellata* to be other than full of bloom in April?

And it is the same with most camellias, though the density of their flower-bud clusters varies noticeably from year to year. But there are other, more special species and hybrids (special because more captious) whose performance is always a toss-up.

I have a *Rhododendron* Polar Bear, a layer given me by a friend, which is now 8ft high and has only flowered well for me once. This year it bore two trusses, last year none. Polar Bear is a large, white-flowered hybrid between *R. auriculatum* and *R. diaprepes* and its average flowering date is mid-August. That, and its wonderfully powerful scent are what really get me, there being few enough such shrubs at that season to make them precious. Its leaves are not inspiriting and its habit is stiff, but once it develops into something like a tree it becomes, in its season, a very exciting object.

Rhododendron Buds

Another intriguing habit in this shrub is the fact that it does not make its new season's foliage and shoots until August and early September, either. And yet by the end of September you can already clearly differentiate, from the fatness or, contrariwise, thinness of its terminal buds, which will be flowering 11 months hence, and which are going to remain vegetative. And there are lots of fat ones. Hurrah! Hurrah! No one shall deny me my gloat.

I know very well that if my Polar Bear received all the water it needed in late summer and at the time of flushing it would flower for me nearly every year, but our ground, although clayey, does dry out at awkward times and it is difficult to reach with irrigation, so the weather must continue to play its enigmatic part.

Magnolia × *veitchii* flowered to beat the band last spring, as already recorded, and I feared it would, consequently, be too inhibited to do much next year but, again thanks to rain and sunshine, it has made new flower buds and new growth, so that its blossom should be plentiful enough, and all the larger for not being crowded.

Of course, with fragile and exposed spring flowerers of this kind, weather at the time of blossoming is all-important: even more so in the snob woodland gardener's forest-tree *M. campbellii* which I do not aspire to grow (sour grapes).

Cornus kousa var. *chinensis* carried few of its white blossoms last June, but is set with plenty of plump, onion-shaped flower buds now. I must remember to cotton my *Viburnum carlesii* against sparrows as soon as its leaves have fallen. Last year I thought the little beasts were looking the other way, but they pecked off the lot, leaving nothing but charred remains. If you thought yours were frosted, I suggest you think again.

Viburnum farreri Compactum has a reputation for shy flowering as do certain of the dwarf forms of large-growing shrubs, for example forsythias. Given a sunny position and a not too dreary summer, I find it reliable, but it has only the one burst of blossom, and that, frequently, before the leaves have fallen. The plant is dumpy like a tea cosy, I fancy its days are numbered.

And I'm wearing very thin in patience towards *Garrya elliptica*, covered with embryo catkins though it may be. The shrub is a picture of introvert gloom from spring to autumn and there's so much of it.

Even in January I can find better cheer than from that. From wintersweet, *Chimonanthus praecox,* for instance, which is carrying a nice quota of its Indian-club buds, and from *Hamamelis mollis*, whose clustered velvet knobs will then expand into yellow antlers.

Even if frost, storm and wrack mar all, there's the comfort that chickens which have never hatched cannot come home to roost.

— November 27, 1980 —

DANGER, PLANTSMAN AT WORK

When you start moving plants around and recreating some patch, gardening suddenly becomes very exciting. Imagination takes over and you have a wonderful vision of how your work will turn out when it matures. Perhaps it does not often turn out that way after all, but sometimes it does and anyway it would be a poor world where hope was not allowed to triumph over experience.

This afternoon's plan (I have now been driven in by early

darkness) originated accidentally. Early this year I bought some plants that were new to me from Washfield Nurseries (Hawkhurst, Kent), that extraordinary quarry for the unusual which you constantly imagine you must have worked to the end of its last vein, only to discover, at the next visit, that by some magic alchemy, everything is fresh and inviting again.

I'm a one-plant man, always being content to work up my own stock from small beginnings until I can make something effective from its increase. And I invariably buy on impulse. Not for me the cool and rational approach. You'll never catch me saying, 'Charming, but I haven't a place for it.' If I like the plant and think I can succeed with it, then I buy and deliberate afterwards.

Often I pot my plants up, pending decisions on their fate. This is not always a good idea. I tend to accumulate collections of potted newcomers; they're not always at the front of my mind when a more permanent place might be found for them, and thus they are sometimes (only sometimes) shelved or forgotten.

The other course is to pop them into the garden, somewhere. If it's where you frequently pass you'll be able, as they develop, to make an assessment of their capabilities. So I had four utterly disparate plants from Washfield Nurseries that February day, and I popped them into a border together, because the ground there happened to be vacant.

There was *Helleborus odorus*, a small plant with one leaf. It is still a small plant with the same leaf. There was *Paradisea liliastrum*, a plant with a lily-like white trumpet flower that I've known for a long time and seen wild on the Continent but have never grown. It has been out of sight all summer, for so long, in fact, that I thought I had a premonition of its demise. So I put a fork in the ground, near where its marking stick and label were, and eased it upwards. A nice young shoot was revealed; I quickly withdrew the fork, apologised and moved on to the third plant, *Campanula punctata*.

Invasive but Fickle

This campanula had flowered in the summer, but I'd already forgotten so much about it that, on coming in, I've had to read it up in Clifford Crook's monograph. From eastern Siberia and north Japan, he says, but, even so, liable to vanish after a hard winter. He evidently lost his after 1939, but before that, it had behaved like quite an invasive, running weed. This was just the way my plant looked to me, making fleshy underground runners. It didn't appear quite strong enough to cope with rough grass, so I've moved it to one of those tiresome bits of no-man's-land, the strip that develops between a lawn and a hedge.

I have long since forbidden the use in my garden of that wicked tool, beloved of so many hack hands, the half-moon edger, but the results of its nibbling before I was in control are still evident.

Campanulas, especially the self-sowing *Campanula persicifolia*, are rather good at occupying such situations and of peering out of hedge bottoms, so *C. punctata* has joined them. Crook says it should be moved in spring and, of course, if its hardiness is in doubt, he's right. Nevertheless I shall sleep well tonight.

Fourth, I arrived at *Polemonium* Lambrook Mauve, a find of Margery Fish's. I hope someone with the fashionable inhibition against mauve as a word won't feel constrained to change it. I suspect they already have. 'Blue Pearl, dwarf and early', in the Bressingham catalogue, might easily be the same thing, or perhaps 'Pink Beauty. Good foliage and purplish flowers for a long time'. Between pink and purple comes mauve, which Lambrook Mauve undoubtedly is.

It is a dwarf Jacob's ladder, only 9in or so, flowering in May. Actually, it has a few flowers now, as is so often the testimony of exuberance in plants that have been newly set or divided and re-set in good ground. We should re-plant more frequently than we do. Valerie Finnis, when I visited her last July, told me that those mixed beds of thrilling goodies (I refuse to call them alpines) that she does so well are at their best in their second year. After their third, they need a complete overhaul.

In front of the polemonium, I had a small patch of the very pale yellow *Viola* Moonlight, an elegant little sweetie that flowers from April till July. The two looked smashing together. What a bit of luck.

The viola had already done two seasons, which is quite long enough. It is best propagated and rejuvenated from cuttings, but I've split the healthiest clumps into two and three and made a 6ft-long, 2 to 2½ft deep patch with Moonlight in front and Lambrook Mauve behind. Not entirely so; a few Moonlight have strayed behind the polemoniums. I know they're short, but we god-like humans look down on them from a great height. Nothing will be concealed from us.

– May 21, 1981 –

FICKLE SPRING

Spring nearly always includes prolonged doses of outstandingly disagreeable weather. This year is no exception, yet every time it happens we feel outraged and personally insulted. When I lift my eyes from writing, I am looking through the windows at *Magnolia* Lennei, and it is very beautiful, with masses of deep pink blossom, but the windows are shut and the sky beyond is grey and watery. Under such conditions one can only enjoy a garden in fleeting snatches.

I am glad for those late tulips that are still in green but that have not been lured into opening yet. The apricot-orange Dillenburg and the parrot Texas Gold are especially useful in this respect. Perhaps when they do expand the weather will have relented.

Pittosporum tenuifolirum is in full bloom with its little maroon clusters that waft such an astonishingly powerful cocoa scent from evening till morning. I'm rather glad it's not a 24-hour effort and that my tree is at some 50 yards remove from our porch, where I most often stand and notice it (invisible round a corner of the house).

Another pungent scent that I find cloying at close quarters is that of the balsam poplar. I like to meet it on a garden visit, but do not want it in my own. The tree is vigorous and rooty and apt to be debilitated by rust. Let others wrestle with it.

Perched on its south-west slope, this garden escapes the worst of spring radiation frosts. Young foliage that has been touched is the gunnera's, *Rodgersia podophylla*, *Daphniphyllum macropodum* and, as usual, poor old *Hydrangea villosa*. But they will soon pull round. The hydrangea can look quite hopelessly blackened and yet still make a fine display in its late summer season. On the other hand it can be killed outright by spring frost, although remarkably winter-hardy, and young plants are particularly vulnerable. A position near a sheltered north wall is as good as any. The long, furry leaves dislike wind from any direction, between spring and autumn.

Bamboos are at their dowdiest now. With *Arundinaria falconeri* I get over this by removing all its second-year, leafy canes, right down to the ground, every April. All that's left are last year's straight, naked rods, some 9 or 10ft long. They have a marvellous texture, so smooth and polished, and their colouring ranges between purple and dark green. Tufts of tiny young leaflets are just appearing at the joints and soon the whole plant will shimmer with delicate foliage again.

It is one of the most elegant species, but none of the hardiest. Mine has a yew hedge to one side of it and a thick espalier pear (clothed in the evergreen *Rubus tricolor*) behind. The canes become very flexible under the weight of foliage and rain, so I tie them loosely (no trussing up) to a post behind the clump.

Running Repairs

The borders are full of lush young foliage. It's as well to see what running repairs may be needed. Bare soil among the monardas, for instance, can be patched up with healthy pieces from some other part of a colony, even though their shoots are quite tall. If too tall, pinch out the tips. By the time they're settled in, new shoots will be breaking from the top of each beheaded stem.

Those lungworts on which we depend for a display of spotted leaves through the summer months – such as *Pulmonaria saccharata* and *P. longifolia* – look tired and stemmy towards the end of their flowering season. It's not a bad idea to cut a whole colony to the ground now and let it reclothe itself with entirely new foliage. You can do the same with brunneras and with *Symphytum*; the comfreys. The variegated *S.* × *uplandicum* is entirely rejuvenated by a cutback when it flowers.

Stachys lanata is now running up to flower in the same way. Since we grow its lamb's lugs as a silvery carpet, the addition of a third dimension can be upsetting. But they are rather beautiful in their pre-flowering state, and I think it's nice to wait, before cutting them down, until the dingy flowers are actually opening. If your colonies need replanting, that's a good time to do it.

I've given up growing this stachys because it gets mildew so badly every summer and it's not a plant I find indispensable. Benlate is very effective against mildew (on clematis, also), so if you badly want your stachys, and can be bothered to keep it in good health all summer, give the plants a good watering with benlate in solution now and repeat it at monthly intervals: half

110

an ounce of the powder mixed to a paste in a little water and made up to 4 gallons.

The new planting on which I wrote at some length in this column last autumn, of *Polemonium* Lambrook Mauve (a dwarf Jacob's ladder) behind the very pale yellow *Viola* Moonlight, has gone adrift because a large proportion of my viola plants are stunted and sick with virus disease. It's no good being disappointed by such reverses, I was probably wrong to divide old colonies rather than replant with young stock raised from cuttings. However, I have some such growing in pots, so the remedy is in my hands. One should always be propagating and rejuvenating. Static situations invariably turn out to be the reverse. Tired gardens have tired (or bored) owners.

– July 2, 1981 –

DOGS ABOUT

After asking me to tell her about my current generation of dogs and suggesting that they be illustrated in *Country Life* (a not very practical proposition, I fear) an old friend of the family, and of my mother, in particular, writes from Somerset; 'Many people seem to think that dogs and gardens don't mix, but they should be converted.'

While preaching to the converted is a delightful self-indulgence, conversion itself is not so easy. We were all brought up with dogs at my home, and yet I have a brother whose antipathy towards domestic pets is clearly physical. It has to be accepted and I wouldn't dream of attempting the impossible task of conversion.

There are many like him, and anyone who starts by disliking dogs can have a field day pointing out their disadvantages. All that we dog lovers can retort in their defence is 'yes, but . . .', and

111

none of our pleading will cut any ice at all. 'Dogs smell. They have disgusting, dirty habits.' 'Yes, but they don't have to smell, and anyway I like their smell and they hate being dirty. True, they eat and roll in rather unsavoury morsels but . . .' And so it goes on.

Yet the other day we had a visiting party of American gardeners, and when one of them said: 'That's the best thing I've seen since I've been here,' she was speaking for most of them (though not, perhaps, for my garden). Up went her camera and she zoomed in on my younger dachshund who was lying relaxed and in a dreamy, semi-conscious state on her bed in the sun (a dog's bed is a necessary piece of gardening equipment in all but the hottest weather), while I was trimming the osmanthus bushes nearby.

Yes, but what are the dogs doing when they're awake in your garden? There's no end to the trouble they can cause. Well, Sweetie Pie is apt to disappear for long intervals, and where she goes I don't really know, but when she returns, she draws attention to herself. 'Here I am,' she says importantly, 'and aren't you lucky. Make a poppet of me as I deserve', and a brief love-in has to follow.

Her mother, Crocus, always sticks near to me, that being her way. She often finds the sun too hot and then disappears into the inner recesses of the nearest bush, there to become too cold and so out into the sun again. Their thermal arrangements seem to be as inefficient as a snake's. There's something distinctly reptilian about dachshunds.

Of course, there are more active garden tasks that also have to be pursued. Digging. Landscape gardening is what this breed is really built for, with their short legs and broad paws. They can move soil with a kind of lazy, unhurried nonchalance, simultaneously using their jaws as grabbers when the going is a bit tough, as in a lawn.

Creative Activities

I believe in creative activities for my dogs. It is simply a question of channelling them in a harmless direction. They usually like to work near me when I'm weeding, and the smell of newly turned earth has an irresistible appeal. How right they are.

And there are certain plants and flowers that they love to eat. Trim is the word, really like I was trimming the osmanthus but a good deal closer and nearer the soil. Short back and sides; very stimulating to neat, bushy growth. Most of all they love eating the hairy bitter cress, *Cardamine hirsuta*, which is picked out of my trug and devoured with relish. What could be more co-operative? But I suppose the main grumble against dogs in the garden is the physical damage they wreak among border plants, dashing about breaking things and treading them down.

As far as standard-sized dachshunds are concerned, I can truthfully claim that I've never had this trouble. You can train a dog to keep out of flowerbeds and borders, but I have never needed to do this. They go into them constantly, but they filter through the plant groups, gently easing the stems aside with their wedge-like snouts. The body follows in due, serpentine course.

I have often held my breath when I've seen the thick barrier of soft vegetation separating my dog from its goal and its clear intention of achieving its object. The great thing on these occasions is not to interfere. If you disturb, or in any way frighten, your animal, it may do something stupid and you'll only have yourself to blame. Just wait, and you'll be surprised at the unseen passages and tunnels that have been explored among the herbage.

The flowers she trod on dipped and rose and turned to look at her.

Well, almost, and dogs are a lot better than Muscovy ducks in the garden, anyway.

Dogs and gardens do mix. Ask any dog. And although I should not wish to upset the cat-loving fraternity or sorority, I must

113

claim that dogs are very much the more controllable pets. The fact that they are mainly diurnal in their habits means that we can see what they're at, while their comparative lack of agility ensures that the dogs in our gardens are mainly our own and not someone else's gatecrashers.

And they do so communicatively enjoy themselves. The swish of claws over daffodil tops as my dogs describe arabesques across our orchard in spring is a sound I should recognise in any guess-what game. Going mad dog, my mother called it.

— July 23, 1981 —

A THREAT OF WORK

The treacherous thought occasionally creeps into me that it would be no bad thing if, instead of writing about the things I should (or you might) be doing in the garden, I got on with it and actually did them.

Those plants I've been meaning to propagate for so long: for instance, the evergreen, self-clinging climber *Pileostegia viburnoides* (a relation of *Hydrangea petiolaris* but less well known). I enjoy its foliage at all seasons, but the plant attracts special admiration each September when covered with a foam of tiny, cream-white blossoms, and I am then asked if I have any stock. I have not, and as there isn't a non-flowering shoot on the plant at that time, it's not in a fit state to make cuttings then, when I'm thinking about it. But it is now, and they root easily (whereas the hydrangea is fiendish, though easy from layers).

And I must make more of my Comtesse du Cayla roses. The few remaining bushes date back 70 years to when the garden was first planted. Not surprisingly, they are weakening, but one very strong specimen, more than 6ft high, has some lovely material

114

on it. The young stems of this China rose are bloomy purple, and the flowers, which are tea-scented, the kindliest shade of coral.

I'm going to scrap my colonies of *Pulmonaria angustifolia*. The flowers are quite pretty, but only quite, and the main point is the elegant and beautifully mottled foliage. This is decimated with powdery mildew. Why struggle?

Some diseases are far worse on some soils than on others. Clay favours botrytis, and this has got into my *Erysimum* Bowles's Mauve wallflowers in a big way. It enters through dead flowering stems, then works back into leafy shoots and branches. Unless you're constantly cutting out infected areas, you can lose a bush in its second year, whereas on a well-drained chalk soil, it'll last five or six years. And yet to listen to some chalk gardeners (they'd be the worst, whatever their soil), you'd think they were the most deprived people on earth.

I long to go on a Roundup round. This is the weedkiller sold to farmers, which you can also purchase in expensive small retail packs as TumbleWeed, and it will kill anything. But you need to go a bit carefully in close country, so as to make sure that 'anything' doesn't become 'everything'. Beth Chatto has told me how she sets about this. She mixes a small quantity in a tin and applies it with a narrow, builder's paint brush, first draining the bristles of free moisture on the edge of the tin so that none drips around. Wearing gloves, she grasps the foliage of each weed in one hand, and wields the brush with the other.

Weeding Acaena

I have in front of me, as I write in the sunk garden, a perfect example of where this treatment might, and no other would, work; an infestation of a creeping legume, *Vicia sepium*, that's rising above and choking a carpet of *Acaena novae-zelandiae*, which is

115

covered with its crimson, young burrs, and which I should hate to lose. At it, Lloyd.

The fish are very active this morning (9.30 a.m.). I'd rather think about them, even though I've no idea why they should be active. Can even a lumbering Far Eastern higoi carp be attracted by the passing fly? I wonder if they will breed this year. They need to. All the youngsters, up to quite a large size, were heron victims last winter and only about nine monster oldies remain.

All the heron deterrents that I've seen, or read about, to date seem to me to be worse than losing my fish on which, after all, my living and peace of mind do not depend. Stretching a cord, or two cords, around the pond's perimeter at heron leg-heights might not be as objectionable as most, but they would still look pretty dreadful around a formal pool, and I can imagine visitors' children charging into them the very first day.

We have at last had the pond, which was leaky concrete, re-lined by Anthony Archer-Wills with heavy butyl. He assures me it'll last for ever. So shall I, at that rate. For years I set my face against any plastic lining, as one sees (or tries not to see) such hideous examples where the lining comes to the surface (it has to do that) and is *not* concealed by the soil or plants that are supposed to do the job.

A. A-W has done a splendid job here, contriving enough overlap of the surrounding flagstone slabs for the lining to be absolutely invisible. The waterlilies were replanted (this was in March) and are flowering away. You'd never think there had been a disturbance.

I've covered the lilies' brick containers with 2in-mesh, brown Nelton. They can grow through this, but the large fish will be unable to penetrate far. All the carp family are devils for burrowing, and before you know where you are, three-quarters of the soil in any planted container has been excavated, and your submerged plants are left with next to nothing to live on at best. At worst they frost away.

A. A-W is also tackling, over a series of visits, the very tricky problem of *Elodea crispa* in our horse pond. I want nothing less than total eradication, since the smallest piece left behind will start our troubles all over again, the water so choked with weeds as to be invisible.

— December 3, 1981 —

AN OLD PLAN RECOVERED

I have been rather thrilled at rediscovering the original planting plan for our Long Border, made, I suppose, around 1912. It was lying in a cardboard cylinder at the front of a drawer that I open every day, but for the last 30 years or so I'd just taken its presence for granted. Then I suddenly wondered if it contained my mother's family tree, also mislaid, and there the plan was.

It is very unlike one of Gertrude Jekyll's, although we are constantly pestered by students wishing to see her work here (a 5th-year architectural student from Oxford rang up only yesterday, but he sounded nice, and didn't mind being corrected on the pronunciation of Jekyll with a long 'e', so he's coming anyway). She never worked at or for Great Dixter, but the contrary has been stated in print and then copied into other books, so I suppose that ghost will never be laid.

Lutyens designed the garden. The planting plan may have been done by a Sir George Thorold (one of the Lincolnshire Thorolds): he certainly had something to do with the garden's early plantings, but I wouldn't ascribe this one for certain. The groupings are all chunky; there are none of the slivers and wedges that Jekyll went in for. And I cannot detect any particular colour scheme, although there do tend to be large associations in whites, yellows and blues. Often it's hard to tell just what the colours were, when you simply read a name, like *Aster* Beauty of Colwall, of a variety long since vanished (though we still have *Aster* Climax, which is on the plan).

The border is 60yd long and was 18ft deep in those days – only 15ft now that the yew hedge backing it is fully developed. There were few shrubs in it, but there were some tree lupins, guelder rose (Sterile), cistuses, *Olearia gunniana* (*O. phlogopappa* now), and three Mme Lemoine double white lilacs, of which we still have one that is a sucker from an original.

The only other plant that is possibly the same, and in the same position as in the original plan, is that marked in as *Eryngium amethystinum*. We now have *E. oliverianum* there, and I suspect that we always did. Eryngiums are not easily moved, and it is much easier to leave them where they are, once established.

Before the First World War we had nine gardeners, so it is not surprising to find that a good deal was bedded annually into the border. There were two large areas devoted to mixed dahlias and many of gladioli; antirrhinums, Canterbury bells, sweet Williams and stocks at the front; *Campanula pyramidalis*, both white and blue, at the back. Presumably the *Oenothera* in the middle of the border was the biennial *O. lamarckiana*.

Perennials in Groups

Otherwise, it was hardy perennials all the way, and this particular designer tended to put in large adjacent groups of different varieties within the same genus – notably *Aster*, *Phlox*, *Kniphofia* and *Helianthus*. I can't see much point in this. A lot of kniphofias together, for instance, don't really help each other. Whether you spread their flowering season or not, there's all that lank foliage. The border tries to cover far too long a season to be effective, from doronicums in spring to *Pyresthrum* (now *Chrysanthemum*) *uliginosum* in October. The latter is the sort of perennial that few of us want nowadays anyway, growing to over 6ft tall, requiring meticulous support, and then flowering for only a fortnight.

Many of the ingredients had disappeared before I began to take notice in the 1920s. Hollyhocks have never done well at Dixter. For reasons I should like to understand, rust takes them (and antirrhinums, since the early 1930s) much worse in some country gardens than in others. Each group of dahlias had a group of the zebra grass, then called *Eulalia zebrina,* but now *Miscanthus sinensis* Zebrinus, behind it. Gardeners like Jekyll had made this fashionable, but my father cannot have liked it. I never saw sidalceas, *Spiraea* (now *Sorbaria*) *lindleyana, Centaurea ruthenica, C. macrocephala, Phlomis* or *Dielytra* (*Dicentra*) *spectabilis.*

There were oodles of peonies, which have steadily been eroded so that not one remains. Disease is their bane, and, anyway, their flowering season is too short. So, too, with bearded irises. Two montbretias, then *Tritonia*, were grouped side by side. It was interesting to note that one of these was Solfatare. With its bronzed leaves and apricot flowers, this is still attractive, but weak-growing and needing the strongest soil. Sited 9ft in from the border's front, I'm not surprised it soon vanished. *Geranium ibericum* was also in this submerged position, with a tree lupin on one side, *Campanula pyramidalis* on the other, and six (presumably herbaceous) *Phlomis* in front. Someone wasn't too familiar with his plant material.

The border looks totally different now, even though I still include phloxes, monardas and perennial campanulas. You can see it illustrated in comparatively recent garb in Mark Girouard's *Life in the English Country House,* with the caption: 'A mediaeval house embellished by Lutyens and Jekyll in about 1910.' Perhaps when I'm dead someone won't be ashamed to ascribe the planting to me, though I'm proud to acknowledge my debt to the

Jekyll heritage. We move on, and Miss Jekyll would have been working very differently had she lived now.

— July 15, 1982 —

IN NORTHERN GARDENS

Returned from Scotland, my notebook is crammed with jottings on things seen in many good gardens visited. It's marvellous, I must say, to be in a profession that is also your (and many other people's) favourite hobby. There will never be a shortage of gardens to look at and learn from, and Scotland is remarkably well off. The style is different from ours in the South, and that in itself is stimulating.

Blue poppies, for instance, are everyday perennials. They make fat clumps, and if you want more you have the alternative of seed or (far quicker and more reliable where a specially good colour strain is in question) simple division. Of the two most grown species, *Meconopsis grandis* makes the better bedding plant. Most of its growers would be horrified to have it so described, but it seems to me to have the soul of a bedder: stiff, large-flowered, flaunting. A spaced-out row that I admired, showing its heads above a low stone wall, looked just right as a feature near a house. Colour varies. If you're not fussy, there will probably be mauve in the blue. If you are, pure electric blue strains are available, notably Branklyn. It is a colour, found also in hydrangeas, that slightly disconcerts me.

M. betonicifolia has more charm. Its habit is looser and informal; the flowers less large and a kinder shade of blue. A friend on the Black Isle, north of Inverness, has established a splendid colony in a newly formed woodland garden. She made a bed up specially with humus-rich fare, but the poppies are self-sowing

120

outside their compound, so it looks as though they'll naturalise like primulas, if weeds can be kept at bay.

Mistakenly, as her husband pointed out, she has planted bugle, *Ajuga reptans*, next to the meconopsis patch. Bugle is all very well in its way, but its stoloniferous habit makes it root through neighbours in the style of creeping buttercup. This sort of competition is hard to combat, especially as bugle self-sows freely and is always staging a comeback when you thought you'd won.

Ajuga pyramidalis is far better behaved, not having a stoloniferous habit, and it is showy in late spring with heads of purple flowers. My friend had it mixed up with semi-naturalised pansies. I saw pansies and violas growing in this do-it-yourself way in many Scottish gardens; for instance, a white one climbing into the pale grey leaves topped by yellow flowers of *Achillea filipendulina* Coronation Gold. Violas have the knack of making a border look settled and established, even though it may only be two or three years old.

Purples in shade

I saw the purple-leaved *Cotinus coggygria* (*Rhus cotinus*) in several contexts, too. Royal Purple and Notcutt's Variety are the most intensely pigmented clones, and they have the particular advantage, shared by few other purple-leaved trees or shrubs, of retaining their colour even in partial shade. This was evident along the side of a tall Victorian building, belonging to Edinburgh University, beside the modern units in its Pollock Halls of Residence. It was a planting of purple-leaved berberis (probably *Berberis thunbergii* Atropurpurea), *Senecio* Sunshine (*greyi* or *laxifolius*) and the cotinus. Because of the building's shadow, the berberis were showing too much green through wan purple foliage, but the sumach was as rich a purple as you

121

could desire. In the north it grows less luxuriantly than down south.

Another way I liked seeing it used was as a background to a variegated *Hosta*. *H. undulata* Univittata, whose foliage was pushing through the sumach's lowest branches, and again, interplanted with *Dierama pulcherrimum*. The wand flower has pink or magenta bells which look super dangling over and above the dark cotinus leaves, but you need to keep the dierama clumps as discretely free of dead and dying foliage as possible.

The Chilean Fire Bush, grown in its hardiest strain, *Embothrium coccineum lanceolatum*, is still a somewhat tender tree-shrub, but on the Black Isle, it remained untouched after last winter and was covered in its startling mantle of scarlet when I saw it. But it was growing in front of a wall which offered protection. The wall was white-harled and made a wonderful contrasting background, a good deal more flattering than you see in the usual mixed woodland setting.

Even farther north there is an east-coast garden, Geanies, near Tain in Easter Ross, that should not be missed if you can make it for its opening on behalf of the Scottish National Gardens Scheme, on Sunday, July 25. The garden has been in the same family for some 150 years, and shows all the marks of loving affection that sometimes comes of continuity. But alas, the exigencies of death duties necessitate its sale, so I may have seen for the last time a garden that I have taken to my heart over the past 15 years.

An astonishing number of shrubs flourish here. Although North Sea winds can be cruel, snow and frost are never of long duration. *Buddleia colvilei, Carpenteria, Abelia floribunda, Crinodendron, Desfontainia*, several eucryphias of tree-like proportions, and many others of comparable hardiness, all do well. Then you can walk along the sea cliff and look down on *Martensia maritima* making a blue ribbon just above the tide line, while fulmars hover in front of you, waiting to be photographed.

THROUGH A FRIEND'S EYES

Although I make no serious attempt at tidying my garden until early spring, when the days are longer and the weather less inclined to interrupt you, there is always much to enjoy in winter. I was interested in the plants that struck Romke, once head gardener here for three years but now starting a nursery in his native Holland. He was over for Christmas, which was mild and dull. This was by no means depressing, but brilliant sunshine on December 28 was immediately lifting to the spirits.

Romke used to be anti-aucuba – the spotted kinds – but has come round to my favourite *Aucuba japonica* Crotonifolia and noticed how cheerfully it shines when its leaves are wet and there is little light about. The plain green Lance Leaf behind it is looking good too, with a generous crop of berries coming on. Crotonifolia is the pollinator.

Within the same grouping under a magnolia is *Danaë racemosa*, another excellent foliage plant, glossy and green. For the first time, last autumn, this bore a few of the bright orange berries that I should so like to enjoy on it as a regular and bountiful crop. I fear, however, that our cool summers are the reason for its light and irregular cropping.

It is the same with *Nandina domestica*, a handsome member of the *Berberidaceae* with large, compoundly pinnate, evergreen leaves that are purple when young. Its trusses of white flowers are pretty, but they open too late, in autumn, ever to set the crops of fruit that pictures of this shrub from abroad sometimes mouth-wateringly display.

Spindles – all the berrying kinds of the *Euonymus* – were particularly free last autumn, and even my *E. fortunei* Vegetus carried a few. I have this in its bushy adult state; its sparse and sinuous growth, to 4ft or so, is unusual and attractive, always thickly set with tiny, green flowers in May, but nothing comes of them. Yet even in Holland the summers are continental enough for a Boskoop nurseryman to be encouraged to mention its 'orange-red fruits' in his catalogue, while Vegetus Cardinal is principally distinguished for its fruits.

I was glad that my adult bushy form of *Hedera canariensis* Variegata gave Romke so much pleasure. Even though its flowers, which I mentioned in November, are finished now, their structure remains, and the whole plant is singularly cheerful.

The *Phyllostachys* group of bamboos are particularly good, too. Not a scarred leaf to be seen on any of them, as yet, which is more than you can say of the arundinarias. I think perhaps *P. nigra henonis* is currently the most presentable. Its leaves are small but abundant on an 8ft-tall clump that retains its elegance by remaining very narrow at the base.

Long-flowering Grevillea

Grevillea sulphurea is such a nice shrub. Romke has taken a young plant back to Holland. He hasn't seen it there, and it may not be hardy enough, but it may. So often one takes the tenderness of plants like this (belonging to the Southern Hemisphere *Proteaceae*) for granted, without giving them the chance to prove otherwise. Its needle leaves are always light, fresh green and the shrub, now 6ft tall, has a pleasing habit.

At their base the branches have a tendency to grow outwards before rising vertically. Its main crop of pale yellow flowers (already distinctly visible as tight bud clusters on the shoot ends) opens in May, but it is never entirely out of bloom from then to the year's end. Propagation by stem cuttings of young shoots is not difficult, but they should be taken singly in small pots, as disturbance of their young roots causes instant death.

The hard shield fern, *Polystichum aculeatum*, is one of my handsomest at the moment. I brought it home from a wood in Northumberland. It now grows under the deciduous *Escallonia virgata*, and this protects it enough to prevent its fronds from being scarred by frost.

Next to it is a clump of *Arum creticum*, the sharp outline of whose leaves takes the eye for months before its yellow flowers expand in early May. This is one of those Mediterranean plants whose growing season starts in the autumn and ends in late spring, instead of the other way round. Others are *Arum italicum* Pictum (the flower-arranger's darling), *Allium neapolitanum*, whose pearly white flowers open in May, *Cyclamen hederifolium* and *Geranium malviflorum*, better known as *G. atlanticum*. The palmate leaves of this cranesbill are particularly fresh just now. You might expect any of the above to be seriously damaged by hard weather, but they seldom are.

I fell, the other day, for a tree heath in a friend's Kentish garden, where it sows itself around; the reputedly none too hardy Portuguese *Erica lusitanica*. Bean says it can flower as early as January, but this colony was already making a show before Christmas. Long upright columns of white, with very fine, light green foliage. What a pity there aren't more hardy tree heather species.

– May 19, 1983 –

SUMMER OUTINGS FOR CONTAINERS

Plants grown in containers for decorating porch, courtyard, patio and various key points in the garden give a specially voluptuous feeling when we enter upon the summer season. The fragility of hisbiscus and morning glory are just what we need now to create an atmosphere of relaxed luxuriance.

Personally I never want to use my containers for decorative purposes except in the summer. If they are movable, I'd rather clear them out of sight for the winter months (they go to my cellar and force roots of seakale and chicory). If fixtures, a lead tank, for example, they are probably enjoyable as ornaments in their own right. Having appreciated them as such from November to May, we shall not, I hope, resent obliterating their exquisite workmanship for the next five months with plants that will surge and flow in every direction – horizontally and downwards as well as vertically.

Before you launch into this kind of gardening, one or two basics need to be recognised. The more height your plants make in their container, the greater will become its instability. I lost yet another terracotta pot last autumn, that my parents bought in Italy 70 years ago, because it blew over. My fault, I know, but I must in fairness to myself add that the base of these pots is too narrow to sustain their height and width at the top. I have lately bought some replacements that are better designed and proportioned, with broader bases. They are supplied by Ann Redington, who has a range of terracotta containers which are a mellow colour even before being weathered. The one I particularly like is decorated with embossed swags, but is not in the least fussy.

I talked to a paying visitor last year who, after kindly observing that, of course, it wasn't fair to visit any garden in September (I had thought mine was looking rather nice up till then), waved at my plant-filled containers and said airily, 'I suppose once those are planted for the summer, they look after themselves.' 'On the contrary,' I replied (with a certain relish), 'they have to be watered regularly *every day.*'

It is true that you can grow container plants, like the succulent sempervivums, that need no watering, but the soft, lush kinds that epitomise the summer season are also those that lap up the most moisture. The situation is compounded by using clay, rather than the modern alternative of plastic, containers. Plastic holds the moisture pretty well, and it does not have to look objectionable if the colour is subdued and the surface matt, not shiny. But a plastic container is rarely a pleasure to behold. You long to obliterate it as quickly as you can.

Wood is nice, but releases moisture just about as quickly as clay. Then as to a compost filling, I use John Innes No.3 potting compost, which is the strongest, and I reckon to include a liquid feed (of Phostrogen), when watering, about twice a week. After all, whenever the water runs out from the bottom of your container it is taking some nourishment with it, quite apart from what the plant uses. Luxuriance is your aim, and that necessitates generosity with the goodies.

A soil-based potting compost, such as any based on a John Innes formula, is heavier and makes for greater container stability than one based on peat. The latter also has the disadvantage that if it should ever dry out, it becomes the very devil to wet again. All your water runs down the gap between the container and its contents, leaving the peat/sand mixture as dry as ever.

Although an accessory rather than a protagonist, I reckon that the most valuable of plants for container work is *Helichrysum petiolatum*, which makes long, branching strands of felted, grey, heart-shaped leaves. There is a certain stiffness in its growth (the tiny-leaved *H. microphyllum* is a pet, but much limper) so that it brackets outwards as well as over and down. It has a further wonderful attribute in that you can, by clipping a shoot as it grows to an upright cane, raise it to a height of as much as 3ft above the container, in the course of a growing season, and this vertical shoot will branch horizontally like a symmetrical tree. (If your helichrysum's leaves take to browning prematurely, it means that it is getting too little water.)

Other more colourful plants can thread their way through this fabric. One of my most successful link-ups was with *Mimulus glutinosus* and *Cuphea cyanea*, both having orange or bronze-red flowers. The mimulus is a rather lax-growing yet brittle shrub with apricot-orange flowers, deep coppered in the variety Puniceus. The cuphea carries spikes of tubular, orange flowers, which colour much more intensely when its root-run is restricted by a container than when bedded out. It is a hardy perennial.

A not-quite-so-hardy perennial with a flowering habit ideal for containers is *Convolvulus mauritanicus*. Its open blue funnels, which close late each afternoon, are borne without intermission (unless the plant be starved) from May to October. Old plants should be saved. To a small extent they can be split up at the beginning of a new season – simpler for the amateur than taking cuttings of young shoots, which is not entirely straightforward.

Tom Shepherd, my head gardener, had a lovely assemblage in a container against his south-facing cottage wall last summer, with this convolvulus at the front, lapping forwards and down some 9ins. Then a blue *Plumbaga capensis*, which enjoyed the hot weather, and at the back, trained up a support, the climbing, lily-like *Gloriosa rothschildiana*, with red, turkscap blossoms. You buy the tubers from a bulb merchant in spring and store them in a frost-free place in succeeding winters.

All sorts of annual or herbaceous climbing plants are admirable for containers, where a wall-face needs to be clothed. They are especially useful if concrete wall footings prevent you planting permanent climbers in the ground. *Tropaeolum tuberosum* overwinters as tubers: the clone called Ken Aslet starts flowering in early July and is huge with narrow, orange-and-red funnels. Condonopsis are tuberous-rooted climbing herbs. *C. convolvulacea* carries blue saucers rather like *Campanula isophylla*, in late summer and autumn, and is easily trained up supports to 4 or 5ft.

Maurandya barclayana is a tender climbing perennial that can be treated as an annual, with mimulus-like flowers varying in colour from pink to a good blue shade of mauve. Some strains are muddier-coloured than others. Save seed for the next year from a good plant. *Cobaea scandens* is a very rapid annual climber, carrying large, purple bells. Neither must we omit the most exciting of the lot, the sky-blue morning glory, *Pharbitis tricolor*, usually listed as *Ipomoea*. Its freedom of flowering positively benefits from root restriction, so a 6in pot is large enough for this.

Petunias and 'geraniums' will ever be the mainstay of summer container planting. In our windy climate it is difficult to emulate the displays of enormous-flowered petunias that you see on the Continent – in Bavaria and Switzerland, for instance. But in a sheltered courtyard one may be successful even with these fragile creatures of the grandiflora strains, as also with the doubles. Blue, purple and white-flowered kinds are the most likely to waft a delicious fragrance in the evenings.

The trailing habit of the ivy-leaved 'geraniums' is immensely useful, and most of their bright pinks, mauves and carmines blend well. For height in the centre of a container you need a bushier 'geranium'. Many seedling strains are suitable but I do relish some of the old named varieties like Maxim Kovalesky, a zonal with clear orange flowers that look especially appropriate in a terracotta pot. Some of the scented-leaved kinds give an excellent account of themselves in containers throughout the summer. I am especially fond of *Pelargonium quercifolium,* with light green, crimped and indented leaves and cherry-red flowers.

Fuchsias deserve a container to themselves, as they are apt to be swamped by such as geraniums and helichrysums. The prostrate, red-flowered Marinka has the gloss of sealing wax, and will do a trailing job. With its clusters of long, scarlet tubes and bronze-tinged foliage. Thalia is one of the best upright, bushy kinds.

In the shady positions, tuberous-rooted begonias, busy Lizzies (*Impatiens*) and nasturtiums, both trailing and bushy kinds, will be happy and free flowering. But I have merely scratched the surface of a huge and fascinating subject.

— August 11, 1983 —

ROOF TOP VIEWS

When it is hot and airless in the streets, I can recommend a round of visits to the owners of roof gardens. The prospect from any one of these in London is amazing. You look across from one roof garden to another, so many people are doing it, and the style varies according to the requirements. If it's just a summer sitting-out area, you will need nothing but ephemerals; annuals and bedding-out plants, all of them grown in containers.

However, roofs often occur at different levels, with part of a building rising above the main roof area. In that case you find yourself, as does Gloria Stacey from her Chelsea studio, with a view that you are contemplating every time you look up for inspiration. A more solid framework of shrubs, including ever-greens, will then be desirable. Colour splashes can be fitted in by planting round the base of your tubbed-up cypresses with bulbs for the spring and busy Lizzies for the summer.

Not only is the intimacy of enclosure desirable where you sit out, from a human point of view, but the plants themselves will need shelter from winds sweeping across the roof tops (buildings cause all sorts of gusts and oddities), especially if they are there the year round. At Gloria Stacey's the outer parapet of iron rail-ings had, within it, first a wooden trellis, then a fine-mesh Netlon net, and finally (what you actually see) a split-cane screen that looks charming but has to be replaced every three years.

The bituminous material with which most roofs are surfaced looks moderately unattractive and gets extremely hot, so Gloria Stacey has paved hers with a herringbone of brick tiling. As this was given insufficient tilt, it is flooded whenever the plants are watered (daily, at this season), and you are paddling until evaporation has done its job.

What unexpected problems do crop up. Chimney pots, like steam locomotives, have developed a charm of their own now that they are obsolescent, but those that remain active can impose a baleful influence. All very well if they're only used for winter heating, but if it is an oil-fired cooker, for instance, and the flue hasn't been cleaned for some time, the smuts may, as Gloria Stacey put it, force you either to offer your guests umbrellas or to enjoin them to eat their food quickly before it gets dirty.

Fallen leaves are another headache, especially in autumn. Then, if not swept up daily, they will forthwith block drains, with disastrous consequences to the building. I need not further dwell on the physical effort of bringing new plants, soil and containers up to a roof, because roof gardeners take all such matters in their stride. The results are so delightful that they deserve working for.

A Gardener's Luck

From Gloria Stacey's eyrie we stepped across a considerable area of unadopted roof (where she also grows her tomatoes in bags) to a tiny garden where the owner, not expecting visitors, was extended sun-bathing in her swimming costume. Not in the least put out, she welcomed us to view her oasis. It was immediately apparent that here was someone who knew about plants and could handle them with confidence. Furthermore she praised her good fortune in being very sheltered. Now, for an indifferent gardener, it is always the other person who has the luck; her/himself, never a shred.

This lady's plants all looked well fed and prospering – it is so easy to underestimate the feeding necessary with container-grown plants that are constantly losing nutrients by leaching every time they are given a good soak. One red-and-purple fuchsia was covered, at a guess, with a couple of hundred open blooms and as many buds. A single plant of *Helichrysum petiolatum* was spilling out of its large pot in every direction. There were roses, a honeysuckle, but, supremely, clematis, a dozen or more of them. All except a Montana, are cut hard back at the end of every season, no matter which pruning category they are supposed to belong to, and they all flower on their new growth the next year, most of them twice; Lady Betty Balfour, dismissed as 'a bore'. Only once.

I must dally here a little longer (although we visited two more roofs) to mention her viola. There wasn't a dead flowerhead on it, and now in its second year, it has been flowering non-stop for most, perhaps all, of its life. It is a fact that if a pansy or viola is never allowed to run to seed and never short of food and drink, it will flower on and on. A winter pansy will become a spring pansy, and then a summer and autumn pansy. But it is entirely up to the owner's persistence. Place it where you are always passing so that your attention is constantly drawn to its needs (my neighbour's is next to where the milk bottles are delivered and collected).

The root and walls of this little garden (I'm sorry I never caught its owner's name) were painted white to show the flowers off well, and it included tomatoes and herbs, in particular tarragon, chives, basil, sage and a bonny bush of rosemary. I liked the sturdy chrysanthemum plant in one corner, a cast-out from her flat. Three storeys down, but worth its position as a foliage plant – almost a shrub, indeed.

– January 5, 1984 –

QUESTION TIME

The beginning of the year, when we're in a state of suspense wondering what the winter has in store for us, while unable, or disinclined, to get on with much on the ground, seems a good time to consider a few queries that have filtered through to me and that raise points of general applicability.

Hints on the cultivation of *Ferula communis* were sought, its new owner being worried that, since planting it in March 'both my plants wilted completely in spite of daily watering during the dry period in July and August'. On reading up what he could do about it he discovered that good drainage was necessary; his soil is saturated most of the time and iron-hard with severe cracking during the rest. Not ideal. However, both plants returned to life in the autumn. What next?

Mediterranean Plants

The fennels are a confusing lot. These ferulas are giants, perhaps 9ft tall when flowering, but they do not flower every year. Their leaves, lacy and a delicious fresh shade of green, are enormous, though being finely divided they don't always look it. As with many Mediterranean plants (think of *Cyclamen hederifolium*, *Arum italicum* Pictum and a whole range of bulbs), their growing season is in the cool, moist period of winter and spring. Then they flower and subsequently rest completely during the hot, dry months of summer. Watering when they are aestivating is no help at all. You only need to give them a sunny, well-drained position, and to remember where the plants are when they've disappeared.

133

Next we have a spry, 70-year-old who has a *Vitis coignetiae* on a wall. She has trained it outwards, on wires, to form a shade canopy 'under which we sit'. Though it is pretty and successful, she worries that the vine's ever-increasing vigour may eventually exceed her own as that decreases, so that she loses all control. She was planning to replace it with a wisteria, but which one? Or would something else be better? et cetera. 'I dread losing the vine,' she concludes, in a typically British gesture of self-inflicting punishment.

I told her to leave it, but I wonder if she accepted my advice. A vine has handsome leaves for half the year. It casts beautiful shadows. It can be pruned hard without loss of blossom (because its blossom doesn't count). A wisteria no sooner starts flowering than it starts shedding its oldest flowers. If you sit under it, they will drop down your neck. I love wisteria, but in the circumstances described, a vine must be preferable. As to the possibility of its becoming uncontrollable, let the future take care of itself. Things seldom turn out as we expect.

Then we have the strange case of a white *Abutilon vitifolium*, which was planted to replace a lovely purple one, lost in the severe winter two years ago. The new one looked happy, was full of bud in early June, but kept dropping its flowerheads as soon as they opened. Black cotton made no difference, so bird damage has been discounted. Had I any explanation?

It is awfully difficult to judge these cases without actually seeing what's afoot. I have had no success when following the first specimen of this type of abutilon with another of roughly the same kind and in the same position. I suspect soil sickness (as with roses and lilies), but have no confirmation of this from other sources. So this problem has to remain with a question mark poised over it.

The demise of a plant is easily ascribed to the wrong cause. Thus, if it dies after a hard winter, the hard winter is blamed, whereas it may well have been a case of post hoc rather than propter hoc. A correspondent in Edinburgh told me of a number of surprising survivals from that hard '82 winter, but added that it had killed her *Elaeagnus pungens* Maculata. I wrote back that this had more likely been killed by the coral spot fungus, which often goes for elaeagnus. 'I think you are correct,' she replied: 'it had the orange spots all over it.'

Then a gentleman with a famous topiary yew arch at the front of his garden. It has become so bulbous and overgrown with the years that part of it is constantly damaged by turning lorries. It has also been damaged by storms (though I can't quite imagine how. Clipped yew is pretty solid and even takes considerable weight from snow, on the chin). How is he to support, trim, feed it?

Youthfulness Restored

It certainly pays to be ruthless, on these occasions. The archway can and should be cut hard back all over into a framework of old wood. Not a leaf will remain, perhaps, but no matter. There will be nothing more serious to endure than the cries of horror from friends and foes alike. Snap your fingers at them. The yew will be restored to pristine youth within three years and its circumference greatly reduced. After administering a shock of this order, keep it well watered in times of drought to sustain the newly-clothing shoots.

As to feeding, a regular dressing at winter's end, of a slow-acting manure, is always good practice on yew or box, or any hedging or topiary that is not terrifyingly vigorous by nature in the first place. We use blood, fish and bone on our yews, every February. It isn't cheap, but they do appreciate the attention, and it is the least one can do in recompense for depriving them, annually, of all their youngest, strongest shoots.

RITUAL ROSE-PRUNING

Back in my Rose Garden for the annual pruning ritual (late this year; the weather was slow to settle down), I was reminded of a period in the early war years when the task of looking after our hens fell to me. They are the silliest creatures, and were never designed for close companionship; yet, meeting them over and over again, I couldn't help getting a little bit fond of them, although I can't at this distance of time, remember why.

So here's old Iceberg again, tall and leggy with its bright green stems. Nearby, Silva; could one cram more thorns onto a stem than Silva has, the stems themselves packed closely together, the habit desperately upright? Does anyone grow, let alone offer, Silva now, I wondered? It is only 20 years since it came, a Peace cross, fresh from Meilland's stable, but such is the constant pressure of new varieties clamouring to oust the less new, that 20 years is a long span in the life of a modern rose.

However, roses are apt to disappear more quickly from catalogues than from gardens. Not every rose-owner is anxious to keep up to date with the latest marvel. I still like the gentle, buff-pink colouring of Silva's flowers.

My rose bushes are a mixed bunch; I can recognise the majority in their unlovely nakedness, but from time to time I come upon a teaser. 'What can you be?' I mutter. There's a good deal of discussion, exclamation, interrogation and agonised yelling in the course of pruning the roses. They have an instinctive habit of finding out my Achilles wrist, the strip of flesh between glove and sleeve.

Their lack of co-operation is relentless, presumably with

136

other gardeners besides myself – for instance, when you've gathered a number of prunings together and want to throw them some distance onto a central heap or into a barrow. You take careful aim, nicely gauge the strength and trajectory of throw required, and toss. But one small thorn has remained embedded in your glove, skin, sleeve or whatever, and the whole handful tumbles in a slovenly trail between yourself and the target.

Don't tell me you never experience the ignominy of pruning the wrong branch. Your eye lights upon an aged, worn-out complex, follows it back, back. 'That's good,' you think. 'I can remove it completely, down to ground level.' And out it comes. But then you realise that you've also removed a beautiful, straight, base-branched young shoot that was hiding until that moment. I usually take my defeats in resigned silence, never having derived any of the satisfaction from expletives that so many people appear to.

Bourbons and Perpetuals

One trap I have learned not to fall into. I never draw a branch towards me the better to see where to make my cut. If the branch is under strain when the cut is made, it will invariably tear.

There's a variation on this theme when you're in a bed of Bourbon or Hybrid Perpetual or similar roses making long, cane-like young shoots which you want to bend more or less down to the horizontal – an effective and economical way to treat such bushes. In which direction will you bend the cane? Well, if it has an inward curve, don't attempt to straighten by bending it outwards. It will snap off at the base, and you'll feel like a murderer when it was a handsome 6ft rod on Mme Isaac Péreire. Increase the curve by bending the shoot in upon itself and you'll be all right.

You will need to remove some of the tip of the cane where the growth slowed down and is softer and weaker than the rest. The clue, here, on how far to go back is how thickly young growth buds are set along the shoot. Where there are lots of them close together, they'll be weak and useless. Go back to where they are quite widely spaced.

We treat our rose beds with simazine to kill off germinating weeds. Applied this month, it will last the season through, but doesn't appear to affect ash seedlings. The seed comes in with our lawn mowings, all of which are used here in a thick mulch.

Just now there are masses of just-germinated seedlings of *Impatiens balfouri*, and these are dealt with in no time by the weedkiller, but there are some cracks and corners that it mercifully bypasses. Here, this touch-me-not can grow and flower delightfully for much of the summer and autumn. It reaches a height of 3½ft, and makes a bushy plant covered with its pinky-mauve, spurred flowers. This is nothing like as coarse as *I. glandulifera* that colonises river banks, and it is easily kept in hand.

Other self-sowers that I like to have among my roses, whenever they can escape the poison-can, are white honesty; *Verbena bonariensis*, which is the tall purple one, and teasles.

In the centre of the Bourbon rose beds, I have four clematis, each trained up a pole. They revel in the permanent grass mulch. I just now pulled up one young shoot of *Clematis viticella* Rubra that had been buried for a few months beneath the mulch, and it had made new roots at four consecutive nodes. Detached and potted, they'll make four new plants. Clematis do layer with exceptional ease. Instead of pruning all those shoots on the later-flowering types hard back, this month, you might try taking a few on an underground trip.

— May 3, 1984 —

ON WITH THE NEW

What is one to do with new plants that are coming in all the time? One must have them – some of them, anyway – but where to fit them in? I am not one of those level-headed creatures that firmly refuses to acquire new plants because 'I haven't the space'. Always seize your chance and let the brooding on what to do with the acquisition take place afterwards.

It helps concentrate the mind if you carry it round the garden with you. I'm not going so far as to suggest you should ask it 'Where would you like to grow, dear?', because the plant, in strange surroundings, is unlikely to have any clear idea about this itself. But you can at least relate your vision (supposing you have one) of how it will look when grown, with the various possible or impossible contexts passing before your eyes. I find it also helps to have someone with me. 'Come and help me find a place for . . .', I say. In the end it's usually me that finds the place, but another pair of eyes tends to sharpen your own.

Shrubs, of course, are more difficult to position than bulbs or perennials. You will often need to remove one shrub so as to make room for another. 'Where shall I plant my *Trochodendron?*', I rang Romke van de Kaa in Holland, to ask. He worked here from 1976 for three years and is a wizard for thinking of the right spot. Pause: then, 'You could get rid of the *Piptanthus*'. I changed the subject quickly.

Piptanthus laburnifolius has grown in the same corner for 35 years. Once or twice I have changed the actual plant, but it would never have occurred to me to get rid of it completely. It is a legume with rather large trifoliate leaves and clusters of

139

substantial yellow pea flowers borne over a six weeks' period around May. Growth is rapid, to 6 or 7ft, and the young stems are dark green with hints of purple and a lovely glossy sheen on them like a dachshund's coat. But this shrub has one vicious habit: for no apparent reason and at any season of the year, but especially in summer, old branches die. They are replaced by others, but this dying back is a continuing nuisance.

However, *Piptanthus* does make a good wall shrub, and not necessarily on a sunny wall. I had a space facing north-west where a long-toothed specimen of *Ceanothus dentatus* var. *floribundus* had been extracted last year. Its charms are of the obvious and flashy kind, and I feel no compulsion to replace it. But a young piptanthus (I always have seedlings by me) could go there. The deed was done and *Trochodendron aralioides* stands in the old piptanthus's position.

Troc (for short) is the only member of the family *Trochodendraceae*. It comes from Japan and looks, to me at least, rather like an arborescent ivy. The flowers are borne in domed clusters in May, and although they are green and have neither petals nor sepals they are charming, each with a circle of prominent yellow-tipped stamens. In its native haunts it will make a tree 60–80ft high. I am prepared to cope with one tenth of this.

Gloomy Contemplation

Richard, who works with me in the garden, generally has an eye for a plant that isn't earning its place, and he's quick to point it out. We both gloomily contemplated *Camellia japonica* White Swan (syn. Alba Simplex), the other day. You had to peer into the centre of the bush to find an unspoilt flower. Admittedly there has been an extraordinary succession of night frosts, this spring,

140

but camellias have a way of rubbing in every real or imagined defect in the quality of our climate. If it isn't the frost that burns them, it's the wind or simply old age and a case of the bloom dying on its feet instead of tumbling voluntarily to earth. And too often the leaves, although glossy, are like 'incredibly leathery plastic', as Tony Schilling put it when I invited him to join me in a hate session the other day.

I admit that a huge old camellia doing its stuff can be an impressive sight, but it happens too rarely and we are too lenient about admitting to the camellia's faults. Besides, we all change. I remember how thrilled I was when my mother brought me this White Swan from Waterer's, who had shown it at the RHS back in the late '40s, I suppose. In 1976 it suffered badly from the drought, and its growth has slowed down since. I had resolved to cut it hard back after flowering this spring (camellias respond well to this treatment) and to mulch it heavily.

Then Beth Chatto, after her recent visit, sent me a small plant of a purple-leaved *Sambucus nigra*, which she loves and thinks I would, and I certainly have a weakness for the elder tribe. Carrying it around the garden in my trug I suddenly thought, why not get rid of the White Swan altogether? Last year, I mused, it delighted me by already being in flower in January. I should have that pleasure no longer. Never mind. There was something about the replacement of a camellia with an elder that appealed to me. Richard has done it and now points out the defects in my *Camellia magnoliaeflora*, which is flowering (and browning) with particular freedom this spring. We shall see.

Beth also sent me a piece of *Petasites japonicus* var. *giganteus,* one of those take-over perennials whose planting you are supposed to live bitterly to regret evermore. I have planted with joy and trepidation on the far side of our moat. It may be a thug but it is also beautiful and must not be disparaged.

141

WHY NEGLECT TALL PLANTS?

Tall herbaceous and annual plants are out of fashion to the ridiculous point of neglect. Humans can go on growing taller and taller and there is no suggestion of treating them with a dwarfing hormone, as we do poinsettias and chrysanthemums, to reduce them to a more convenient height. But where plants are in question we endlessly hear that smaller gardens require smaller plants and anyway the tall ones need staking, which is itself an insupportable imposition on any heroic, leisure-hungry so-and-so.

You'll read few garden journalists on tall plants, Tony Venison and myself apart. They like to make themselves popular by writing about fashionable favourites – heathers, hostas, herbs, dwarf conifers and cottage garden flowers.

Not all gardens are diminutive yet, thank heavens, and tall plants will suit the scale in larger settings, not merely at the back of deep one-sided borders, where they tend to be drawn and to need the maximum amount of staking, but in open situations where they can relieve or rescue from monotony an expanse of smaller units. Even in a one-sided border I like to bring some tall plants to the front. So long as they are not too solid and barrier-like, they'll have a leavening influence.

A border can be too carefully graded for tallest at the back, smallest at the front. The stemmy *Verbena bonariensis*, a short-lived 5ft perennial, flowering with purple heads from July to November, is my favourite front-of-border ingredient, and this is also its own favourite position, into which it constantly self-sows.

Another self-seeder which you'll often be glad to leave in an exposed position among much lowlier plants is orach, *Atriplex hortensis*, an annual related to spinach, with ruby red and deep purple-leaved seed strains. It is an elegant plant, tall and slender, and looks particularly good among grey foliage like santolina and artemisia (but that would upset your orchestration of a symphony in grey and white).

Get a tall plant into an open situation and it will often prove to be more or less—at any rate sufficiently – self supporting and in no need of help. The 7ft *Rudbeckia* Herbstsonne (Autumn Sun) is a plant of which I am very fond, with its chrome yellow rays and a tall, green, central cone, but at the back of my border it was an awkward cuss to manage. I saw it outside the gate into a small front garden, however, where it was an unsupported feature and in perfect control of itself and its surroundings.

I have never been able to extract much sense from hollyhocks, *Alcea rosea*, annual or perennial, in my garden; they always go down to rust. But no one has ever denied their being an ideal ingredient of the small cottage garden, rising proudly to the second storey against a timber-framed building.

The very fact of being on a narrow path, plunging through a jungle of tall plants, is really rather exciting. You don't always want to stand back in order to admire. The accepted concept nowadays in gardens much opened to the public is an open area of lawn (with one off-centre fastigiate tree), a surround of narrow borders backed by shrubs, and a long, heavy teak seat in front of each border. Visitors can look across at each other, but the plants are rather out of it.

The sort of plant I like to be near in all its phases is the giant *Ferula* fennel. There are quite a lot of similar species, but you are most likely to acquire it as *F. communis*. Its leaves appear in winter; not many of them but conceived on the grandest scale. They are the freshest imaginable green and subdivided into a filigree of thread-fine leaflets. For several years, perhaps, while the plant builds up its strength (but much depends on how well you feed it), leaves are all you see and they die away in summer. Then comes a year of flowering and your plant soars to 10ft.

Don't back away from it; there's nothing to be frightened of. It is an umbelliferous plant with the same construction as hogweed, parsley and many another, pale lime green and marvellous in silhouette against a blue sky, which is the reason for staying close to it. A beautiful structure in death, too. Then the plant will take two or three more years to build up its strength for another flowering. There is no need to site it at the back of anywhere. Plant it where you'll always be seeing it; that's the important thing.

Ferulas, like many other early flowerers, let you down at midsummer. A skeleton of ripening seedheads may not then be sustenance enough. Interplant them with fast-growing annuals. *Cannabis sativa*, the Indian hemp, would be one of the most appropriate, except that its cultivation is nowadays frowned upon in this country. It used to be offered in all the seed lists and no doubt will be again, one day, when we've finally realised how laughable we make ourselves (ask them on the Continent).

It has fingered leaves like a horse chestnut and shoots up to 6ft in a few weeks. It also makes an excellent pot plant to stand in front of your porch. Some bird seed mixtures contain a proportion of cannabis.

Another quick space-filler is the zinnia-like Mexican, *Tithonia rotundifolia*, listed as *T. speciosa* Torch. It has orange, sombrero-shaped flowers of the most intense shade, and in a warm summer the plants grow to 5 or 6ft. Each is the better, in case of gales, for one stake and one tie at the 2½ft level, and you can space your plants 3ft apart. The new strain called Goldfinger is dwarfer, more congested and less graceful in habit. It's the usual old breeder's story; there'll be a Thumbelina tithonia only a foot tall before we know where we are.

Ricinus communis, the true castor oil plant, is another good

144

filler that depends on a warm summer to give of its best. The purple-leaved strain Gibsonii is more interesting than the green, but no castor oil leaf is ever boring; the palmate outline sees to that. With all the talk of dwarf plants for small gardens, no one has ever suggested that a row of annual sunflowers rising to 7ft above a cottage garden fence is other than delightful, even if comic. It is the patterns made by their seeds in the enormous disc that always fascinates me.

If yours is not too cold a garden, and you are prepared to take a bit of trouble, do try the glamorous cultivar of *Helianthus atrorubens* (which has a red-skinned, tuberous rootstock) called the Monarch. Its black-centred, semi-single flowers are of the largest if you will practice a bit of disbudding, as for dahlias.

Frequent division and replanting in improved soil is also a help and should be done in spring. Outsize sunflower blooms are not in the least vulgar, I do assure you, when they are borne on a tall plant of matching height.

Obviously I can only dip into the long list of tall plants that I have in front of me. Grasses of the genus *Miscanthus* make splendid internal garden barriers and divisions. I like them even better, I think, as single plants rising fountain-like among jowlier neighbours. Their elegance is better appreciated like this than in a grouping. At 9ft *M. floridulus* (still incorrectly listed as *M. sacchariflorus* in this country, but not on the Continent) is the tallest and most imposing. It seldom flowers.

With narrow leaves striped silver along the central vein, Gracillimus deserves its name and grows to 5ft. Zebrinus and Strictus are both crossbanded in yellow and indiscriminately dubbed zebra grass, but the former is the taller and more arching. Strictus is quite stiff and upward-pointing, 5ft tall and the more brightly patterned, when in a sunny position. Silver Feather – 6ft to 7ft – is the one to have for reliable flowering. From late August till Christmas it is always worth looking at.

145

Aruncus dioicus (*A. sylvester* and formerly *Spiraea enuncus*) is a proud space-filler, entirely in command of itself, clump-forming, 6ft high with large pinnate leaves and creamy flower panicles in July. It enjoys moisture and shade, but will grow anywhere. Its main drawback is a short flowering season (one week), but whereas the male plants fade brown, the females turn green as the seeds develop and remain presentable.

I saw this wild as a roadside plant when I was in the Carpathians of Romania, three years ago, so thought I should be safe to take a slide of it to the Pacific north-west when lecturing there last year. My picture showed it infilling beneath a planting of lilacs in Alan Roger's garden in north-west Scotland. Blow me if aruncus wasn't growing like a weed in the wilds of the western States and British Columbia, also. No one there would have dreamt of deliberately planting it in their gardens. In Britain we need have no such inhibitions.

Try it with the tall, silvery mauve panicles of *Campanula lactiflora* and with the feathery pink 'spiraea' *Filipendula rubra* Venusta – all moisture-loving and July flowering.

– September 6, 1984 –

BRINGING BULBS INTO THE PICTURE

The bulb catalogues are surely the most tempting that reach us during the year. I can easily lose my head over them. This year I have a plan, if I can find a reasonably cheap source so as to be able to use several hundred of them, to interplant Nanus gladioli among perennial dianthus, which I raised from seed last spring. They are still lined out in rows, to grow on, and I shall treat them as biennials, like sweet Williams. These little gladioli, which grow through the winter and therefore need to be planted in autumn, flower in June, and should look charming among the pinks.

That is my dream, anyway. Normally, in the principal piece of bedding out in front of the house, here at Great Dixter, tulips would be my first bulb choice, as they would also be yours or any parks department's – tulips among double daisies (*Bellis*), wallflowers, polyanthus or, most commonly, forget-me-nots (*Myosotis*). These themes are not really hackneyed, and they work. There are endless colour variations that can be experimented with as between bulb and carpeter, so there is no need to become stereotyped.

Last year I used little-known carpeter, the mauve *Erysimum linifolium*, which you raise from midsummer-sown seed as you would Siberian wallflowers, to offset a strong, mid-May-flowering red tulip, Halcro. But as Kew, where assistant curator Brian Halliwell is always experimenting, I greatly admired a bed in which the lily-flowered China Pink tulip was interplanted with *Brunnera macrophylla*. That is a blue-flowered relative of forget-me-nots, but perennial and therefore has greater substance as a plant. You would cut your plants back, after flowering, break them up and line them out in a spare plot against replanting in the autumn.

But tulips also look very good when offset by foliage rather than by flowers, and this is where their use in mixed borders comes into its own. They can often be left *in situ* for years on end and, if your soil is stiff, which is what they like, they will carry on without dwindling. I liked the effect when I had a brown-and-yellow-streaked broken tulip, Absalon, in front of the metallic young foliage of *Leymus arenarius*.

This is a take-over grass reminiscent of couch, with a wicked rhizomatous underground network, but I enclose my colony in an old, galvanised iron bath (one we used when we had cocker spaniels, on the frequent occasions when they rolled in carrion and needed drastic remedial treatment).

Bulbs among spring foliage is a theme worth pursuing. Hyacinths, for instance, look good among the ruby-red shoots of June-flowering lactiflora peony hybrids, when they are less than a foot tall in April. At Sissinghurst Castle, last spring, I was particularly impressed by a large, permanent colony of the white-starred *Ipheion uniflorum* among peony shoots of this kind.

Daffodils, on the other hand, go especially well among the young foliage of *Hemerocallis* clumps. *H. fulva* is a particularly bright lime-green at this season, and would offset a yellow daffodil of (let's hope) a not too coarse structure.

One of my favourite narcissus for border work, because it flowers as late in May as the pheasant's eyes, is the yellow jonquil hybrid, Tittle Tattle. Back-planted by *Erysimum* Bowles's Mauve, it was certainly striking, this year, but I shouldn't want to overdo this rather pushing contrast. It needs plentiful surrounding green to tone things down. A little earlier, *Arum creticum* (which behaves like a bulb) was showing up against the same background.

At one time I had an excellent summer combination in a border planting, with the white Cape hyacinth, *Galtonia candicans*, rising among self-sown plants of *Lychnis coronaria* in magenta and grey, and the dusky pink foliage of *Fuchsia magellanica* Versicolor. The galtonia is a stiff plant that looks unnecessarily gawky on its own, and anyway its leaves are no asset and need masking.

Such also is the case of many alliums. By the time they are in flower, their leaves are dying off and need to be concealed. In May, the tall, lilac-coloured *Allium aflatunense* looks good rising above or behind glaucous hosta leaves. A little later, I enjoy the pearly white *A. neapolitanum* with the pure yellow trumpets of *Hemerocallis fulva*, but if I were starting again I think I should use the bolder, yet otherwise similar *A. cowanii* instead.

At Glyndebourne this year I thought the big, mauve globes of *A. christophii* looked super among the fleshy young shoots of a

148

colony of *Sedum* Autumn Joy. Try giant chives, *A. schoenoprasum* var. *sibiricum*, in your borders. They are great self-sowers, and if you don't immediately hit on the best place to show them off, they will soon find it for themselves. In my Long Border, this, in one case, was among the magenta mat of a *Geranium* Russell Pritchard; in another, less permanently, among self-sown plants of the five-spot, *Nemophila maculata*, which is a purple and white annual.

Some of the late-flowering alliums are a valuable standby: *A. senescens* spp. *Montanum* Glaucum, for instance, opens its pinky-mauve globes in August. Butterflies love them. Its spirally twisted, grey leaves are an asset long before this, however, and one idea I had for extending the season of interest in May–June was to interplant with the vivid scarlet *Hippeastrum pratense*, which, considering its name and appearance, is hardy beyond all expectations. Don't ask me for the name of a supplier.

Where bulbs have a winter flowering season they can make their picture in a setting that will be utterly transformed later on. Snowdrops, for instance, can be tucked in underneath deciduous shrubs, where it will become too dark for anything much when spring foliage has expanded. I have a clump of *Galanthus nivalis* Samuel Arnott growing through a rather loose mat of purple aubrieta, and this itself is growing through the lower stems of the white Persian lilac, *Syringa persica* Alba. The three have made a stable trio for many years now, and provide a succession of interest for several months.

Crocuses and winter aconites will put up with the same conditions, only asking to be left undisturbed. There will be no difficulty about that under a tree like a beech, for instance. Or you can combine them with summer flowerers that also dislike disturbance, such as the already mentioned peonies, or with Japanese anemones. One of the most surprising and successful plantings I know, in a chalk garden, is of winter aconites and

Crocus tommasinianus among romneyas, the Californian tree poppies, which are cut to the ground at the end of their season.

I particularly enjoy crocuses, as I do so many other bulbs, in grass, where they will not be disturbed by premature haymaking and can seed themselves to their heart's content. In front of our house I have all the small crocuses, mainly February-flowering, such as *Crocus tommasinianus, C. aureus, C. sieberi* and *C. chrysanthus* in its many variants. Behind the house, in the orchard, the larger, later-flowering Dutch hybrids are concentrated, and here, too, are the larger daffodils, though nothing outsize.

Snakeshead fritillaries, *Fritillaria meleagris*, take over in April. They are naturals for damp meadowland so long as the ground is not stagnant and the soil not too acid. *Leucojum aestivum* is good at the same season, but, exceptionally among bulbs, this snowflake is tolerant even of drowning. I grow the Gravetye Giant from among the dogwoods (*Cornus alba*) at the boggiest margin of our horse pond.

Blue is a particularly welcome colour in a green grass sward, especially if there are specks of yellow around to complement it, as is usually the case from dandelions, cowslips and buttercups. Our native bluebells are closely followed by the slightly paler Spanish kind. Their botanical naming is always in a state of flux, but they are usually listed as *Scilla campanulata*, and also come in pink and white, all at their prettiest in grass.

All bulb books, nowadays, include besides corms any sort of tuberous-rooted plant like orchids, arums, anemones and cyclamen that take the author's fancy, so I need not apologise for doing likewise. Hardy orchids are quite freely available, especially from Avon Bulbs of Bathford, Bath. The spotted orchid, *Dactylorhiza fuchsii*, is a particularly successful garden plant, and is quite bold enough, in a good strain, to make its mark in flower borders, as are the even showier *D. elata* and *D. foliosa*.

The gratifying thing about this group of orchids is that they multiply quite quickly, under border conditions, by clumping up. They are easy to divide, and from these beginnings you can experiment by trying them out in turf. This is where I find the spotted orchid does so well, self-sowing freely. By the horse pond (in the same area as, six weeks earlier, the Gravetye Giant snowflake flowered) I have it near to flag irises, water dropwort, *Gunnera chilensis* and to Bowles's golden selection from the wild of the sedge, *Carex stricta* Aurea.

Quite other kinds of pictures can be made with bulbs in pots stood in a strategic position (outside our porch, in my case) and moved around as their seasons come and go. There are various kinds of anemones in spring, narcissus and bulbous irises, and the yellow and white *Iris bucharica* is a special success, grown in a deep pan. Another success of a bulb that would, I fear, be liable to disappear in the hurly-burly of border life is the green *Fritillaria pallidiflora*.

Later there are lilies and also some tuberous-rooted climbers, like *Codonopsis convolvulacea* and *Tropaeolum tuberosum* Ken Aslet. The lily-like turkscap, *Gloriosa superba*, would also be good in such a position if really warm, but my site faces rather coolly to the north-east.

– January 24, 1985 –

BEYOND THE SNOW BLANKET

While ice and snow remain in charge of the garden, I can take a look at more general problems that have preoccupied my correspondents. Two of them wanted to know how to manage *Eucalyptus gunnii*, whose rate of growth takes many people by surprise. One had made the mistake common to all impatient gardeners of buying 6ft-tall specimens. In a season these two had already doubled their height but were leggy, spindly things, and I have no doubt they were heavily dependent on their stakes. This lady really only wants bushes for juvenile foliage anyway, not trees.

Cut back to the ground is the answer. If this is likely to bring on a serious attack of nerves, spread the job the first spring (best time). Then, when you see how well it has sprouted on different parts of the stem during the ensuing season, finish the job off the next spring. I have never heard of a E. gunnii being killed by this treatment, but if it should perish (no, really, it won't), a replacement will grow so quickly that our own personal wound will recover almost immediately.

I know many readers will take no notice of my next recommendation. 'Pooh to that,' they will say. Never mind. You should always plant a eucalyptus that is no more than one foot high. Not because this will be the cheapest buy, but because it will establish quickest and be root-firm so that you don't have to worry about it blowing over the whole time.

A subsidiary question was when to prune ornamental cherries. I don't know what aged trees were in question and wherein the purpose of the pruning lay, but generally speaking mature cherries don't respond graciously to being hacked about. They look awful and can go down to a variety of diseases. Ask yourself or a trusted friend whether it would be more sensible to remove the tree altogether. Cherries are generally on a vigorous rootstock, and they frequently grow too large for their positions. If it is merely a question of needing to remove some low branches that get in your way, the safest time is after flowering and when the cherry is in leaf. I don't always take my own advice. I once butchered a standard Prunus subhirtella Autumnalis in March, reducing all its branches to 3 or 4ft stumps. It responded with masses of new growth and never looked back.

152

Figs and Prunes

Now as to a fig. The problem child was planted eight years ago against a south wall and in a box, but it has nevertheless run up to 12ft and has long, spindly branches bearing an insufficiency of fruits to satisfy any self-respecting fig pig. How and when to prune it so as to create a compact and productive bush?

Evidently a too vigorous variety is being grown. In my experience (and I have always lived among figs) the more you prune a fig, the less it fruits. You *can* reduce its vigour without forfeiting too much crop by confining its roots in a tub or other container, but constant attention will need to be given to feeding and watering, because a fig can easily be starved under these conditions. By the sound of it, the one described has got away – I mean, rooted through.

Brown Turkey is not usually too vigorous, but I suspect that any fig will grow too large for its owner's peace of mind in the position described. It may be more satisfactory to grow one out in the open (we are speaking of near the sea in Kent) where it could make a large bush without causing anxiety. Wall protection is by no means obligatory in the south.

Fired by my description last month of growing winter sweet, *Chimonanthus praecox*, from seed, a reader wishes to do the same if she can, for preference, find seed to sow or, at the least, a plant to plant. The snag is that she gardens at Golspie in the north-east of Scotland. Would it flower in her climate? she asked. My firm and repressive answer had to be no, and she accepted this, though with a small voice of protest. Her *Wisteria sinensis* flourishes and flowers, which is quite an achievement.

So does *Camellia* × *williamsii*, which I find less surprising as the williamsiis are much readier to flower well in north Scotland than the *C. japonicas*. And *Desfontainia spinosa*; that is no surprise either, as I knew a garden not 15 miles from Golspie, as the hooded crow flies, where ancient bushes would flower regularly up till Christmas. *Eucryphia cordifolia* (reputedly tender) did well there too, as also *Carpenteria*, *Garrya* and *Abelia floribunda*. In these coastal regions the North Sea winds are poisonous, but snow seldom lies nor does frost become deep, so plants that can be given shelter will thrive as they would not in the English Midlands.

But the winter sweet needs not only to grow but to ripen its wood, if it is to flower. I have seen it doing the one but failing in the other respect in Scotland, and it is such a dull shrub unless it will flower well that it seems to me a waste of precious warm wall space to attempt it so far north.

What about north wall space in Surrey, where concrete footings mean that whatever is chosen must be grown in a deepish tub? A climbing or rambler rose was preferred. But I should be against this. I think its legginess would be hard to conceal. I should like an ivy. The variegated kinds are so lively and never have a dull season. Or a *Clematis montana* with an evergreen bush in front of it: a camellia or *Choisya ternata* or *Daphne pontica*, or *D. odora*. All would flower well in shade in Surrey. Feeding and watering would need to be generous.

— March 13, 1986 —

THE FICKLE GARDENER

February was a wicked month, the coldest since 1947 I have read, and I can remember that one. But here we have had little snow this time, which at least has merits of convenience. Indeed, it has been incredibly dry, these past weeks. Many of the doors in my house which I expect to stick are working free; it's quite unnerving and certainly has nothing to do with central heating.

The temperature in my kitchen is 37 deg. F this morning. I know that if I put the blow-heater on for a couple of hours it will rise a couple of degrees, but that is hardly a refuge. Excluded from garden and kitchen, I'm left with chilblains in the inglenook, and lofty thoughts divorced from current ills.

I have just been reading a long article on roses in *Horticulture*, the bestselling American monthly gardening magazine. It is by Henry Mitchell, gardening correspondent for the *Washington Post* and, far more important, one of the few enjoyably readable authors on our subject today. His book of articles, *The Essential Earthman*, was published by Faber & Faber as a paperback the year before last.

He is great on gardeners as well as gardening, and must, I feel, be a disciple of La Rochefoucauld, so neatly does he turn an aphorism. 'Gardens in the "Japanese Style" tend to be particularly vulgar and unsuccessful, by the way. As far as that goes, no style of gardening should be aped.' When all around us Japanesque we see, a corrective makes breathing easier.

Nearer to what I'm approaching is 'You will notice that fashionable trees (which change with the generations of mankind) never have their faults pointed out; it is only the unfashionable ones that you hear gossip about.'

On the subject of roses, he points out how especially fickle the public are – but then the publicity attached to roses makes no pretence of sanity and level-headedness. Mitchell, however, dissociates himself from crowd treachery. 'When I say all the roses I mention are glorious I mean it, and I meant it five years ago and will mean it when I die. No fickleness here.'

But it is easy to confuse fickleness, which goes with a yearning to be in the mainstream current of fashion, with a continuous development in your tastes, which is necessary to your dying day, if mental sclerosis is not to overtake you. Just think of all the books you used to read with avid enjoyment when you were

155

young. There are not many you could face again now, but that's no reason for regret over time wasted. It wasn't wasted; it was simply developing your tastes.

Not to be Repeated

And so with flowers and with the styles of gardening we adopt for using them. Many readers will know John Treasure's gardens at Burford House, on the borders of Shropshire, Worcestershire and Herefordshire. They are not merely beautifully kept, they are packed with original ideas. When I first met John in 1952, he had a small garden at nearby Tenbury Wells, and I remember a bedding-out combination with scarlet nasturtiums and the bright, rather hard purple *Verbena rigida* (*V. venosa*). He never repeated that or anything like it. It was just something he was working out of his system.

He moved to Burford House two years later and, an architect himself, laid out entirely new gardens there, large, informal island beds (so big they didn't look like islands) with many promontories and re-entrants. The promontories were largely devoted to heathers relieved by vertical conifer accents, the sort of thing that every landscape architect today has been brought up on like mother's milk.

But John is a plantsman, and he is also fascinated by the ways in which plants can be made to help each other. The heathers were interplanted with clematis, using them on the flat, which had never been done before, I believe. And so many other shrubs were grown besides conifers that these melted in with their associates. Heathers are still around, but any kind of addiction has been entirely outgrown. The garden has moved on and the prolonged experiment in how to grow a wide range of plants together continues. It is not a question of being fickle to one kind of plant in favour of another.

Imagine a formal parterre (attached to an old house; I won't say where) that is outlined in box hedging and well kept. So far so good, but the beds are filled with rose bushes, and this is a disaster. They are out of scale with their formal surround, many being far too tall, and the flowers are mere agitated spots of colour offering no kind of unity.

There are many formal gardens for which bedding out is nowadays impossibly expensive, and so roses have been used in lieu. But they are too fidgety. Even heathers, restricted to just a few varieties, could offer a better solution. Or heather in some of the compartments and other kinds of evergreens, kept clipped so that they didn't grow too tall, in the others. The grey *Helichrysum splendidum* could be an excellent choice where climate is too harsh for the majority of greys, as is the case in this instance.

One would need to experiment, to try various ingredients out on a small scale for a start, but at least to make plans beyond those roses, which have proved themselves impossible, and not to declare yourself helpless.

– August 7, 1986 –
SUMMER COMMENTARY

What a difference a really summery summer makes to a garden and to one's own enjoyment of it. The problems are as nothing to the pleasures. Actually, with all the warmth, there was a good deal of cloud cover in July, and this is a kindness to certain flowers, roses in particular. And verbascums. On a hot day the mullein flowers will be limp from midday onwards and not recover until the next morning, but if it is reasonably dull they will remain in good condition throughout.

Growth has been lush this summer. My giant reed grass, *Arundo donax*, dripping with dew after a foggy night (I am writing before breakfast), has risen from zero in April to little over 6ft, but it will more than double that height in the coming weeks. Especially if I ply it with the water it so relishes. I make my watering as liberal as I can, but most border plants cannot be visited by my sprinklers more often than once in two or three weeks.

If you were to judge our summer by the weather forecasts, you would think that it rained every other day, so often is rain mentioned and so little account is given to the fact that most of us will receive none. I started irrigating in mid June and have not let up on a single day in the five weeks since.

Thrips have been quite a plague as a consequence of dry weather, and pollen beetles have been tremendously in evidence, as also this time last year. If you pick any sort of a daisy flower, you need to shut your eyes and then blow very hard into the centre of it to remove some 80 or more of these small, black creatures. We had a visitor in the garden recently who was strikingly dressed in yellow with black trimmings. The quantities of pollen beetles walking conspicuously over the yellow background looked as though they were an intentional part of her get-up. My companion and I couldn't help giggling, and luckily the lady, who had noticed her condition, thought it comic too.

I don't remember such hordes of these beetles until recent years, and I've heard, though with what truth I cannot substantiate, that the build-up has occurred as a result of the huge acreages of rape grown on farmland these days. Rape blossom in May would give early generations of these beetles a great boost.

Fragrance from Roses

There has been more fragrance on the air from flowers and plants, on dewy mornings and at other times of day when humidity has remained high. I hadn't, until this summer, noticed the scent released by two rose bushes in my garden. *Rosa* × *cantabrigiensis* has sweet-smelling foliage and young stems. Its ferny luxuriance is most attractive, so there is no need to resent the brevity of its early flowering season.

Then there is *R. ecae.* Another early, yellow-flowered single rose. The bush is no beauty, but it gives off the same incense fragrance as *R. primula,* which is the one that is always written about for this property. I grow that too. I wish I could propagate it from stem cuttings, though. I wonder if any readers have had better than my nil success. It does sucker a little, when on its own roots, so I should try it from root cuttings.

I am not keen on having to give thought to bulbs at this time, but the arrival of bulb catalogues is a pointed reminder. Some bulbs have a desperately short dormant season, and if you want to sort out your own stocks you need to make the mental effort of thinking about plants that you can't even see. I was gapping up with annuals near to my patch of Tête-á-Tête daffodils, a few days ago, and turning up some of their bulbs reminded me that I wanted to make a panful of them to enjoy next March. They were already sprouting new roots.

Colchicums can leave quite big, bare patches in a border, and I have interplanted some of these with *Helichrysum microphyllum,* which does a quick job of creeping over and covering the ground with its slender, grey shoots. When the colchicums come on to flower, very soon now, they will have a ready-made background. Not that I mind seeing them appear without leaves, as some people do.

Having flowered, alstroemerias look pretty dreadful. I need the seed from mine, so I have to put up with their dying growth. Some *Verbena bonariensis* in front help to mask them, and the advantage of this tall, stemmy plant is that it develops late but then keeps on growing.

When you don't need the alstroemeria seed you can simply

yank all their stems out, in a very few seconds. They will break cleanly away from the tubers several inches below the soil surface, so that you can plant annuals or tender bedding plants over their heads.

Another bulb-related job that I'm boiling up for is where I have *Scilla sibirica* planted among fuchsias. The bulbs do very well, the fuchsias do not, and the ground needs improving for them. The scillas are completely dormant, so it is only a question of collecting them in a box. The fuchsias won't mind an upheaval as much as you might suppose. I've done this to them in August on a previous occasion. I shall water them heavily before cutting back and lifting them. Their roots are thick and woody, and these, again, will make new plants, treated as cuttings. But the variegated kinds must be done from stem cuttings. From roots they will all come green. It's surprising the number of jobs that can be successfully accomplished at the 'wrong' season.

– March 5, 1987 –

HEART OF DARKNESS

Many people grumble about how small their gardens are, but few take full advantage of the space available. I know I don't, so in a way I'm preaching at myself.

I remember a visitor who was used to my Long Border in summer exclaiming, when he saw it in early spring for once, that I had massacred its contents. But it was simply that summer foliage, which would later blot out the soil from view, had not yet appeared. Even evergreen shrubs are considerably reduced as shade-makers by the end of winter. Either they are only semi-evergreen, like *Eucryphia* Nymansay, *Viburnum* × *burkwoodii*

160

and *Piptanthus laburnifolius*, or winds and cold weather have stripped them of their largest, softest leaves, as with *Phlomis fruticosa* or the bamboos. Under deciduous trees and shrubs, even under a beech which later causes the darkest shade of any tree, a great deal of light penetrates up till May under a gunnera, whose leaves are the largest of any plant hardy in this country, full darkness is not reached until the end of June.

On the other hand there are many plants, bulbs especially, that flower and make their growth between autumn and spring. They can take full advantage of ground that is light in their season but Stygian in summer. Other plants, like hellebores, will flourish in places that are pretty dark for most of the year. I noticed today, for instance, a healthy clutch of *Helleborus foetidus* seedlings at the foot of a pillar rose in my mixed border. I probably shouldn't have thought of planting these right up against the rose's ugly stems, but the hellebores had taken excellent advantage of their opportunity.

Wedged between a bamboo and a clump of hydrangeas, there is quite a swarm of stinking iris, *Iris foetidissima*, seedlings. Although evergreen (so that in summer, when the hydrangeas are in full leaf, they will receive precious little light), their light requirements are very low. They are not beautiful plants, but their vivid scarlet seeds are welcome in winter.

Many variegated plants need light to bring out their colour contrasts and patterns. Not so the dead nettles, notably *Lamium maculatum*. This has many cultivated forms. The trouble with Beacon Silver is that it mildews badly. White Nancy has no such weakness, and the whiteness of its flowers perfectly tunes in with the white leaf markings. The pinky-mauve flowers of *L. maculatum* Aureum, however, can be a bit hard to swallow in the company of its golden leaves.

161

Filling the Gaps

Pulmonarias, the lungworts, are flowering already and they need little light, even though their leaves are made in summer. The silvery areas on *Pulmonaria saccharata* Argentea are just as well defined in darkness as in light, and the plant is happier in shade, making larger leaves. *P. longifolia* is so well spotted and has such elegant lance leaves as to be arguably the handsomest in this respect, but with me it falls prey to mildew.

Keith Wiley, from the West Country, who has just been visiting, points out that rodgersias and hostas, great shade-casters in their season, are excellent hosts now for such plants as snowdrops, crocuses and spring-flowering anemones (he particularly mentioned *Anemone blanda* and the double forms of *A. nemorosa*). I looked in shame at my *Rodgersia pinnata* Superba colony. Besides its rhizomes, there is nothing to be seen but moss. Moss is a sure sign that the ground is undisturbed. You rarely need to tamper with rodgersias; a good autumn mulch is all that is required.

Where the ground lies peaceful for years on end, early bulbs will revel. Winter aconites also. It is the same among hostas, although I do find that the quality of their flowers and foliage benefits from not too infrequent division. But if you do this in early autumn and replant the bulbs immediately, even though they will have started making roots they will hardly suffer.

Behind my rodgersias I have two enormous plants of *Euphorbia palustris*, and I have at least done something about them with that prolific, early-flowering snowdrop, *Galanthus* Atkinsii. I dug up a big clump for a neighbour a few days ago, and took the opportunity of planting some in the now hollow centre of the euphorbias. *Euphorbia griffithii* lends itself no less to planting with early bulbs and it is easier still with an area devoted later

162

on to *E. polychroma*. Each plant remains compact. You are aware of a series of undulations when it is flowering, but earlier on the interplant furrows are free for crocuses and such like, and once established they will seed themselves into crannies where you couldn't plant.

Keith Wiley also pointed out that we don't think nearly enough about making the most of plants in paving. A large part of our sunken garden, in the paving around its octagonal pool, is covered with a mat of *Acsena novae-zelandiae*, whose crimson burrs are at their liveliest in July. Now, there is nothing except its tentacles, which form a dense canopy over paving slabs as well as cracks. I only need to give crocuses a start by pushing a few small corms into the cracks among the acaena roots. The rest they will do by self-sowing.

Nature has helped here, however, with numerous clumps of *Dactyloshiza fuchsia*, the spotted orchid. Its dust-fine seed has blown in from our meadow areas and competition from the acaena worries it not at all. It flowers in June. I need something there now.

– June 25, 1987 –

NEVER A QUIET MOMENT

Just in case you think you have the garden sufficiently organised to be able to relax in it, I'll apply a few jabs at your conscience. To mine equally, of course; I can't look at my garden without being assailed by febrile pangs. I've already dived into the thick to comb out threads of goose grass. If that seeds, the problem will grow worse from year to year. Perhaps ground elder is your problem, or bindweed. Tickle them up with TumbleWeed while their growth is strong and lush.

163

Make sure that your borders will look full at midsummer. Some gardeners don't need to be told; theirs are crammed already. But that is preferable to the great expanse of carefully weeded, heavily mulched ground that I saw recently in a famous garden where every plant or small – much too small – group of plants was isolated in a carefully cultivated waste. That is a depressing, negative way to garden.

If there are self-sown or direct-sown annuals in your borders, thin out well so that those which remain do justice to their potential. In my borders the purple orach – *Atriplex hortensis*, related to spinach and likewise edible raw or cooked – is presently drawing a lot of comment. Much has sown itself in the wrong place or too thickly, but what I leave will look handsome as it rises to 6ft. I particularly liked it last year where it had sown itself among mauve *Phlox paniculata*, the wild form which I originally had from Margery Fish.

When your self-sown annuals and biennials are finishing – *Limnanthes douglasii* will be one of the first – pull out the majority as they run to seed, so that you're less likely to have an excess of them in future seasons. Welsh poppies in orange and yellow are pretty in early summer, but you should have a grabbing session to break off their main stems at ground level as soon as the main display is over.

When your violas are looking tired, shave off at ground level; feed Growmore and then give a heavy watering, followed by further watering to get them going again. Other early flowering perennials can be treated likewise, for instance geums, giant chives and various comfreys. If the plantings are worn out, overcrowded or woody, make this your opportunity for lifting, splitting and replanting pieces in ground that you have improved with garden compost or other humus-rich manure. Bergenias, polyanthus and other primulas, irises, pyrethrums, earlier flowering cranesbills like *Geranium macrorrhizum*, come to mind. Don't let their roots dry out while you're getting their bed made for them. Drop them into a big plastic bag in a humid atmosphere.

Watch out for variegated plants reverting in patches to plain green. They are easiest to spot now: the odd branch on *Weigela florida* Variegata, on Dickson's Golden Elm, on variegated sweet chestnuts, on *Acer platanoides* Drummondii and on the box elders, *Acer negundo*.

With a fuchsia such as *F. magellanica* Versicolor, yank green shoots out from below ground level by grasping firmly and giving a sharp tug. *Astrantia* Sunningdale Variegated will need to have reverted crowns winkled out individually with a sharp-pointed trowel. Where green leaves spoil your comfrey, *Symphytum × uplandicum* Variegatum, the trouble, as with fuchsias and other plants that will shoot from damaged roots is that your cultivations have at some stage broken the top of a root and this will produce a new, green-leaved plant henceforth and for evermore. *Phlox* Norah Leigh is another case in point. Sometimes the simplest course is to lift the original, variegated plant and transfer it elsewhere.

Perennials that you know will grow too tall (often self-sown) can still have their leading shoots pinched out at 18in or 2ft. They will then branch and bush out, flowering at a much lower level than usual. Such are border phloxes, Michaelmas daisies, perennial sunflowers and the tall *Campanula lactiflora*.

If you have any daffodils or narcissi that need to be moved, there is no better time than the present, not just because you can still see, from dead leaf remnants, where to find them but because they start making new roots so early. The pheasant's eye, *Narcissus poeticus* var. *recurvus*, has only a few weeks of dormancy following its very late flowering. So if moves can be made before those new and fragile roots have started growth, they'll settle in the sooner.

I was asked, during the daffodil season, why some that had

been planted a few years back were now coming up blind. I said that dry conditions were usually the cause. Bulbs in general need plentiful moisture during their growing season, even if they are baked in summer.

Lilacs, *Syringa vulgaris*, will often get into a biennial flowering habit in middle and old age. Or parts of the bush will flower heavily one year, and take a complete rest the next, while other parts are green and unflowered this year but do well next. No lilac is ever too old to be restored to regularly productive youth. If you have one that has flowered heavily and that you know from experience will rest next year, seize this opportunity to prune it heavily. It still has time to make new shoots, and these will be further reinforced in 1988. But if you don't do it at once, leave your pruning till next winter.

Don't bother to dead-head your rhododendrons unless the sight of spent flowers is offensive (as with lilacs – on the double white Mme Lemoine they emphatically *are* offensive). There is a school of thought which believes you cannot expect rhodos to flower well next year if they were not saved from ripening seed this year. In fact, no experiment to test this theory has ever been carried out, and I feel confident that dead-heading makes so little difference to future performance as not to be worth the time and energy, not to mention the danger of falling off your ladder as you reach for seed heads at the top of an enormous old bush.

Watch your hellebores, if you're hoping for seed from them. They make a habit of ripening and spilling when your thoughts are elsewhere. Where seed heads are carried in clusters, as with *Helleborus foetidus* and *H. corsicus*, you can catch the crop by making a bag around them with an old nylon stocking. Seed collecting started with winter aconites and crocuses in May, and you need to think about it right through to the latest ripeners, like certain lilies, at the end of the year.

CHASING RAINBOWS

By mid-July when the weather broke (on St Swithin's Day) I was glad to see the rain. I had been irrigating the garden like mad but could not reach every part with sufficient frequency (except for the Florence fennel, which I was determined to give no excuse for not making fat 'bulbs' before it bolted).

But as is the way with rain, once it starts it does not know when to leave off. After a week of it, the garden, from being my pride, had turned into a bedraggled mess. A German lady told me that last time she had visited, it had been early July, and the garden then had been better. There is no reason why it should not have been just as good in late July, I said, and now she could see the Mount Etna broom, which she would not have seen early in the month. Just going over, said she. Not at all, said I. She was silent. When I went to look at it (which I did, in some haste) all the blooms left were shut and a kind of wasted shade of yellow, totally lacking in the vibrancy of a few days earlier. Yet it was only half way through its flowering season with buds to open. Instead of that, they were falling off.

I was mortified. It was the *pièce de résistance* in the Long Border. Devilish truthful, these Germans.

The annuals were nearly all pathetic. Thank goodness I do not have many petunias. The geraniums in their display pots were posing as scarecrows, even the less susceptible single-flowered kinds. All daisies, annual or perennial had a chewed-up look. Not a flower on verbenas or daisies. The new blooms on hemerocallis scarcely less depressed than the faded ones I had not removed

167

(what a boring necessity that is: like bearded irises they need going over every day). I suppose campanulas were near the end of their season; this was their *coup de grâce* and no mistake. Even the clematis were battered, while *Asphodeline liburnica*, which open its starry yellow flowers at four o'clock on every sunny afternoon, refused to open them at all, day after day. I could not blame our garden visitors for looking glum.

But there were oasis, if you looked for them; islands of hope and pleasure where the plants, their flowers included, were palpably revelling in this sopping fare. Hydrangeas were in the van. There is quite a bit of substance in their flowers. On a hot afternoon they quickly lose it and flag, even if moist at the root, but in rain they gleam. If a hydrangea could purr, my garden would be full of the sound, because I grow a lot of them. Despite its harsh weather, last winter (in contrast to the previous one) hardly affected them at all, so there is a good display.

Phloxes are their equivalent in the world of hardy perennials. The two flowers are excellently matched in partnership. Heavy rain at the end of the phlox season will deflower them totally, but they were just coming out and loved it. So did the annual *Phlox drummondii*, of which I have a big bed.

Hostas are moisture-lovers and that includes their bells and trumpets. *Hosta ventricosa* and *H. undulata* are good in their July season as will be *H. lancifolia* and Royal Standard this month, but greatest staying- and flower-power comes from Tall Boy, which lasts through much of July and August.

Rodgersias love it wet. Their foliage is, in most cases, of greater importance than their flowers, but not so in *Rodgersia pinnata*. Superba is the most sought after clone of this but it is a slow, weak grower, even though in perfect health, and it remains an expensive plant because there is a limit to how much it can be divided (micropropagation could be a help, here). I have a much more vigorous clone, originally given me by Maurice Mason,

168

which I find a far easier and most satisfactory plant. The pigment is not so heavy, the flowers being pink rather than red, but it is handsome and grows to 4ft. I am sure that if plant-breeders turned their attention to this species, improvements would soon follow.

Astilbes enjoy moisture from tip to toe. *Astilbe taquetii* is my favourite because the whole plant is handsome and, being rather later in flower than the average, you have plenty of time to watch it coming on. Also it self-sows freely, so that in time it makes a far more imposing colony than you had envisaged, with outliers in various unexpected places. The strong mauve colouring is to my liking, as are the narrow, upright panicles.

For the back of a border or in woodland conditions, *A. rivularis* is excellent, too, with specially large and well presented leaves and a widely branching 6ft inflorescence. It soon passes from cream to green, but you scarcely notice the difference.

Eryngiums are so stiff and bony, they do not seem to notice the weather, although they never look their best in shade. Spurges are carefree, too. Just now I am getting particular enjoyment from the clean, bold lines and clear, sharp colouring of *Euphorbia schillingii*. The waxy bells of galtonias are weatherproof; white in *Galtonia candicans*, green at little more than half the height in *G. Princeps*, which is 18in tall or a little over and carries a long, dense raceme set off by neatly prick-eared leaves. In *G. viridiflora*, the flared green bells are spaced and very striking, but this species loses out on its tousled foliage. One must have it, especially as its season is a little later than the other two.

Verbascums bounce back from a deflowering by heavy rain within 24 hours. They love cool weather and grey skies or the freshness of a sunny morning after a dewy night, but wilt in noontide glare. *Verbascum olympicum* and *V. chaixii* are my two mainstays in this genus, the former especially statuesque. Some of them are in a rather dashing combination with pink phloxes

169

backed by the rich, purple foliage of the deepest *Cotinus coggygria*. This one is a non-smoking smoke bush, so I can prune it entirely with foliage effect and the height I want it at in mind. Moisture with warmth suits it, with a sunny position to bring out the richest colouring in its leaves.

– August 20, 1987 –

BACKS TO THE WALL

Recent hard winters have undoubtedly sorted the sheep from the goats among the wall shrubs. The only evergreen ceanothus that I now have is one that I planted last spring – *Ceanothus impressus* Puget Blue. If that falls victim next winter, I shall consider giving up ceanothus altogether. After all, there are other things.

Surprisingly, *Dendromecon rigida*, the shrub poppy with grey lance leaves and luminous yellow flowers, survived. It returned to life from ground level, where snow had protected it in the coldest period. Being a quick grower, it is flowering (a little) now.

So is *Mutisia oligodon*, which turns out to be a remarkably hardy member of its strange South American tribe of evergreen, tendril-climbing composites. I can't say that my plant has regained any height to speak of, but it has already carried a long succession of its pink daisies. The species that I should most like to possess is *M. decurrens*, with marvellous flame orange daisies, but this suffers from lack of hardiness and difficulty in propagation.

Both *M. oligodon* and the *dendromecon* root quite easily and we shall be taking cuttings of them any day now. Like other poppies, the *dendromecon* is extremely tricky in respect of the slightest root disturbance, so we root these individually in small pots. A cold frame (snug, with solid walls) is warm enough to get them started.

170

Another wall shrub that we are propagating now is *Schizophragma integrifolium*. Some people find this difficult, and indeed it is impossible if you try to root mature, flowering wood. You must use soft, non-flowering shoots of this year's growth. If yours is an old specimen, there may be none such on it. In that case cut it hard back to its supporting wall this coming winter. That will force it to make young growth and will have a generally rejuvenating effect on the shrub as a whole, which can otherwise subside into the condition of flowering well only every other year.

The possessors of old schizophragmas (*S. hydrangeoides* is the other species in cultivation and that is good, too, though less dramatic than *S. integrifolium* with its large, creamy oval bracts, tapering to fine points, each of them up to 3in long) are probably fairly thin on the ground, but there are a lot of wall shrubs and climbers that can do with the rejuvenating treatment from time to time. At worst you will lose the next year's blossom.

For instance, a pyracantha that has served you for years will probably be standing a long way forward from its wall by now. The annual clip back that you have to administer to keep it in order also prevents it from flowering and hence fruiting as freely as it otherwise would. Besides which, old pyracantha growth, as also old ivy and old garrya, becomes a noisy, messy roosting haven for squabbling house sparrows. Lop everything back to the wall at the end of next winter.

The climbing *Hydrangea petiolaris* will certainly benefit from an occasional hard cut back, and even a wisteria can be so treated if the distance it stands forward from a wall has become an embarrassment, but it could take a couple of years to regain its flowering potential.

The aftermath blossom that my *Wisteria sinensis* is now, as usual, carrying, gives me almost as much pleasure as the main crop. True, it is only scattered and makes no great visual impression, but the colour seems richer to me, its season is more

171

prolonged and it is such a treat to welcome back that incomparable scent.

It is generally supposed that the wisteria of which I write stems from a single, vegetatively propagated clone that came to us from a Cantonese merchant's garden in 1816 and is by far the most satisfactory example of the species grown in Britain. There are other clones around, but most of them disappoint in one way or another.

If your wisteria carries the aftermath flower crop now but nothing to speak of in spring, you may be certain that bird damage – sparrows pecking out the dormant buds – is the reason for the maincrop failure. Cottoning works against this trouble: black cotton or nylon thread, put on in December or January after the wisteria's late leaf fall.

The genus *Bomarea* could become quite popular if only it were available. It behaves like a climbing alstroemeria, carrying trusses of blossom at the ends of its twining shoots. In winter it dies down completely, but despite its South American origin, there seem to be some encouragingly hardy species about. Only their names and naming are in a state of confusion. Pink, red and salmon are some of the commoner flower colours. There is a famed hybrid, *B. × cantabrigiensis*, at the Cambridge Botanic Garden that has been going for many years. Bomareas have tuberous roots and these can be divided to a limited extent or they can be raised from seed. It would be good news if Chiltern Seeds would tap a source for us. *B. caldasii* is a name to be looked out for.

Bomarea is the sort of plant that will fill a wall gap quickly and so is *Solanum jasminoides* Album, if you start with a strong specimen planted out in spring. That same year it will crop well with its white jasmine-like (but unscented) blossom. If it can bring its old growth through the winter, it will get away to a flying start the next year, flowering profusely from June to October and covering a large area of warm wall surface.

172

But if it is killed back to (and has to start again from) the ground, subsequent renewal will be too slow to be useful, and you had better start again with a strong young plant rooted from an early summer cutting taken the previous year and brought through the winter under glass.

The gap this solanum is now filling for me has been left by *Abutilon megapotamicum*. That is still alive, but has been forced to come up from ground level these last three years, which doesn't give it a chance to get going. A mild winter would provide the necessary break in its run of bad luck.

— January 28, 1988 —

GOOD OLD JANUARY

Writing about mild weather in winter is always dangerous because by the time my piece is read, two weeks later, the situation may have changed completely. But I believe in living in the present, when it is agreeable to do so, rather than worrying about a problematic future. The 'we'll pay for it later' school (and I've heard plenty from them of late) are so engrossed in their forecasts of doom and gloom as to forget entirely that the present is actual. It cannot be taken from us before being converted into the past. So why not extract its pleasures?

What a contrast between now and a year ago. The temperature in our porch dropped to 9 degrees F. The dog's bowl in the room where I spend my evenings froze solid. There were drifts in our drive that kept me (quite a willing prisoner) from taking my car out for 10 days. Whereas, from the porch, I have just been enjoying a song thrush's full-throated performance from the naked branches of *Eucryphia* Nymansay (it was stripped by the great storm but is none the worse) and the garden is full of activity,

173

although so wet, on our heavy soil, that it would be foolish to stodge about.

I can add, however, that a few days without rain would transform the situation, and most of all in the many areas where we have lightened the clay with heavy dressings of crushed grit, which I buy by the load (at a price) from the local builders' merchants. This and the worms between them keep the soil pretty open, so that weeding is quite possible for much of the time.

Annual meadow grass keeps growing and flowering. There are masses of willowherb seedlings, and now we see germination of two spring specialities, the ivy speedwell, *Veronica hederifolia*, and goosegrass or cleavers, *Galium aparine*, which I reckon to be just about the most insidious weed that can take charge in any border.

Other early germinations are honesty (*Lunaria annua*) and violet seedlings. The giant fennel, *Ferula communis*, is already germinating in a pot, and hellebore seedlings are always precocious. It is worth lifting some of those that appear around favourite parent plants and pricking them out into a seed tray as soon as they are large enough to handle, which is, for the neat-fingered, as soon as they are large enough to see.

The *Helleborus orientalis* hybrids (and *H. orientalis* itself, which I had from a wild source) have caught me napping by coming into flower before I have got around to cutting away their derelict old foliage. I hate that job. If you lose patience and give an old leaf a tug, it comes away together with the young bud at its base.

So do the related peonies; I refuse to go along with revisionist botanists who would take them out of *Ranunculaceae* and put them into a family of their own. Everything about them that matters proclaims *Ranunculaceae* and a close affinity with hellebores. If you cut the leaves as low as you can, which is only right and tidy, sooner or later you find you have inadvertently cut a young flowering stem. Maddening.

174

There is great activity among plants that we might prefer to remain dormant. I don't mind the daffodils being several inches high, but when I saw the fat snouts of *Eremurus robustus* poking up, I had them thickly mounded over with grit (another use for it). Their precocious appearance can be lethally blasted by frost.

Around my *Hydrangea* Ayesha, which was killed to the ground two winters ago, we have fixed a plastic envelope (made with canes and old fertiliser bags – not a pretty sight), leaving the top open. Over-protection does more damage to an only semi-dormant plant (and full dormancy is practically unknown in our climate) than no protection. As long as the weather remains open, I will keep the hydrangea, but I shall stuff old male-fern fronds bountifully between its branches and heap them over the top if it turns frosty.

Many gardeners are worried about the growth on their large-flowered clematis, as well they might be. If those that flower early from their old wood have their growth frosted now they will not flower as much later on, if at all. Such are Nelly and Marcel Moser, Miss Bateman, Lasurstern, Vyvyan Pennell and others with double flowers, and many more. Each of the short side shoots that they make from last year's wood contains a bud, so it is vulnerable if exposed too early. That is why people living in the north so seldom see the double blooms that Vyvyan Pennell is famed for: they get only the single blooms made later, on the young shoots.

In many cases this doesn't matter. The President, Marie Boisselot, Ville de Lyon, Rouge Cardinal and others have an unending capacity for making flowerbuds through the growing season. Loss of the first crop will scarcely be noticed. This is why they and later-flowering Jackmanii and Viticella-type clematis, which unequivocally make a practice of flowering on their young wood, are so much the most rewarding garden plants.

They, too, are shooting strongly now, 'What shall I do?' cries the anxious gardener. Wait now till March or even April, and then cut them hard back so that not a green shoot is left. There will be nothing lost.

As for Vyvyan Pennell and other early large-flowerheads, the best you can do is to hang some netting in front of them in cold weather. You may still lose those fat buds. If that happens in successive years, give up and concentrate on the later clematis.

I'm giving up most of my hebes this year, and a number of ceanothus and olearias. There comes a stage when being a devil for punishment is merely pigheaded. If the climate fluctuates, we must take our cue from altered circumstances. At least I am encouraged, by the recent absence of bullfinches (killed off in hard winters), to plant a few plum trees again. Their flower buds may be spared, as they used to be in the 1940s. Mild or cold, there will be advantages somewhere.

Meanwhile it's mild, and the scent of *Mahonia japonica*, *Sarcococca confusa*, winter sweet (*Chimonanthus*) and Chinese witch hazel is wafted to me as I go round the garden. When they are picked for the house and placed in a cool room (our Great Hall is ideal), the waft continues. Who said January was evil?

– September 1, 1988 –

EXPERIMENTAL BEDDING

The art of bedding out is much abused, both by those annually perpetrating a dull (though often blatant) routine in public places and by those of the public who fancy their own exquisite taste and imagine that bedding can never be other than vulgar.

But, like most art forms, bedding can be well done or badly done. It requires thought and it requires experimentation. If you are gardening for and paid by the public, it is politic to do your experimenting in a back-up area where mistakes can be noted and quietly buried while the successes can, in a future year, be exposed to the public's critical, appreciative or unheeding eye.

But always to play safe and never to experiment is unforgivable. At the Royal Botanic Gardens, Kew, the assistant curator Brian Halliwell has never been afraid of criticism and has always made a point of stirring the pot. Either in spring or in summer I have usually gone to see what he is up to, and have never come away disappointed. Besides his singularly unusual bedding-out with vegetables, as a final flourish before his retirement he has bedded the most important area in front of Decimus Burton's magnificent Palm House with an ornamental display of vegetables and herbs.

Besides this Palm House area I very much liked, in the large roundabout at the head of the Broad Walk, the combination of *Kochia childsii* and of the rambling yellow, coreopsis-like composite *Bidens ferulifolia*. Kochias make rather formal blobs of fresh green colouring. The bidens weaves among them and softens their outlines. Those two alone would have been enough for me. The jacarandas, grown as foliage dots, were a motley crew.

In the Broad Walk, the opposite pairs of beds often have the same contents. Not so this year; the contents are similar or comparable but not the same, and this is interesting. Two of the most successful ingredients are *Argyranthemum maderense*, 15in tall and smothered in pale yellow daisies, and the *Verbena × hybrida* clone, Silver Anne, which is not silver at all but a pretty shade (or shades, according to the age of its generous trusses) of pink. This verbena has the pale grey foliage of *Centaurea gymnocarpa* dots to set it off. The argyranthemum has a fringe of the purple heliotrope Marine, rather smothered by its exuberant team mate. I would not mind combining the pink verbena and the yellow daisy in the same planting. I might try that next year.

The daisy, which is a half-hardy perennial, propagated from cuttings and (like the verbena) overwintered under frost-free

177

glass, would until recently have been known as *Chrysanthemum*, like the Paris daisy, *Argyranthemum frutescens*, here represented by some excellent clones, all a mass of blossom. Jamaica Primrose, more than 3ft tall, had swamped its blue partner, *Felicia amelloides*.

The double pink, anemone-centred *A.f.* Vancouver (so named by Mr Halliwell, who found it in Vancouver) is an excellent bedder, here edged with the grey foliage of *Helichrysum petiolare*. Standards of *Plumbago capensis*, which should provide columns of blue, were engulfed. But it didn't matter, they probably would not have been flowering in this chilly summer anyway.

Mr Halliwell has long refused to bed out with 'geraniums', which he feels are quite sufficiently represented elsewhere, as indeed they are. But they can still be excellent bedders and I strongly recommend a visit to the Victoria Embankment gardens (next to the Embankment Underground station). There, the geranium seed strain Pulsar Red is strikingly combined with Blue Mink ageratums (which make a decent-sized plant and are not too squat) and an edging of Silver Dust *Cineraria maritima* (*Senecio cineraria*).

Preparations for next year's bedding have already been made with late summer and autumn sowings. Particularly useful, if you are short of heating facilities in the early months of the year, are sowings now of antirrhinums. They will germinate readily in a cold frame kept closed. The seedlings can be pricked off into trays as soon as large enough to handle. Ideally, you will then pot them individually in late October, into 4in or 5in pots (I use 4in Long Toms), and they can be grown hard enough to be overwintered, at least in the south, in a cold frame. That is, provided it has solid walls and can be kept snug, with hessian on frosty nights.

At low temperatures, darkness will not harm green plants for several weeks on end, and this is what will happen if snow falls. Don't clean it off; it is a marvellous insulator. But as soon as a thaw sets in, brush it aside, open up your frames and spray the contents with a fungicide. Your antirrhinums will make fine plants for bedding out by April. If overwintered in their trays, they should be potted in March, and will be ready for bedding a little later. That will suit you if they have to follow spring bedding.

Year after year I have been plagued with antirrhinum rust, even though it was not visiting the antirrhinums of many of my friends. This year I was ready for it. Tumble Blite exercises excellent protection. However, the rust must have heard the rumour and has stayed away. If it does strike, it can do so as early as April, so it is as well to be prepared. I am also sowing Viscaria seeds now to get big plants, some for display in 6in pots, others to bed out in the spring. Rose Angel is a particular favourite with me.

Dianthus are close relations. Autumn sowing of those best treated as annuals will make for stronger plants than sowings delayed until February or March. Such are Queen of Hearts, Brilliancy, Orchid Lace, Queen's Court, Telstar and Princess. The last makes large, bushy plants which flower with commendable persistence. Princess Scarlet is similar to Queen of Hearts. Princess White is dazzling, but I know of no retail outlet offering it as a separate colour. Write and ask them to do so. They need pressure from the customer.

Dianthus Rainbow Loveliness is a deliciously sweet-scented strain with lacy flowers in rosy purple, pink, mauve and white. Sow it now. I usually save my own seed and sow it forthwith.

— November 10, 1988 —

THE POND IN AUTUMN

I love my ponds at this season of the year. I love them at every season, but their charm in autumn is less heart-on-sleeve than at other times. On a calm day they seem to be musing; the double meaning of 'in a reflective mood' is altogether apt. When the wind blows, there is more light in the water and it is busy. One way or the other, there is far more water visible now than in the summer. The cover of waterlily pads is patchy, though the deep red Escarboucle keeps on flowering in all weathers.

In our octagonal sunk garden pool, the water soldier, *Stratiotes aloides,* has been a great feature all the summer. Like some great sea anemone with tentacles extended it makes a purple underwater rosette. In summer this rises to the surface and the projecting two or three inches of leaf are a festive bright green. These past two months they have sunk again but the purple rosettes make a beautiful pattern at slightly different levels and are thus three dimensional. It is a living tapestry design. Meantime, the pond's surface has been swept clean.

Of course there are leaves about, blown from the trees. Especially noticeable are the jagged outlines of my red oak, *Quercus rubra* (*Q. borealis*), which I took as a self-sown seedling from a neighbour's garden 30 years ago. Its parent blew to bits in a subsequent gale. It is a soft-wooded, fast-growing species so I am glad that mine is in poor soil. Its growth is good – it is quite a tree, now – but not too soft. It stands on a bank 40ft from the horse pond, so quite a lot of its leaves will never reach the water. That is good. If there are too many leaves from overhanging trees they form a thick mat at the bottom which is inimical to much pond life.

By and large, trees should be kept back from ponds so that plenty of light reaches the water. Any shading that this needs to prevent too much algal growth can be provided by waterlilies and by oxygenators within the water. Some of these last, especially the elodeas, can become pestilential weeds, but some are reasonably restrained. The water violet, *Hottonia palustris*, is my favourite

180

and is looking its best now. Its bright green filigree leaves are arranged in rosettes and these again are seen at varying levels, as if it might be an underwater cumulus cloud.

The only tree I have that is really close to the water's margin is a swamp cypress, *Taxodium distichum,* a deciduous conifer with bright green pinnate foliage all summer. Now it has changed to warm, foxy brown. I much prefer it to the fashionable dawn redwood *Metasequoia,* and it grows far more slowly, an advantage if you're not looking for great bulk.

The other pondside plant that has changed through yellow to warm rufous is the royal fern, *Osmunda regalis,* but I wish it was happier with me. It seems to relish the most acid soil and water conditions available. Huge old colonies more than 6ft high are the most interesting feature in Newick Park, 30 miles west of me in mid Sussex, which I visited for the first time in September. Once well established, osmunda colonies live happily without attention for centuries. Their range in the wild has been greatly reduced, partly by collectors but mainly, I should have said from observation in north west Scotland, by sheep grazing. Their strongholds in the Outer Hebrides, for instance, are on small islands within lochans, where the sheep cannot reach them. In June, the brilliance of their lime green fronds proclaims them from afar.

Even if they are not yet frosted, the pondside gunneras subside into dormancy now and I collect an inflorescence, covered in ripe seed, from each species, *Gunnera manicata* (the larger) and *G. tinctoria,* to dry off in a light window, indoors, and sow next spring, *G. tinctoria* always germinates with great freedom but I never know what results to expect from *G. manicata.* Certainly it must have plenty of light, for germination.

The dormant buds of gunneras enclosing next year's foliage are like huge udders. They are well protected with layer upon layer of pink, fimbriated scales. In a very hard winter the main bud may be killed but there are nearly always, at least in an established colony, smaller, better protected buds beneath the rhizome that supports the main ones, which will survive. It is common practice to fold the old, frosted leaves back into the centre of the plant as added protection.

After many years, a gunnera colony – which is always travelling outwards as do other rhizomatous colonisers, like irises – becomes naked in the centre. Here, by the horse pond, I planted a bamboo (at John Codrington's suggestion), *Arundinaria tesselata*, and it has made an excellent contrasting feature. It is a restrained clump former, some 9 or 10ft tall, well furnished with grey-green foliage. As the gunneras die off, the bamboo assumes greatest prominence and its leaves are at their smartest in autumn. By spring they will be horribly battered, but you can't expect an evergreen to smile at you year round.

I was interested to read an article by Allen Lacey in the *New York Times* magazine in which he describes Oehme and van Sweden's landscape architecture firm's pioneering work in the United States, wherein they lay increasing emphasis on large plantings of perennials, especially of ornamental grasses. But also on the use of water and water margin plants. 'Ninety per cent of the gardens their firm has recently completed or has on its drawing boards involve water, and in 60 per cent it is something other than a swimming pool.' (Swimming pools are not easy to integrate harmoniously into the garden scene.) 'Oehme points out that the fastest-growing segment of the nursery business in the US is that which specialises in aquatic and bog plants for the edges of ponds.'

Here, too, there are so many situations in which a pond would give more pleasure than a lawn. With water reflections our pleasures are doubled. That makes sense in the smallest garden, so long as young children are not an anxiety.

182

ANOTHER COUNTRY'S SPRING

In the middle of March I went to Georgia and North Carolina for nine days. Their winter has been as notably mild and their spring as early as ours, but being a good deal farther south (latitude 35 degrees rather than our 51), daffodils were already going over.

What struck me, however, as we flew into Atlanta, was the brownness of the countryside; much forest, not yet in leaf, and no green fields as we know them.

The temperatures during the first few days were in the upper 60s and lower 70s and there was something almost spooky about the nakedness of deciduous trees. A friend tells me that he got the same feeling at the other end of the season when visiting Minneapolis (west of Lake Superior) in early November. There was a heatwave taking temperatures into the 70s but the trees were already bare.

On large continents, big temperature swings can be expected in spring and autumn. During my last four days, it was cold, overcast and wet so that my eventual emergence at Gatwick airport on Good Friday seemed warm by comparison.

The principal early greenery in Atlanta is provided by the, of recent years, ubiquitously planted Bradford pear, a clone of *Pyrus calleryana*, whose homeland is China. Its flowering was already past and it was in young leaf. Its rapid growth and compact habit have recommended it for crazily widespread planting. It makes an unattractive ball-shaped specimen of no personality, with narrow-angled branching which now, in early middle age, is being discovered to constitute a serious weakness. A high wind or late snowfall when the foliage has already expanded causes the trees to break up.

183

Early interest in the woods around Asheville, in west North Carolina, is provided by our own familiar pussy willow, *Salix caprea*, which we also know as palm. It was, as in England, at the height of its flowering on Palm Sunday. There was also an early flowering *Amelanchier* species in bloom, but the field layer at the margins of and within such forest as I saw was without a single flower. This came as a surprise, seeing that our own woods were already a carpet of blossom from primroses, violets and anemones and of greenery from such as dog's mercury and bluebell foliage.

In this part of America there are similar wild flowers about, but one has to know where to find them. We visited one garden where the late owner had made a practice of naturalising native plants in a steeply sloping, north-facing section of forest where his home was located.

This is a charming kind of wild gardening and not too exacting. The only restraint necessary is in curbing the development of self-sowing scrub beneath trees that have been sufficiently (though not obviously) thinned to allow a little extra light to penetrate to floor level. One of the worst and most strangling of such invaders is honeysuckle. Now that the owner has gone and there is no one left with his interest in the project, it is sad to think that the colonies he had so successfully established will gradually be choked.

Already in bloom were a *Shortia*, a *Hepatica*, *Mertensia virginica*, not quite out, and blood root, *Sanguinaria canadensis*. In Britain one normally sees the double form of this which looks like a miniature white waterlily. It doesn't last long in bloom but perhaps for a day or two longer than the single-flowered wilding. I had thought, on this account, that the single was scarcely worth growing but its particular charm has gradually become apparent to me. One sometimes sees it in London at one of the RHS shows. I had hoped to be able to raise it from seed, but with no success.

Now the curator at the Atlanta Historical Society's gardens tells me that whereas fresh sanguinaria seed will germinate immediately, like hellebores, it quickly loses vitality, so is already dead by the time it comes into the customer's hands. I must find a way round this.

Another early flowerer in the late Mr Shinn's garden is *Erythronium americanum*, which had built up into a most satisfying and extensive colony. If there is a dull erythronium (the dog's tooth violets, or trout lilies, as they are called in America), I have yet to meet it. This one has mottled foliage and is yellow flowered, but dusky brown on the outside of the three outer segments, the most visible part of its flower when seen from above. It is available in the trade, at a price, and is said to be amenable to cultivation in this country, which is more than can be claimed of snowmelt erythroniums like *E. grandiflorum* and *E. montanum*.

There were wonderful colonies, here, of two club mosses (*Lycopodium* spp.), not at all dissimilar to the two species we commonly find on our hills. But I would never have expected them to flourish beneath trees. I wonder if ours would, or be otherwise adaptable to garden conditions. Has anyone tried them?

There is tremendous interest in America now in hardy perennials, which were the main subject of the talks I gave. Many new cultivars are coming in from Germany. I feel that the British have not sufficiently trained their eye in that direction. There is always a danger of our becoming complacent in our assumed role as the leading gardeners of Europe, possibly of the world.

One flower that could easily and quickly be improved in East American gardens is the Lenten rose – hybrids mainly deriving from *Helleborus orientalis*. They grow well under their conditions, but the flowers are unnecessarily small.

The highly developed kind that are being bred over here by Helen Ballard and Elizabeth Strangman (to name two grower enthusiasts), are not easily purchased because these hellebores lend themselves so reluctantly to being pulled to pieces in the way that most perennials can be divided. Neither can one take cuttings from them. Seed is the way: seedlings will not precisely replicate the parent, but, if of good lineage, they will make excellent plants. What the Americans need is fresh seed taken from good stock.

– May 11, 1989 –

UNDEMANDING LABOUR

One of our guides to parties who want to be shown round the garden is sometimes asked whether, as Mr Lloyd gets older, he is changing his style of gardening to be less labour-intensive. The answer is no. I do less actual labouring myself (because I spend a lot more time cooking and being sociable with house guests) but I have some excellent helpers in my garden. In any case a lot of my gardening is not demanding at all.

I don't grow plants because they are troublesome or because they are not, but because I want them for themselves. Many are undemanding. That is not to say they never require attention. Nearly all plants are the better for that, now and then, whether for feeding, pruning or splitting and re-setting, but for much of the time they are looking after themselves.

Apropos, I have just been looking at one border which is 6ft deep by nearly 30ft long. It is backed by a 5ft wall and by the bulk of the house in its southern corner. As it faces a little north of north-west, it receives no sun in winter, and late afternoon sun in summer. But there are no overhanging trees so there is plenty of sky light.

Ferns, hostas and epimediums head the cast. Self-sown hart's tongue ferns grow along the bottom of the wall. Four hefty clumps

186

of the soft shield fern cultivar, *Polystichum setiferum* Acutilobum, are spaced 3ft apart on a salient corner, with white martagon lilies and purple spiked orchids. *Dactylorhiza foliosa*, filling in behind them. Then there is *Hosta ventricosa* Variegata, whose yellow edged plantain leaves remain in good condition for longer than most hostas. The lavender bell flowers are good in July.

Behind that there are two more ferns, *Athyrium filix-femina* Plumosum Axminster, a form of lady fern with very finely divided pinnae (two plants of this), and *A. f.f.* Victoriae (found wild in Stirlingshire more than a century ago) with long, narrow fronds crested at every division. The pinnate leaf of *Epimedium pinnatum* subsp. *colchicum* is simple by comparison. Its butter yellow flowers in April match *Narcissus* Liberty Bells behind it. There is a plant of the evergreen, non-spreading *Sarcococca ruscifolia* behind these and hard up against the wall. Six feet is not, after all, a great border width.

Farther along is a patch of snowdrop species *Galanthus plicatus*, which I have to keep the evergreen epimedium from invading, and beyond that a pink 3–4ft filipendula, which is deciduous and so late into growth that it can mingle with the snowdrop as much as it likes. This is a kind of meadowsweet, and I moved most of it to a piece of boggy meadow, where it flourishes, flowering in July. But a bit got left behind and has made a new colony. It is better when given discreet staking and tying, the spot being draughty. But I sometimes hope to get away with omitting this attention.

There are two spurges: one, *Euphorbia amygdaloides* var. *robbiae*, an evergreen sub-shrub, is happiest against the wall. It is a curious species, it gets tired, after a while, of the spot in which you planted it and strays to nearby territory. The best course is to adjust your plantings to its progress. The other spurge is a dense clump-former, *E. wallichii*, only 2ft high with me, though taller in its native Kashmir, with a pale medium stripe on its leaves and a bold lime green inflorescence. That will be flowering soon but last a long time.

The border is mainly herbaceous but there are two more shrubs. *Rhododendron viscosum*, the swamp honeysuckle of Eastern America, is a June-flowering azalea, sweetly scented but lasting in good condition for no more than a week. *Clerodendrum bungei* is a suckering sub-shrub and I never quite know where I shall find it next, but as its growth is sparse, this doesn't much matter.

If its old wood is cut back by frost to the ground in winter, it starts up too late the next year to flower properly in its autumn season, but the proximity of Dixter allows mine to escape serious damage most of the time. This year it should be wonderful, from late August onwards, with dense, domed heads of rosy purple buds opening to wetly scented, paler flowers. Butterflies love it.

There are several other plants which seed or stray around. Forget-me-nots – they are in nearly all my borders, and so is the peach-leaved *Campanula persicifolia*, with blue or white bells in June–July. I see that that has seeded into the crown of one of the ferns, but it won't hurt. I am trying to eliminate purple-flowered honesty (*Lunaria annua*) seedlings here, as the sparrows strip their flowers. Welsh poppies in orange or yellow have to be controlled, but are good infillers, lovely and fresh at this season.

I also notice I have two fat, self-sown clumps of the candelabra *Primula bulleyana*, which is soft orange and quite welcome near the ferns if it doesn't overdo it. These primulas are liable to do their own thing incontinently, so I try to make a point of dead-heading when the top-heavy seedheads start to lollop sleazily around. *Saxifraga stolonifera*, excellent in damp shade, has beautifully patterned, shell-shaped leaves and open panicles of lop-sided, bluish white flowers at midsummer. It spreads by overground runners. It is such a grateful plant and really you need to do nothing to or for it, ever.

But most of the border's contents do benefit from a little

attention at one time in the year or another. Probably the reason it usually receives it is that it is very much in my line of passage from house to potting shed and frame yard. Bits of garden that you have to visit on a loop line tend to be a little more neglected, though even writing about my garden reminds me of jobs that need doing or that it would be nice to do. For instance, I should like to spread *Galanthus plicatus* a bit more deliberately among the meadowsweet before the snowdrop disappears from view.

And there is a bare patch from where I removed the handsome blue lungwort, *Pulmonaria* Lewis Palmer, to make a larger group elsewhere. I could replace it with a Himalayan golden saxifrage I have been given. *Chrysosplenium davidianum.* It looks a little more important than our native species, and that is the kind of emphasis you need in gardens.

– June 15, 1989 –

A FUNNY OLD YEAR

To anyone who works on the land, every year, without exception, seems exceptional. Nothing, or not much, works out as we had planned or expected, and it is the surprises that we remember – if we remember anything correctly, and that is not to be taken for granted.

This year is odd for two reasons. The winter was exceptionally mild and frost-free. The spring was exceptionally mild, dry and sunny. I take spring as ending on the last day of May, which is the day on which I am writing. As I walk around my garden, I am rather amazed and, I have to add, often delighted by what I see. After all, the mild winters of this and last year followed three in a row of great severity, so one felt a remission was needed, if gardening was not to become an endurance test.

Just look at the *Solanum jasminoides* Album. It is a twining climber of great vigour, but if, as usually happens, it is cut to the ground in winter, it takes so long to recover in the next year that it will hardly flower, if it does at all. In this expectation, it is sensible to take cuttings now, overwinter the young plants, by then in 3½in pots, under frost-free glass and plant them out next spring.

Treated thus, as half hardies, they will have a chance to give a reasonable account of themselves. Leave them *in situ* over the next winter in case you are lucky, but take a new batch of cuttings each June in the more likely eventuality of the old plants being crippled.

However, if spared, as this year, they will do a fantastic job, making a curtain of white, yellow-eyed, jasmine-like (but not fragrant) blossom from early June to November. My plant is 20ft high on the side of a barn, but the curtain is narrow. At Glyndebourne Opera, where several plants forming a single unit have been trained against the end of the Green Room, the curtain is a vast tapestry; a wonderful sight.

I should add, apropos this climber's hardiness, that, given fairly average winters, it is a notable success in London, and should be seen in lieu of rather boring Japanese honeysuckle (*Lonicera japonica* Halliana) in a great many urban gardens.

In the same family of *Solanaceae*, a shrub of similar hardiness, *Cestrum parqui*, is flowering now whereas in a normal year it will not start until July or even August. *C. parqui*, when performing, covers itself in a profusion of small, tubular, bright yellow-green flowers which have a most exotic, nutty fragrance at night. The easiest way to savour this is by picking a sprig to enjoy indoors, where it will perform for about three nights before becoming disgruntled by its treatment.

After the first crop, which is borne on the previous season's growth and has just started as I write, your shrub will make a lot of new shoots and flower terminally on these in late summer and

190

autumn. So, if old wood comes through the winter unscathed, flowering continues, with short pauses, from June to October. If frost cuts your shrub to the ground, its season will be halved. In the north it won't flower under any circumstances, because there is insufficient warmth to ripen its shoots. But if it likes you, it will tell you so unequivocally.

I have another cestrum, *C. fasciculatum*, in full bloom now, its old shoots wreathed in pinky red blossom – no scent in this case. Later, vigorous young growth will take over and it becomes a handsome foliage plant of a coarse and florid kind. Cestrums are generally rated as conservatory plants, but it is worth experimenting with them in warm corners outside, and this is a good time to get any such plant established.

The best-known shrub under the popular name of Californian tree poppy is *Romneya coulteri*, with big white poppy flowers and yellow stamens. That is pretty hardy, and flowers well in most parts of Britain, at least as far north as Edinburgh, but the other tree poppy from California is *Dendromecon rigida*. If you are anyway a poppy addict and don't know this yet (or even if you do), you will marvel at the sight of a healthy plant in bloom. Its vivid yellow, four-petalled flowers open to the sun in the mornings and are made doubly seductive by their background of glaucous lance leaves (their shape, undivided and with smooth margins, is unexpected in a poppy).

If this shrub is maimed in winter, it either dies or hangs on into another year with lack-lustre performance. This year the succulence of its juicy young shoots is fantastic. You should always insure against accidents by taking some stem cuttings in summer. Insert only one to each pot so that root disturbance, to which it is particularly sensitive, is never necessary.

I am glad that I started another plant of *salvia microphylla* var. *neurepia* last autumn (after a long interval). I took no precautions in case of hard weather and was vindicated, although nothing

191

could be easier than rooting cuttings of this shrubby sage. There are several similar salvias, and perhaps this one's foliage is the least interesting but its bright carmine pink flowers, borne in short spikelets, are a joy, and they are carried abundantly from May till late autumn, during which time the shrub will double or treble its size. It makes, on average, a 3ft bush each way, and can be pruned in spring as much or as little as you like. It is another of those plants that helps to give summer its voluptuous feel.

South African daisies do that too, and they are a confusing lot, especially the osteospermums, once dimorphothecas, of which more and more are being produced. The shrubby or sub-shrubby kinds are nice because they can, if necessary (which in most cases it is), be kept going from cuttings taken in autumn and over-wintered under barely frost-free glass. The one irritation in respect of many of them is their propensity to vegetate in summer, after a burst of spring blossom. Not all of them do, and shy flowering may simply be caused by capsid bugs damaging the young shoots.

The one that has spilt over with blossom in my garden this year is *Osteospermum ecklonis* Prostrata, white with a blue eye and bluish reverse to the rays. Its prostrate habit is especially good at a border's margin. It brought its old growth through last winter; hence the explosion. Then it will make a lot of new growth, and flower quite well, if not ecstatically, for the rest of the summer and autumn.

— August 3, 1989 —

IN SEARCH OF ORIGINALITY

One of the visiting public asked me to recommend any clematis that would thrive in a hot, dry garden in the South of France. Not knowing the area, I felt incapable of giving advice. Clematis like plenty of moisture in the growing season and to be cool at their roots. Most come from climates having abundant summer rainfall. All I could say was, take a look at gardens in the neighbourhood and see which clematis, if any, are thriving in them. Grow those.

I might have said, why bother to grow clematis at all? You could be growing exciting climbers like bougainvillaeas and begonias (*Campsis grandiflora* et al.), which we find difficult but which would bask and revel in the extra heat. Why not garden with your given conditions instead of against them? Yet that is perversely the way we so often carry on.

This is largely a matter of sentiment. We want to grow the plants we were familiar with at home or in our youth. British expatriates in East Africa, I remember from 40 years ago, all wanted to grow roses. Seeing that there is no winter in equatorial regions, the roses have no resting season. They exhausted themselves by flowering non-stop throughout the year, and within a short time, fresh stock had to be imported from temperate climes.

Despised cannas, on the other hand, grew and flowered prodigiously. If they needed a rest, they could be lifted and allowed to dry out on the soil surface for a while. I haven't seen cannas in their native West Indies and Central America, but plants such as these and dahlias, which form a fleshy rootstock, whether rhizome, bulb or tuber, are not merely providing for uncongenial growing conditions but, by so doing, actually need them. The tulips and irises of the Middle East are geared to a summer baking. Doubtless some similar condition (though not the subsequent blanket of winter snow which many bulbs receive) affects dahlias and cannas.

Be that as it may, I fell for cannas in Kenya where I once saw a big planting of different varieties in groups on either side of a stream and beneath the dappled shade of trees. Their normally horrible bedded treatment at the hands of parks departments is

193

quite unnecessary and puts most gardeners off them. But is it climatically sensible to grow them in England at all? I think so. Their leaves look splendid whatever happens and the flowers are a bonanza if the summer obliges.

Life would be humdrum did we not live on the borderlines of what is sensible and what is stupid. No one can yet tell us, in advance, what kind of a summer we are going to have, but it is as great a shame to miss out on all the flowers that will benefit from a corker as it would be asinine to grow nothing but.

Thanks to heat and drought, it is a bad season with me for rust on the antirrhinums and red spider in the primrose plants; but it is super for zinnias (on which I laid a tiny bet), tithonias (first cousins of zinnias) and petunias. Next year (*pace* the greenhouse effect pundits) it may be the other way about, with the lovers of cool, moist conditions coming to the top. We have to hedge our bets.

But to take one's gardening traditions abroad is dubious practice. Box hedging is almost worshipped in New England, where a special society exists for its promotion, yet it is grown under duress and needs special protection against snow in winter.

Australian gardeners, I am told, are only just coming round to a greater appreciation of their amazing native flora, while in the more populated areas of New Zealand one can travel for many miles seeing only plants of European, Asiatic and American origin. No doubt this is an exaggeration, but certainly their native plants, so widely cultivated in Britain, are far less regarded at home.

We most of us have a tendency to take what is native for granted and there is an element of snobbery in this. The exotic has greater appeal. The wildlife enthusiast would like us to grow nothing but native plants as these provide food for the whole range of native fauna, which are in need of protection. This would provide a rather unstimulating diet, seeing that, for geological and climatic reason, our native flora is singularly restricted, and anyway, some of our fauna are sufficiently adaptable to be able to thrive on exotic food.

Cabbage white caterpillars appear to be as fond of nasturtiums as of brassicas. Elephant hawk moths can be successfully reared on fuchsias and death's heads on potatoes. But if we had a flora like Turkey's or New Zealand's I should revel in making a garden feature of it.

Probably not of it alone, not having a pigeon-hole mind. I do enjoy combining plants experimentally which could never have got together in nature. And that is possibly a less unnatural way to carry on than planting all the roses in one place, all the hostas in another, the ferns in a fernery, the shrubs in a shrubbery, the bedding plants in beds for them alone.

Meantime, the botanical gardens, in which there is only a limited horticultural driving force and design is at a discount (most botanical gardens are a visual mess, although packed with interesting detail) – these places are justifying themselves by educating us. Their plants are arranged by continents. Thus we can discover what grows in other parts of the world (supposing it does not object to growing in ours) without being obliged to visit them.

Gardening fashions are epidemic. They are largely controlled by officials trying to do a good job but lacking inspiration. Bureaucracy is the enemy of inspiration and individuality. It is in private gardens that we must seek and shall sometimes find these qualities. And what a joy that is, but it has little to do with fashion or with the worship of ancestral practices, with nostalgia or with a desire to educate or even to emulate. It is that intangible something which immediately proclaims that behind the scenes there is an original, whose guiding hand has created something ephemeral, yes, but with the magic of a sunset. This is unlikely to be achieved by trying to grow clematis in conditions that they loathe.

OFF TO A FLYING START

Large pots and tubs planted up last May for display through the summer and early autumn months have done particularly well this year. To date, there have been no howling gales to tear them apart, and they mostly comprise plants that have revelled in the prolonged sunshine.

The gardener has to accept that watering is a daily chore, but it is something that the willing guest will give you respite from. In any case it doesn't take very long, especially if there is a dip supply – so much quicker than awaiting the pleasure of a tap. Once the contents of a pot, tub or trough have covered the surface with a tangle of vegetation, you can simply tip the contents of a can on top of everything; no need to use the spout. A large pot will take a daily gallon.

Feeding, which needs to go hand in hand with watering, takes a little longer, stirring the stated dose of Phostrogen into each gallon. 'How often do you feed your plants?' visitors often ask me. I suppose it's about once a week in fine weather when I'm watering a lot. I start off with a strong John Innes compost, No.3, so feeding doesn't become necessary or desirable until there is good plant cover. That is quickly achieved by close planting, which I'm all for.

Enthusiasts are apt to over feed, with the result that they get enormously lush leafage and little flower, especially noticeable with nasturtiums and 'geraniums'. You soon learn the right balance. In shady situations, flowers are generally less prolific anyway.

Most of the plants used for ornamental pots and tubs are tender perennials. Rather than trying to save old plants, which are apt to become woody and gnarled with age, it is generally preferable to renew your stock from cuttings, taken now and over wintered under frost-free glass. There are exceptions. Old plants of *Convolvulus mauritanicus* (correctly *C. sabatius*) get you off to a flying start the next year. We pot these into large pots, and they do take up quite a lot of space on the greenhouse bench (rooted cuttings are more economical of precious winter space).

Next year, these huge old plants can, if necessary, be chopped into more manageable chunks. Wait till they are actively growing before you do this. In fact you can wait till May, when you are planting your tubs up for the summer. There will be a noticeable check to their growth but it won't last long.

Still, I should recommend taking some cuttings of young convolvulus shoots now. Keep them under close, humid conditions in a frame or propagator until they have stopped flopping. Then harden them off and leave them in the same pot they were rooted in over winter (you can fit a dozen or more cuttings into one 3½in pot, but there will be some misses). Pot them off individually in March or April.

This is the treatment for all cuttings taken now. It is generally unwise to pot them off as soon as rooted in the tail end of the year. Quite apart from the fact that this takes up a lot of space, they will have little inclination to make new growth with shortening days, feeble light and falling temperatures. Many losses can occur through getting busy at the wrong time. Wait till the year is on your side again before disturbing young plants and offering them new potting compost.

Convolvulus mauritanicus carries a long succession of flowers that open almost blue in the morning turning mauver in the afternoon before they close again around 4 p.m. It has a good, mat-forming habit that droops over the margin of its container. So have cascade lobelias (*Lobelia erinus*), and the clone called Richardii, excellent for its sky-blue colouring, is easily struck from cuttings.

197

The blue daisies of *Felicia* are also much to our purpose. I have grown *F. pappei* (*Aster pappei*, as we always knew it) for many years, and I do prefer its near linear foliage to the coarser, oval leaves of *F. amelloides*, but its flowers are not quite significant enough. In this respect *f. a.* Santa Anita is the one to grow: sizeable blue, yellow-eyed daisies presented on long stems. Both stems and faded flowers need dead-heading regularly.

In the 'geranium' (really pelargonium) field, the ivy-leaved kinds are the floppers, and although there are seed strains, such as Summer Showers, they are not as impressive as some of the named kinds kept going from cuttings. Among the most prolific in flower is the elfin Roi des Balcons (alias Ville de Paris), so widely used on the Continent.

In the centre of your pots you will need a bushier, more up-standing geranium. A strong red, orange or magenta will often be just what the position requires. It can be offset by the grey foliage of *Helichrysum petiolare* or the smaller-leaved *H. microphyllum*, which we now have to call by the hideous name *Plecostachys serpyllifolia*.

When rooting these woolly-leaved plants which are apt to damp off in the early stages, keep them close only as far as is necessary to prevent wilting. I find cold frame protection under a single light and with the dappled overhead shade of ash trees sufficient. As soon as the cuttings will stand up to ventilation, give it them in increasing doses, and over winter on an open greenhouse bench. Gas or paraffin heating where the fumes circulate within the greenhouse is particularly damaging to these plants. Stick to electricity if you can, though a second source of heat is a wise precaution in case of power cuts.

All the spreading kinds of verbena are excellent tub plants. I have a display of the scarlet *Verbena peruviana* in a sink, mixed in with the little white Mexican daisy, *Erigeron karvinskianus* and a bit of lime green spurge, the biennial *Euphorbia stricta*. This is charming, but the last two ingredients have sown themselves into a planting which I originally made last year with the verbena alone. In its first season it hardly flowered at all, but the plants overwintered and this year it is abundant and much improved by its companions.

Verbenas root easily, not only from the usual nodal cuttings (trimming the base of your cuttings just below a nodal pair) but, giving you twice as many plants from the same material, from intermodal cuttings, making your lower cut just above a nodal pair. This pair will form the top of your next cutting. Fuchsias will respond to the same treatment.

– October 26, 1989 –

GLORIOUS ANTICIPATION

I never feel I have enough bulbs and I specially enjoy the freshness of those that flower in autumn when so much else is going to rest. Having, effortlessly, worked up quite large stocks of colchicums in our borders, how wonderful, I thought, it would be to have a great carpet – tufted – of their clumps in a piece of meadow. They grow naturally in meadows and short grass makes the best sort of background, since they have none of their own, producing foliage only in spring.

We have a sort of no-man's-land enclosure, with a horseshoe of ilex (*Quercus ilex*) hedging round it that was originally intended as a small formal garden. The soil was horrible and the intention lapsed in 1934. Since then it has just been meadow.

How wonderful it would be, I first thought, some 15 years ago, to plant it all over with purple-flowered English iris (*Iris xiphioides*) bulbs, which always accumulate enormously in the garden proper. Their performance varies from year to year but they

199

have done rather well and they come as something of a surprise at the end of June.

But in this patch, black medick, a wretched annual weed which is leguminous, drags down much of the herbage, including the irises, with its long, lanky growth. If I remember to water its young seedlings, in October, with a selective weedkiller such as we use on the lawns, there is no trouble in the following year. I don't always remember.

However, at colchicum time the turf is tight. The problem with colonising them is that when you want to plant them, in August or early September, just after the grass has been shorn and just before they start flowering and growing themselves, the ground is iron hard and won't take the bulb planter.

I don't know how many gallons I put on that patch from the sprinkler, leaving it on all night as well as by day. At the end of it, the planter still penetrated only two inches. So I repeated the treatment. Now the colchicums are in and sweet anticipation takes over. I have a glorious vision in my mind's eye, not for this year or next but years hence when (if) they have clumped up. It could happen. It often doesn't, but never mind. Many of our best moments are spent fantasising, and this is by no means pure fantasy.

In 1976 I had the same kind of vision in respect of *Crocus speciosus*, the blue-flowered autumn species which multiplies at a great rate in cultivated ground – hence my spare stocks – but is also as happy as any crocus can be in meadow. It was the area near our horse pond that I had in mind to go to town with, and I planted when the ground was still soft in April and the turf still short. These crocuses are showing their 'grass' then and it is a convenient time for spreading them around.

Thirteen years later I am still awaiting realisation of my dream. The ground was extremely badly drained and rushes took over much of the area. Their roots and rhizomes are pretty exclusive to other plants, and anyway few bulbs like to sit in water for any length of time. Now we have put in some efficient Barflow drains. Combined with the past dry summer, the rushes have almost disappeared and there are still signs of the crocuses, although they have barely increased. They could do yet.

Another autumn-flowering bulb that I was anxious to establish in the garden was the Scarborough lily, *Vallota speciosa* (now *Cyrtanthus elatus*, if you can bear it). Although it is normally a window-sill bulb, Robinson in his great work stated that it could be flowered outside. I found a baking position, but for several years only foliage materialised. After the hot summer it must flower this year or never, I thought.

In early September a flowering stem poked through. I was overjoyed. The stem was dark purple with a spiral twist on it. Odd. The buds were pale, not bricky red. Odder still. It soon transpired that I had planted *Amaryllis belladonna,* not vallota at all. This was annoying, but as I'd failed to flower amaryllis when I last tried it as a boy, I'm quite pleased in a way. But the Scarborough lily question remains unanswered. Have any readers tried it in their gardens?

Blue tropical waterlilies have been tantalising me for some time. With the help of my vet friend, Nick Mills, who knows a lot about fish and aquaria, I installed a cylindrical tank within our sunk garden pond, filled with soil and warmed by an immersion heater connected to the nearest power point (that cost £90 to rig up, which I didn't resent at all).

My first lily, Blue Beauty, came from a botanic garden. It flowered well, from August to October, but I was unable to overwinter it. I felt I couldn't keep on begging for fresh pieces so I missed a year but was then put on to a firm which sells them. Blue Beauty from them didn't flower at all.

So, from them again, now in my fourth year, I tried another blue variety, Pamela. It didn't arrive till July, when half the

201

summer was over, but by September it had woken up. The first bloom is open as I write and there are a number of buds to follow. The flowers are small, but if lots of them came out together they would make a lovely contrast to the pink hardy kinds. So I feel I'm getting somewhere, especially as the supplier told me to leave the plant *in situ* through the winter. They generally survive, he said. I shall leave the heater on also; it can't be costing me much.

Enthusiasts for rhododendrons, camellias and magnolias will by now have summed up the prospects for their favourite shrubs, whose flower buds become clearly differentiated from six to nine months before they actually flower. That allows plenty of scope for mouthwatering anticipation.

I remember how keen 'Cherry' (Collingwood) Ingram was that his own rhododendron crosses should flower before he died. He lived to 100 but some of the crosses were made quite late in life and seedlings tend to be a long time coming to maturity. When one of them flowered and realised his dreams, its proud creator named it Immensity.

I was given a camellia called Drama Girl and it is covered in buds, but such a coarse thing, large leaves, woody stems. I think exasperation may get the better of anticipation in its case.

– November 16, 1989 –

DIFFERENCES DOWN UNDER

I learnt a lot in the Antipodes. For instance, the small garden requiring minimum maintenance can be described as 'a human comfort zone'. In it, you go in for back-yarding. That expression came up from one of my phone-in radio interviewers – I forget if it was John, Matthew, Malcolm or a fourth gentleman whose name I never did learn. Anyway, I became a hardened interviewee and even protested that back-yarding didn't give a very flattering notion of a garden. Beth Chatto, who was in the same expedition, said it conjured up an image of dustbins, washing lines and children rushing around on tricycles. I wish I'd thought of that.

The fact that I saw and heard so many British birds in every garden was less surprising after we were told that they were deliberately introduced by settlers in the mid-19th century and that there was a Bird Acclimatisation Society for this very purpose.

Gardens were packed with both familiar and unfamiliar plants, sometimes making strange bedfellows. Thus, in a garden near Auckland, *Strelitzia reginae*, the bird of paradise flower, was close to a carpet of water forget-me-nots, while the lose-growing 'tree' fern, *Dicksonia squarrosa*, which one had supposed to be a shade lover, was intertwined with *Helichrysum petiolare*, generally accorded an open site. However, one has to remember that in a hot climate, plants which we regard as sun lovers will often bake brown, and are much more comfortable in shade.

Orange clivias were flowering abundantly in many gardens, but where exposed to sunshine, their old leaves were a sorry mess and made a poor setting for the flowers. The best planting I saw, at Dalvui in West Victoria, was beneath a tree and in the company of ferns, both terrestrial and epiphytic on the tree's trunk – our old conservatory friend, *Platycerium bifurcatum*.

Fashions are evident there as elsewhere. Almost every suburban garden in Christchurch (and theirs was a high standard of maintenance) had its quota of clipped *Photinia* × *fraseri* Red Robin. The bushes look lumpy and the red young shoots are numbingly assertive. With us at their season you'd have been getting an overdose of double pink Kanzan cherries.

Rock gardens were much enlivened by self-seeding colonies of ixias, freesias and the closely related *Sparaxis* and *Babiana*. In one garden there was a great carpet of browny red and yellow sparaxis beneath an oak tree in young leaf.

Freesias were also common in paving cracks, together with the familiar Mexican daisy, *Erigeron karvinskianus* (*mucronatus*). Freesias also colonised and went feral on rocky roadside banks. They were old-fashioned, deliciously scented kinds.

On roadside verges we saw colonies of the pale green, sweetly scented *Gladiolus tristis* in full bloom. Clearly this was accidental but it would be easy to start meadow gardening with plants such as these, albeit not natives. What they called onion grass – *Babiana rosea* – neither an onion nor a grass but a bulbous plant with pink star flowers, was universally reviled as a weed, but in turf it could surely be welcomed. Whenever I admired a flower that seemed to be doing really well, I was told it was a weed. Also, if you ask an expert the name of a plant he cannot name, it is likewise dismissed as a weed.

In frost-free gardens, which they all were, cinerarias of the kind we grow as spring-flowering pot plants will flourish and self-sow. In the course of years, they lose some of their man-bred squatness and outsize blooms, becoming much more natural and relaxed. Their colours are still brilliant and can look excruciating among evergreen azaleas. On the other hand, they make a lovely surround to lemons, whose branches are dripping with fruit down to ground level.

Macadamia (*M. ternifolia*) nuts have only recently become popular in Britain. I think that, as much as its flavour, it is the way the nut crunches and crumbles between your molars that makes it so attractive. But the bush is attractive too: evergreen like a laurel and hung, in spring, with chocolate-scented, dusky pink racemes of blossom. The nut shells are so hard that specially strong nutcrackers with colossal leverage are required if you are to deal with them on a domestic scale.

Seeing that spring was already well advanced, I was a little surprised in an Auckland garden centre to see a forsythia, still leafless and covered in blossom. It had, I learnt, been fetched up from the far colder south and would never again flower as well in Auckland, where the winters are too mild for these shrubs to set flower buds freely.

The owner of this chain of centres finds it worth his while to take trained students from our own Horticultural College at Pershore, where there is an excellent course in garden centre management. These Britons enjoy the life in New Zealand and often remain. This suits him better than having to train them himself. Well done, Pershore.

Camellias were still in full bloom in Victoria and they did not endear me to the large-flowered cultivars any more than hitherto, although there was one garden, in the Dandenong Hills east of Melbourne, where a single white *Camellia japonica* was radiant, from top to toe, with yellow-centred blossom. It looked like Alba Simplex (or White Swan) but I was told a different name and certainly it had not held on to a single browned bloom.

How different from the double white camellias I saw, hideous with unshed browned rosettes, and they were at the peak of their flowering with plenty of buds to come. It beats me how the owners can remain blind to such a fault. It is just the same here.

I described the sage-leaved *Buddleia salvifolia* in this column, earlier in the year. We have to treat it as a wall shrub. In Victoria you see it as a splendid tree, up to 20ft high and 30ft across, a dome, laden with lavender grey blossom trusses down to ground level, and scenting half the garden. Another scented flower that blooms prodigiously and as we never see it is *Clematis armandii*. Extra summer heat does tell when it comes to ripening tree and shrub wood in preparation for next year's flowering.

205

BLACK AND WHITE

The smartness of black and white has always appealed in men's and women's dress and on stage; so why not in the garden?

Start with a grove of white-stemmed birches, *Betula jacquemontii*, and underplant with a carpet of *Ophiopogon planiscapus* Nigrescens, with black strap leaves. (This has already been done but not yet overdone.) That will last all winter and to it, if the site is reasonably moist, one could add the black-stemmed form of common dogwood, *Cornus alba* Kesselringii. Large clumps of snowdrops interspersed will be *de rigueur*. I should recommend the bold *Galanthus nivalis* Samuel Arnott, which clumps up quickly.

To this winter assemblage add the darkest-flowered *Helleborus orientalis* hybrids, having cut their tatty old green leaves away well before the display. They, too, can be highlighted by snowdrops, preferably a rather later-flowering strain, such as some of the *G. elwesii* hybrids or *G. ikariae* subsp. *latifolius*.

That will set your winter garden up nicely, a complete feature in itself. For the other seasons you will need to allot another area and various snags need to be discussed. First, how far can the rules be stretched in defining black? There are some truly black berries, although they may be hidden among green leaves, as in the blackcurrant, but black flowers and leaves are deep maroon or purple.

Despite their optimistic naming, flowers such as *Delphinium* and *Buddleia* Black Knight are flagrantly no darker than purple, while *Magnolia liliflora* Nigra is not even as dark as Ribena. Then, again, one must accommodate oneself to the fact that most of the plants that do have acceptably black flowers have green foliage.

A good planting of black tulips will not show too much leaf, which is well below the bloom, and anyway one can engulf them with a white carpeter. I suggest *Anthemis cupaniana*, whose leaves are grey. Its white daisies are at their peak in mid May, which will call for a May-flowering tulip. I find the shape of Black Parrot disappointing, while the square-shouldered black Darwins are stodgy; I suggest using the sulky purple Greuze. One could, alternatively, give it a background of white wallflowers – White Dame or Ivory White (the ivory of yellowing old tusks).

Meanwhile, in April, I should like a patch of black fritillaries, and would choose *Fritillaria pyrenaica* because it is an easy garden plant – which is more than can be said of most. That could be shown off by white button pomponette daisies or by a white-flowered mossy saxifrage (*Saxifraga hypnoides*), or a wood anemone such as the double *Anemone nemorosa* Vestal.

Very dark foliage is going to be an asset as background to white flowers. Two shrubs which can be stooled back annually (thus achieving the boldest foliage effect on their young shoots) are *Sambucus nigra* Purpurea, a selection of the common elder, and *Prunus cerasifera* Nigra, a selection of the cherry plum. The latter is darkest when its leaves are mature.

A group of cape hyacinths, *Galtonia candicans*, would look handsome in front of it. Their leaves, being low down, could be masked by a planting of *Sedum telephium* Maximum Atropurpureum, which is a stonecrop growing 2ft tall and with dark fleshy leaves. It is a somewhat gawky perennial and I like to see it filled around with the pale, felted foliage of *Senecio cineraria* (*Cineraria maritima*) in a clone such as White Diamond or Ramparts. This is a not very hardy shrub. If it survives the winter, be sure to cut it hard back in April, otherwise it will carry its unprepossessing yellow daisies. We don't want to be made a laughing stock.

The dancing, insect-like flowers of *Gillenia trifoliata*, 3ft, would make a pretty foreground to the elder in early summer, or the white dittany, *Dictamnus albus*.

As a low, marginal feature one could grow black-faced violas. The annual, self-sowing *Omphalodes linifolia* would make a charming contrast in early summer, its upright, loosely spiky habit in contrast to the lolling viola. *O. linifolia* has grey leaves, and its white flowers have more substance and personality than the comparable annual gypsophila's.

In *Papaver orientale* Black and White, you have an oriental poppy combining both our dominant colours, that black forming big basal blotches on each petal. An amorphous plant like this needs a structural companion. It could be *Crambe maritima*, our native seakale, whose cloud of honey-scented white blossom opens at the turn of May and June above glaucous foliage. It has a stiffly branching habit. You could even grow the poppy in the centre of a grouping.

Any plea for *Geranium phaeum*, the Mourning Widow cranes-bill, falls on deaf ears. It has a miserably insignificant flower on a weedy plant. The white-flowered Album is more significant, but I should far prefer *G. sylvaticum* Album, of which we could create a 2ft carpet beneath *Paeonia delavayi*, which is deepest maroon. Plant several of this 'tree' peony, if you can spare the space.

And I shall turn a blind eye to the genus *Hemerocallis*: Black Knights, Princes, Dragons, Magic, the lot. They surround themselves with far too voluminous a luxuriance of green strap leaves for any white, contrasting flower to be able to approach closely.

The 6ft *Veratrum nigrum* we must attempt, whatever inroads the slugs may make upon its foliage. That will flower in July, with panicles of black stars. They would not go amiss with its white counterpart, *V. album*, both liking moist soil. So does the dragon arum, *Dracunculus vulgaris*, another July flowerer but at 2½ft.

White border phloxes would be in contrast, and I should like to see the elegant cones of *Phlox maculata* Mrs Lingard in a neighbour planting to the blackest possible form of *Iris chrysographes*. Again they are moisture-loving, but it is pointless to site black-flowered plants in shade. Herb Christopher, *Actaea spicata*, will revel in damp, humus-rich soil, but its gleaming black berries will show to advantage only if they can reflect sky shine.

We must have the cocoa-scented *Cosmos atrosanguineus*, but my vulgar instinct would be to contrast it with strong yellow flowers, so I had better stop writing.

— January 4, 1990 —

RETROSPECTIVE

Most people look back on an old year with distaste, aware of the shortcomings in their own behaviour and blaming them on hideous fate. The new year will be different.

Gardeners moan as much as the rest, but should surely recall with lingering affection the prolonged summer, warm but seldom excessively hot, when we could really enjoy our gardens as a garden is meant to be enjoyed, either by ourselves, when we are most aware of the feel of plant and animal life around us, or in the relaxed company of friends. There were even a few evenings (not many), when biting insects were in abeyance, although the midge season in Scotland was phenomenal.

Neither was spring, of which expectations tend to run so much too high, the customary disappointment. There were some beautiful warm spells and following an exceptionally mild winter everything was, and continued to be, absurdly ahead of normal. Our village spring flower show was held on April 15 and this would normally have been a peak date for daffodils. In the event, most were well past it, but the show was the prettiest I have seen in years.

There was so much else in bloom that might normally have been backward; notably tulips, polyanthus and wallflowers. Daffodils arranged for exhibition, three to a standard vase (those vases have much to answer for), at best look stiff and sparse, so I felt no regrets for their being thin on the benches.

Although it was not a vintage year in the pleached lime walk at Sissinghurst Castle, there was much inspiration in their spring garden. For instance, the white bells of *Leucojum aestivum* Gravetye Giant in front of Crown Imperial fritillaries. In the nut walk, there was a singular freshness from the combining of white Spanish bluebells with Bowles's golden grass, *Milium effusum* Aureum. The latter can also team up charmingly with blue forget-me-nots.

Woodland Shade

The young foliage of shuttlecock ferns, *Matteuccia struthiopteris*, contrasted strikingly with the broad, plain, pleated leaves of *Veratrum nigrum*. Again, this was beneath the nuts, and it is worth observing that this shady walk is by no means heavily shaded. The nuts have been rigorously thinned, greatly to the advantage of all the ground flora beneath them. They always flower most freely after the wood has been coppiced.

A mild winter followed by a hot summer is uncommon in Britain and one way we notice its result is in the freedom of many plants' flowering; especially shrubs, that are often costive. Thus, *Cestrum parqui*, which brought its old growth through the winter, flowered magnificently from June until late autumn. If you like to sit out after dark, plant this green-flowered beauty where its night fragrance will be carried to you on the air. Alternatively, bring a succession of cut stems into the house to savour there.

The summer jasmine, *Jasminum officinale*, is night scented and its larger-flowered cultivar, Affine, which is inclined to be less free than the straight species (although flowering over a longer period) was prodigal this year.

There has been a great bud set, thanks to the summer, on plants whose flowering we are enjoying now (*Iris unguicularis* and *Chimonanthus praecox*, the winter sweet, for instance), or have yet to enjoy. If your *Clematis cirrhosa* does not flower generously this winter and next early spring, move it to a warmer spot (or throw it out). The bud set on rhododendrons is phenomenal.

Our main trial, however, has been, and continues to be, drought. For all that we often curse it, rain is as great a benediction as sunshine. Water restrictions played havoc in many gardens in the south. But nature has a way of compensating for its deficiencies and excesses. It will be interesting to see what 1990 has in store. Perhaps the wettest spring and summer ever.

– April 26, 1990 –

LICKING OUR WOUNDS

All right, so it was a stinking frost and most of our gardens caught it, but at least we had enjoyed some exceptional flowering tree and shrub displays before it came. And somehow, it seems to me, those great moments are the more intensely felt in the almost certain knowledge that they will be brought to an abrupt end.

The promising young figs that I wrote of last week have every one of them been reduced to pulp. Hopes are now deferred to 1991. The young cones on *Abies koreana* were also frozen. What about premature clematis flower buds? I haven't dared to scrutinise them yet. But this kind of damage is a reminder that the later-flowering clematis – those that do it from late June onwards – are the most reliable rent-payers.

Of the hydrangeas, *H. villosa* was, as usual, the worst hit. This is

211

a winter-hardy shrub, but spring frosts on its tender young shoots can play merry hell. An old, established plant will recover, but I am expecting no blossom. John Treasure tells me I'm wrong: from past experience he expects Phoenix to rise from the ashes. I hope he's right. *H. quercifolia*, interestingly, scarcely suffered on its young foliage at all, while the tough *H. paniculata* types have not yet made leaves to be frosted.

I know that this is not a kind time of year to be judging evergreens, which always look their worst in spring, but I wonder how many gardeners have had a joyful experience from *Choisya ternata* Sundance since it took the horticultural world by storm two or three years ago? It is amazing how gardeners can lose their heads over a plant like this, whose charms depend on its being brought on fast, under protection, and then being launched from garden centres as though they were hardy shrubs. Hardy after a fashion, they may be.

Given the last three mild winters, few are likely to have been killed. But the tender lime-green of their young foliage, for which we buy them, is not made for exposure to the sunshine and wind of an al fresco existence. I think, and indeed hope, that this nurseryman's bonanza is near its end, although one has to remember the proverbial fools (and novices) that are being born every minute. And there may still be a place for Sundance in protected London patios. I should prefer a fatsia or a stately bamboo, any day. Or the spicy scent of a myrtle. Young myrtle shoots were blighted by that frost, but I think they will bloom well this year, come August.

Actinidia kolomikta, that climber of the pink, white and green young foliage, must have a great resilience. Its young foliage is dreadfully susceptible to frost, and yet the shrub is tough, as happy in Scotland as it is much farther south. In Sweden I have seen it effectively grown as an unsupported shrub without wall protection. You don't have to treat it as a climber. It would make a good lawn specimen.

212

I was telephoned by an anxious gardener yesterday, to ask how he should plant a summer jasmine, *Jasminum officinale* Affine. His literature told him all about clematis – making a hole 2ft square and deep, excavating uncongenial subsoil and replacing with a mixture of good top soil, old potting soil and well-rotted farmyard manure or garden compost – but nothing on jasmines.

At first I couldn't see the problem. As with *Clematis montana* (they would be a good match, planted together), excess vigour is more likely to arouse anxiety with this jasmine than failure through lack of adequate preparation. He was planning to grow it over an arbour. Having discovered that his soil was a sandy loam, I suggested that he just add some organic matter and plant it. But this didn't satisfy him. Only when I allowed him to give it the full treatment, was he happy enough to ring off. 'Warum einfach wenn es kompliziert geht?', as the Germans say. (Why take the simple course if a more elaborate one is on offer?)

It is rather pleasing when crime (mine, not yours) fails to be visited by punishment. The Generaal de Wet tulips that I forgot to extract from the bag they arrived in last October, until I planted them in early March, are now coming into bloom as unconcernedly as if they had received princely treatment. It is amazing what you can sometimes get away with. Narcissi would dry out far more readily. I have just discovered another over-looked bagful of sprouting tulips. Must pop them in somewhere. The trouble is that they do so well in my garden, with its stiff clay soil, that I am already overflowing with them. A delightful kind of overflow.

I am sometimes asked how deep I plant tulips, and my answer – just below the surface – arouses surprise. I took that tip, years ago, from Brighton Parks department and it certainly works well. Also it's so simply and quickly done. If the tulips are to remain through the years, they have their own devices for going deeper should they need to. Many of the species produce dropper bulbs, at the end of stolons leading from the original bulb, and these can quest 9in to 12in deep. There, in their native Middle East habitats, they are protected from heat and drought and also, in some circumstances, from the plough. However, most hybrid tulips are happy near the surface, and there they remain.

There was a dianthus in bloom here at the beginning of the month: a new one to me, Monica Wyatt, which I had admired on the RHS trial grounds at Wisley. Fully double, soft lilac pink with maroon base and an excellent scent.

The young, non-flowering shoots that your pinks have made by now are excellent material for cuttings. Detach them *in toto*, trim the base and shorten the leaves, with a single chop, by a third, so as to cut down on transpiration. Stick them into a gritty cutting compost in a closed cold frame. They mustn't be allowed to shrivel or wilt, but on the other hand too humid an atmosphere destroys the natural waxy coating that makes dianthus leaves look blue and exposes them to fungal disease. So, as soon as you detect, from new growth, that roots are being made, give them a little ventilation. Increase this until they are hardened off and can be potted individually into a more nourishing compost.

— October 18, 1990 —

RICHES OF AUTUMN

This is the time of year when I most enjoy writing my weekly piece, while sitting in the sunshine in our sunk garden. I am reluctant to switch on the central heating before I must, knowing that it will be piling up the bills for the next six months, and the sun makes it feel warmer out than in.

Besides which, there is still so much colour to be enjoyed in the garden. More than usual, in fact. Around my feet, red valerian is flowering as freshly as though it were early June (it was cut hard back after its first flush), while behind me the little, wall-inhabiting Mexican daisy, *Erigeron karvinskianus*, which started up in May, seems to have taken a fresh interest in life.

Hardy fuchsias could have been flowering since early summer, and so, to an extent, they were, but on the whole mine were not. What with drought, which they detest, and the damage by capsids to their shoot tips (I really cannot be bothered to spray), they remained largely blind until a huge surge of blossom started developing last month.

They are at their best through October, given an open autumn, and fortunately we are seldom afflicted by frost before November. Cool, moist conditions suit fuchsias ideally. Genii is particularly pleasing, with lime green foliage, red veining and abundant red and purple blossom. I cut it to the ground annually, well before winter's end, so as to highlight the snowdrops which are colonised through it.

Another bone-hardy fuchsia, particularly stylish just now, is one called Voltaire given me years ago from Nymans by Mr Nice, the head gardener. Again it is the traditional red and purple, but presentation is its strong point. The habit is upright to 3ft without being stiff, and the foliage is small and neat.

I find that, mild winter or not, most fuchsias are the better for being cut to the ground by early April at the latest. They perform far better on the young wood. Hedge-like *Fuchsia magellanica* has been looking a wreck all summer, what with the drought and patchy dieback, caused, perhaps, by battering from last winter's storms. Only now is it glowing in the autumnal sunlight. Come the winter I shall cut it level with the ground.

I have two rows of F1 Fanfare chrysanthemum seedlings. The first is in its second year from seed, the second was sown last April. Old stools left unprotected could be decimated by a hard winter but came through unscathed, so they are nearly 4ft high now and twice as tall as the youngsters. They have a good range of typical chrysanthemum colour and flower forms. Individual plants come into flower at widely differing dates, and this is ideal from the picking point of view, which is their purpose. The smell of chrysanthemums is so much part of the season.

I am arranging vases of them with sprays of white *Ammi majus* to give lightness. This pure white annual, closely resembling cow parsley but far more refined and without the sickly smell, is more highly regarded on the Continent than here, but it is an ideal cut flower, lasting for as long in water as the chrysanthemums. The best treatment is to sow it in a row, but commercial seed packets contain too little seed for this to be possible. So, having successfully raised the few crumbs allowed by sowing under protection, potting the seedling individually and then lining them out, save your own seed each autumn.

A number of salvias are at their best in autumn, notably, in my garden, *Salvia microphylla* var. *neurepia*. This soft-wooded Mexican shrub needs sun and shelter. It should be tidied over with secateurs, not too severely in spring, after which it will flower from late May onwards, but most freely (after capsids have gone into hibernation) in autumn. The flowers, borne in short racemes, are a bright, clear shade of cherry red, richer in autumn than in summer.

Verbenas are a great autumn standby, although not some of the modern, annual, mixed-coloured seed strains. They go down like ninepins to mildew in a year like this. No, the mainstays are *Verbena rigida*, with small, bright purple flowerheads at 18in and the 5ft to 6ft *V. bonariensis* in soft purple, which has been flowering with increasing abundance since July.

In the South, where it can ripen its seed and self-sow, this species gets around but seldom looks out of place. Indeed, it often gives one new ideas for plant and colour combinations, as where some of mine are growing through a low, 18in bank of the single-flowered *Zinnia* Chippendale, which is bronze with yellow ray tips. That is a winner, with a tremendously long season.

After a couple of hot summers one feels how underrated cannas are and how important it is that nurseries should be offering a range of them. Not just the big, muscular kinds – although, used in the right way, these can be monumental, their leaves like sculpture – but a range of quite petite varieties, with smaller, slighter foliage and flowers. These are delightful plants, especially when seen growing in shallow water.

Canna glance is one of my prettiest at the moment, with narrow, glaucous foliage and small, pale yellow flowers. *C. musifolia* which I had from a Dutch botanic garden, is a dramatic foliage plant with banana-like leaves, 2ft and more long by a foot across. It is wonderful to see autumn sunlight slanting through it and picking out the veins, which are purplish. The margins are distinctly purple but the leaf is otherwise green.

One of autumn's greatest offerings is the freshness of the bulbs and bulb-like plants that are flowering now – amaryllis and nerines, crocuses and colchicums, sternbergias, zephyranthes, cyclamen and the tiny white bells of *Leucojum automnale*.

Some of these await the rains of autumn before they will start flowering. If you get impatient, give the ground a good soaking and they will be up within a day or two. *Nerine bowdenii* takes a bit longer, but that also responds to a soaking when its flowering season is upon it.

– December 20, 1990 –

FOXGLOVES IMPRESS

Not until early this month did we get around to planting our foxgloves in the borders from their rows in the vegetable garden

217

where they had been making size through the summer and autumn. I had sown them in pots in April and they had subsequently been pricked out.

It may sound as though I grow them in great variety and numbers. Not so; there are too many other good things claiming space, and anyway there will be a whole lot more self-sown foxgloves in the garden, so all together they will be making a considerable impact next June.

And foxgloves do make a tremendous impression. At the Australian Garden Design Conference in Melbourne last year, lasting three days, I was amazed how many of the speakers, who were mostly landscape architects, showed slides in which foxgloves were the dominant feature. Those lean and elegant spires queen it over the rounded, softer shapes of their associates. If there tends to be an amorphous element in your garden, these will correct it.

There are, of course, many species of *Digitalis* – all poisonous to humans and generally rabbit-proof – but it is of our native, biennial *D. purpurea* that I write. Most species are perennial, which is a convenience, and they have other merits, but none have the presence or force of *D. purpurea*.

Its habitats in the wild are varied. We associate it with woodland, but seed lies dormant for many years until the wood is coppiced, or until large gaps are created by a storm, and light is at last admitted. Foxgloves need a good deal of light and reasonable freedom from competition at their own level.

In open woodland, plants grow 6ft tall and more, but another favourite habitat is shingly, reclaimed coastal land, where they are fully exposed to sun and wind. There they grow to half their woodland height, the spikes are much more densely packed with flowers, and the rosy purple colouring is more intense.

Wild Albinos

This, the normal colouring, is frequently varied in the wild by albinos, entirely devoid of red pigment. I remember one wild stand, near Tummel Bridge in Perthshire (foxgloves are notable in Scotland and frequent among moorland rocks), which was white throughout.

In the garden, the common pinky purple foxglove tends to be despised, and the aim is to have them either all white, or all white with purple spots (which is rather fun) or in the Apricot strain which is offered by several seedsmen.

The two strains I am growing this time are Apricot, from Thompson & Morgan, and a white of my own saving. If there is a range of foxglove colours in or near one's garden, one cannot expect saved seed to give rise to the same colouring as the seed parent. There are quantities of pollen arriving from nearby parents of different colouring. But sometimes a plant flowers late on one spike, when all the others have finished, and it was from one such that I collected my seed.

We rogued the seedlings before planting them out. It was from Graham Thomas that I learned that if the leaf stalk and main vein, examined from the back, show any flush in their colouring, they will carry pink flowers. We found two or three of these and discarded them. The rest were pale green and should carry white flowers. It is obviously by similar selection that the foxgloves at Mottisfont Abbey, which freely self-sow throughout the Rose Garden, are all white.

If one finds the odd foxglove that is opening pink flowers one can pull it out, but that may leave a tiresome gap. I do not think we should be fussy all the time. A mixture of pink and white foxglove spires is charming among the 4ft domes in mauve and white of sweet rocket, *Hesperis matronalis*, in an open woodland setting, and would scarcely be improved if the whole lot were white.

219

CROCUSES IN THE MOOD

Much as I dislike the many depressing grey days that we endure in our northern winters, I have to admit that they have a kind of negative virtue in reining back plants. Early forms of *Crocus chrysanthus*, such as Gipsy Girl and Snow Bunting, were already showing colour early in January, as usual, and many others had joined them by the end of the month.

But crocuses are moody flowers. That is one of their great attractions. An unexpanded crocus reminds me that I am not feeling in the least expansive myself. Even if there is a touch of sun, and even if the crocuses are not sitting glumly in one of those long shadows, there is insufficient warmth to coax their petals apart.

February can be totally different, depending on which way the cat jumps. This year it swaddled us in snow. But I know exactly what will come next; will maybe already have arrived by the time this is printed. There will be that glorious morning – the first of several if not of many – when the sun, now markedly higher, feels almost hot.

Perhaps that is stretching it a bit, but anyway the crocuses and I think it is hot, and out they come, some scattered, some in bunches and others (*C. tommasinianus*) making a carpet; and out come the bees, and down I go on my knees (having forgotten a kneeling mat, that means a couple of dark patches on my corduroys) to sniff the honey scent that comes so generously from Snow Bunting, but not quite generously enough to reach me without my performing the genuflexion. The rite is anyway well deserved.

If the air as well as the sun is warm enough, all the crocuses

220

will open out, in shade as well as sun. What is more, having been delayed up till now by chilly weather, there will be an exciting concentration of blossom. The early kinds like *Crocus chrysanthus* in some of its manifestations, *C. sieberi*, *C. tommasinianus* and *C. flavus*, not forgetting the big, clump-forming Dutch Yellows, will overlap with the late kinds, in particular the purple, mauve, white and stripy, large-flowered Dutchies.

All are delightful; I cannot feel snooty about any of them. However much you coarsen a crocus in the pursuit of size, it is still a lovely flower. I shall not describe it, because I assume that most readers have seen a crocus before, but next time you see any expanded some way beneath your nose, take a closer look. It is worth it.

My garden is just about as full of crocuses as it will later be of tulips (I closely associate the two flowers), but whereas I find it hard to keep tulips going for more than a few years in our several meadow areas, this is where the crocuses predominate.

And here I have a piece of luck on my side: our heavy clay soil inhibits the movement of mice and voles. They do not like it and so, in the main, they leave my crocus corms to increase, although these are their favourite food. Rabbits are, potentially, another major pest. Their numbers and location fluctuate from year to year. They crop off the crocus flowers and foliage. The foliage keeps on growing, even after being cropped, so the plants are not seriously weakened for the next year, but you lose your display for this, which can be maddening.

If you have a daffodil orchard, it can, no less, be a crocus orchard a few weeks earlier because the daffodil foliage is still short enough not to count as an obstruction while the crocuses are having their innings.

Once you have given them a good start, they should do most of the work for you and you will have the pleasure of seeing more and more of them from year to year. The principal self-sowers

221

are *C. tommasinianus*, the deep orange-yellow *C. flavus* and all the purple, mauve and white *C. vernus* forms. Because they are so busy setting seed, these crocuses tend to make carpets, rather than clumps.

The clump-formers are typically represented by the sterile Dutch Yellow crocus. If you would like more of that, the best course is to dig up a few old, established clumps as soon as they have finished flowering, separate the corms and replant them scattered, forthwith. The turf will be short and soft enough to make planting easy, as this will be at the end of March.

Among the many different varieties of *C. chrysanthus*, some make clumps – Snow Bunting does – while others do so less obviously, but they also self-sow and they interbreed like crazy. In time you will find all sorts of intermediate flower forms and colours appearing among the named varieties that you originally planted. That is great fun, even without imagining that here you have something so special that someone (not you) should work up stock of it and put it on the market for posterity, with your wife's or daughter's name attached.

When he had named a few after himself and his family, Ernest Bowles tended to use bird names for his *C. chrysanthus* selections. But the trade is not always too particular about marketing the same crocus under a good selling name, like Snow Bunting. 'Here's a much whiter crocus than that old thing,' you can imagine someone saying, and out it goes, masquerading as the original.

I am suspicious of the stock I bought from one dealer as Snow Bunting last autumn because, although I am growing it under glass, it is not yet in flower, yet it was as early as always in the garden. This has happened to me before, from the same source. I was served with a late-flowering chrysanthus hybrid *without any scent*. Never mind that it was whiter; the earliness and the scent are my principal reasons for wanting to grow the true Snow Bunting in a bowl so that I can savour and ogle it in comfort, indoors and at any level near to my nose that I please, without getting wet knee patches.

When you do grow crocuses in bowls, it is important not to force them at any stage. Then, when they come into flower, bring them into a warm room to open out, but only for a few hours at a time. I like to put mine on the luncheon table when I have guests. If this is done at the start of the meal, they open as we watch. But they must, as in nature, have a cold, resting period in between bouts of warmth, otherwise they get tired and cease to open properly, but are neither one thing nor the other. '*Il faut q'une porte soil ouvetre ou fermie.*' So, I rest my Snow Buntings in the larder, which has been cold enough recently to make ice cubes without my bothering with the fridge.

— March 7, 1991 —

TRICKS OF THE SEASON

No season plays more tricks on us than spring. It is not so much the way in which the weather see-saws from day to day as the general trend in holding back or pushing forward. The plants tell us what is going on, and I think it is worth keeping a few notes on when such and such a flower puts in its appearance, for comparison with other occasions.

In an exceptionally late spring, 1970, my *Magnolia denudata* was at its best in early May (I photographed it on the 8th). Last year the corresponding condition was reached in the second week of March.

I was out in the garden with my camera a lot last March, and the magnolia, with its pure white, lemon-scented chalices, made part of a pretty grouping. Behind it, the wall-trained apricot was still in bloom (it is always ahead of the peaches); in front, an apron of Lenten roses, *Helleborus orientalis* hybrids, while to one side the female *Acuba japonica* Longifolia was laden with its newly ripened crop of crimson berries. These do not colour until the new year. Their freshness contrasts quirkily with that of spring blossom. But the acuba hated last summer's drought and scorching sunshine, so it is not performing at all this year.

My March 1990 photographs remind me of pleasures soon to come. The lush, squeaky foliage of *Eremurus robustus* expanded so prematurely that, first, half was torn off by fierce winds, and then the rest, as well as the flowering stems, were decimated by the April 4–5 frost. This year its buds are still snug beneath their dome of protective grit, although that cannot last for much longer.

Berberis linearifolia Orange King was glamorous a year ago (no colour yet). Given its upright habit (scrawny unless you cut it back quite severely immediately after flowering), you can plant appropriate bulbs close up to it, to flower at the same time. I use hyacinths.

And the pale yellow, usually rather late hyacinth, City of Haarlem, goes well with the sharp blackcurrant purple of the clump-forming *Lathyrus vernus*. Seed of that offers such an easy method of raising new stock, as also in its milk-and-roses variety Alboroseus.

My F1 Crescendo Red polyanthus had almost finished by the end of last March, but have not properly started yet. I may need to protect them against sparrows. They make a carpet for the early-flowering Fosteriana hybrid tulip, Purissima. It is such a lovely shape. Like White Triumphator, it opens cream and fades to white, but is quite short-stemmed, and that is really de rigueur if these early flowerers are not to be utterly bashed.

Another Fosteriana hybrid I am fond of, and again it flowers early, is Orange Emperor. That sounds brassy but the shade, although bright, is soft, starting with green down the centre of the outer segments, and the petals are long. That looks good over a carpet of the celandine (*Ranunculus ficaria*) Brazen Hussy. Its shining yellow flowers, which open to the sun, are backed by light-reflecting, purple, heart-shaped leaves.

Ranunculaceae are strongly represented in early spring. Of the kingcups, the most commonly seen is our native *Caltha palustris*, which makes tremendously bold splashes of yellow in its double form. I don't have that; I do grow the white Alba, which is first of all the pondside flowers to bloom, although it never makes a great display, for me. But a colony of *C. polypetala*, with wood anemones on the bank in front of it (they arrived accidentally), is a great asset. Individual blooms are large when it first comes out, although it is not a clumpy plant: more of a wide-spreading coloniser in shallow water and the nearby margin.

My stock was given to me by Walter Th. Ingwersen, on a visit with my mother to his garden and nursery years ago, and he told us of Farrer's acquisition of this species, described in typically flowery language in *The English Rock Garden*. ' . . . there is a romantic legend that it was for long known in Europe in the ponds of the Vatican, where the old Pope refused to let it go forth from that sacred seclusion into an heretic though horticultural world; but that one day some hero ventured thither on the high quest, enshrouded in a bevy of aunts, whom he discharged upon the custodians to hold them in talk, while he himself hooked out some fragment of the caltha with his umbrella.'

Before March is out, even in a normal year, I expect the anemones to be joined by snakeshead fritillaries, *Fritillaria meleagris*, and both these consort with Lent lilies, *Narcissus pseudonarcissus*, in the crowns of *Gunnera manicata* at the pondside. You can make a considerable spring garden in what will later be the shadow of the giant. The gunnera, in fact, unscrolls its first leaves at the first warm breath of spring. These are invariably punished by frost, but an established gunnera has in its quiver a plentiful supply of

225

further embryo leaves with which to replace the unlucky scouts.

Back to *Ranunculaceae*: the Blackthorn strain (developed by Mr White) of *Helleborus* × *sternii* has an excellent, compact habit and appearance, with its firm, evergreen foliage on a sub-shrubby plant. The flower trusses are dusky purple on the outside, green within the bell. I felt that something around the plant was needed to highlight it. I rejected pulmonarias and have settled (at a young friend's suggestion) for *Anemone* × *seemannii* (now *A.* × *lipsiensis*) which is a cross between our own wood anemone and the bright yellow *A. ranunculoides*, with pale sulphur-yellow stars of great appeal.

As I write, snowdrops are flowering among the crowns of my male ferns, *Dryopteris filix-mas*, which we cut back in the new year. They will be succeeded by *Scilla bithynica*, a pale blue, early-flowering bulb which is an enthusiastic, self-sowing coloniser. There are many spots, dark later, where it will colonise beneath deciduous trees, shrubs and plants like these ferns. Yet, easy though it is, *S. bithynica* is seldom offered and you do not often see it in gardens.

– May 9, 1991 –

DOING IT ALL YOURSELF

One of the inane questions that I least enjoy hearing from casual visitors is 'Do you do this all yourself?' Mine is a highly complex garden, totally unstreamlined, intensely demanding – just the way I like it, in fact. But without help I should be lost, as should be obvious, surely, to anyone of average intelligence even if not a gardener.

However, a close friend after a day's visit wrote: 'How lucky you are having that charming Edward (a student working here during his vacation) – energetic, intelligent, loves gardening and Dixter. The only thing that doesn't make me envy you is that I really like doing it all myself, or with Giles, actually, though, there is too much, so we don't manage it . . . Of course, I don't want to do the grass, or that sort of thing. Best, I like making piles of rubbish and not clearing them up.' Yes, piles of visible rubbish do give one a sense of achievement.

I am sure she sometimes has to clear them away before Giles returns from the City, because he is a great preserver, and cannot bear the idea of shrubs being curbed, let alone removed. These things sometimes have to be done by stealth, when the spouse's back is turned.

But being ruthless yourself is quite different from someone else being ruthless for you. When their gardener cut back the tree peony, so that it produced none of its fat buds and blowsy blooms that year, it was an upset. As also in autumn, when the odd golden rod and three Michaelmas daisies were the only promise of flowers left, and Sonia caught him in the act of cutting them down before they had started flowering. She now keeps all cutting tools out of his way, to the extent of his having to bring his own.

The more you do in your garden, the better you are aware of what needs to be done. Time was, when the greenhouse was heated by hot-water pipes, that I used to light the fire there every evening that frost threatened, having first glued myself to the wireless for the latest weather forecast. It was a relief, when March came round, to have enough light left after the five-to-six forecast, to be able to light up while there was still a little daylight.

Nowadays, one of my helpers listens to a phone-in forecast. The greenhouse is electrically heated, but cold frames may need covering. All goes well, by routine, right through the winter, but on the night of April 20–21, at the weekend (always

227

a danger period), there was a quite heavy frost, the greenhouse was left open, and so were all the frames, even the young hydrangea cuttings. I was around; I should have checked but, being at one remove from the job, I did not. So much the worse for me.

Edward has been an enthusiastic helper on all sorts of jobs, but again the hydrangeas were at the sharp end. He pruned them, excellently, then mulched them with mushroom compost. Chalk is used liberally for mushroom casing, so you need to remember to keep it away from rhododendrons, camellias and the like.

Hydrangeas do not object to a certain amount of lime if they are already growing in acid soil, but alkalinity does change their colour from blue to pink or, in the dark-coloured varieties, from deep blue or purple to red. My soil is, to judge by the hydrangeas' colouring, fairly neutral, and, on the whole, I am as happy with pink hydrangeas as with blue.

But in three cases I am not. If a hydrangea is named Blue Wave, it saves a lot of explaining if its flowers come blue, not pink; if Bluebird, blue is preferable to mauve. Générale Vicomtesse de Vibraye is such an entrancing shade of pale blue, when it is blue, that I am prepared to take trouble to have it that way, rather than pale pink.

So, from February to July last year, we applied dressings of aluminium sulphate, to acidify the soil round these varieties. Now, inadvertently, because I forgot to warn Edward, we have applied a dressing of chalk, and are back where we started. Oh well, worse things can happen.

There was the time when we attempted to shift the branch system of our enormous apricot, trained against the house wall since before I was born, over to the right. It has become lop-sided. On the right, it used to go from the south-west aspect to the south-east, turning the corner of the house. About a quarter of the tree gradually died at this point, but the rest was as vigorous as ever.

If we could just redirect it, we thought, swing it across, a little. Every tie, years and years of them, was released, in preparation. Every tie but one would have been wiser. Uncontrollably, the tree crashed forwards.

I like to think that, had I been present, this would not have happened, but perhaps it would. Either way, I was responsible. Years later, I am glad to say that the apricot has forgotten its accident, although we have still not got it round to the south-east aspect.

Machinery causes the worst accidents, and not just to humans. As I have never had a macho image of myself operating a noisy, smelly machine, even if I could ride on it, lord of all I surveyed, I have always left this side of gardening to real men, frequently with disastrous consequences.

Those frightful gashes that are left as permanent eyesores in the trunks of young trees are not the whole story. Entire saplings are destroyed. For years I have been unsuccessfully trying to establish a central feature in a horseshoe area surrounded by an evergreen 'ilex' hedge. First, in my brasher days, a forsythia; that was mown off. Then, still brash, a *Robinia pseudoacacia* Frisia. That simply turned up its toes (quite a relief in retrospect). Then a white-stemmed *Betula jacquemontii*, which I saved, as a tiny seedling, from being devoured by sheep, cows and horses in Kashmir, 20 years ago. I doted on that birch, but although it grew to 50ft, machinery sliced it off like butter (grass-cutting is the official object of the exercise, I should add).

I forget what the next victim was, but the latest to be beheaded, last year, was a rather special sumach, a handsome foliage shrub, *Rhus chinensis*, given to me by Dr Jimmy Smart. I am contemplating a piece of inanimate sculpture, now, but I reckon a machine would charge into even that, and I should be paying for a new grass-cutter.

— July 11, 1991 —

THE RAIN CHILDREN

What a blessing summer rains are. Never mind that they wreck the tennis, cricket and picnics at Glyndebourne, not to mention flattening farm crops. There is no more soothing sound than the steady swishing of purposeful rain. Or so I thought until, one night, the sound seemed exceptionally close and I discovered that it was dripping onto my bed, but a dedicated repairer of old roofs and a bill for £1,300 have settled all that, I can enjoy the rain once more.

One Sunday last month it never stopped and, for once, there was no wind, I spent hours (it seemed) going round the garden with an American first-time visitor. I do not know what his impressions were, but I could not conceal my rejoicing. More than an inch fell, and next morning the horse pond was above its overflow. That does not often happen in June; lately, after two desiccating summers and autumns, not until December or January. It is heaven not to have to think about hoses, whether banned or not.

The borders are incredibly lush. The stems on my sow-thistles are like tree trunks (although hollow). Not everything is suited, of course. Any roses with too high a complement of petals are brown, and squeeze out like sponges before they have had the chance to open. A reflection on the breeders, surely. Single roses are a picture. The buds of Irish Elegance, opening soft coral, have never looked better. The bush that carries them must be all of 80 years old.

Annuals like petunias and zinnias, not to mention the bedding 'geraniums', could be in trouble, although there is plenty of time for a change in the weather pattern yet. But many plants that were desperately unhappy this time last year and the year before are radiant, making a quick recovery from this year's dour spring drought, when it seemed that north winds would never cease.

The bergenias are one example. My favourite is the deciduous *Bergenia ciliata,* whose furry leaves will grow to a whopping size, when there is plenty of moisture around, yet without a trace of coarseness (although a little of that commodity is gladly accepted in my canon). Perched on and overhanging a low ledge, they are ideally displayed, but ledges tend to be dry spots in south-east England.

Drystone walling is ideal in Scotland for *Tropaeolum polyphyl-lum,* where its deliciously cool, glaucous foliage, followed by swags of yellow blossom, will hang in festoons, colonising every crack, so that the owner complains, as owners will (hard to get it right), of being over-blessed. 'It's a weed,' you will hear. The retaining wall that I allotted to this lovely plant became its grave.

Still, my heavy soil suits many things when they are down at ground level, and when the rains oblige. One thoroughly stodgy border faces north-west and *Aralia cachemirica,* with huge pin-nate foliage, is a marvel of lushness. For the last two years it has burned and dried off when in mid career. This time, surely not. Rodgersias and hostas nearby have never looked better, although I should go out on snail-catching forays before retiring to bed, for the hostas sake. Rodgersias never suffer from slugs or snails, but they do from drought.

If a plant is moist at the root, it is far less likely to suffer from blazing sunshine on its foliage. That is especially true of yellow-leaved cultivars, such as golden marjoram, golden conifers, *Ber-beris thunbergii* Aurea or the golden cut-leaved elder, *Sambucus racemosa* Aurea. This last was a horrible sight in my Long Border for much of last summer and autumn, while Dickson's Golden Elm was as bad. They are wonderful now and I am hoping their contentment will last a while yet.

Fuchsias love moisture. Even the common hedging *Fuchsia magellanica* Riccartonii was a mess last year, not flowering until September, and then there was much dead wood through the bushes. That was partly because, following the previous two mild winters, they had remained untouched by frost, and I had not pruned them. This was probably unwise. I had hoped for early blossom from their mature wood, but drought put paid to that plan.

Even before last February's frosts, all the Riccartoniis were sawn to ground level. They are now 2ft tall again, growing apace and carrying a little blossom. That normally becomes prolific only in late summer or autumn with me, probably because of capsid bug damage, and I cannot be bothered to spray.

Cimicifugas, the bugbanes, demand moisture. The foliage of *Cimicifuga racemosa* is as great an asset as its September plumes of fluffy, white blossom, especially in the purple-leaved forms. *Eupatorium purpureum*, which I mentioned last week, should now be called *E. maculatum*, I see from *The Plant Finder*, if we are to follow its directives. The clone Atropurpureum is a little less inconveniently tall for some situations, but has a more intense purple flower colouring. I have a new planting of this at the back of my Long Border. As it is naturally a marsh plant, the rains have gladdened it and helped to get it established.

It was not until May that we implemented my decision to cut *Magnolia* Maryland back into old, bare wood. This grandiflora-style hybrid carries its waxy, fragrant, cream-coloured bowl flowers in succession from early July to late October, and it matures at an early age. It is lovely to bring into the house, but the habit of the plant is tall and stringy, so that most of its blossom was being carried far beyond convenient reach.

232

If you cut a greenhouse shrub back into old wood, you syringe its stems with water, often twice daily, to encourage them to break into fresh growth. The principle is the same in the garden, although less easily organised. In fact, we hope that the weather will do the job for us. My magnolia's bark was dark with rain damp when I looked at it before starting this piece, and I think I can spy some tiny, green snouts appearing high up. I hope there will be more of them lower down shortly. If not, it will not be the weather's fault.

— November 28, 1991 —

RETROSPECT ON BEDDING

Looking back, I do not think I was very clever with my bedding this year, although at the time it did not seem too bad. But I seem to have ordered a lot of seeds that never materialised as plants. And yet, as usual, I sowed more than 100 different kinds. Some of my best results were with own-saved seed.

The single French marigold, Cinnabar, for instance, is dropping from the lists; there is so much competition among marigolds, with whose improvement the breeders continue to be obsessed. But D. T. Brown still offer it, and they are noted for the quality of their seeds. It is open-pollinated, with deep bronze petals having the thinnest margin of orange. It is meant to be no more than 9in tall, but I have been saving seed over the years from the tallest plants and now have them large and bushy at twice that height.

The other marigold whose seed I save is the original *Tagetes patula*, from Mexico, parent of all the so-called French types, whose seed I obtained from a Dutch botanic garden. This will grow 2½ft tall and has small, single flowers which are light orange right through. This blossom looks light and airy when

233

interspersed with foliage and not too densely presented. That is my preference, anyway, although it may not be yours.

It suits the way I grow my bedding, which is not in beds of their own – these usually look self-conscious – but integrated into mixed borders which give them a background of other plants and other neighbours. The small, single zinnia Chippendale associates well with the last two, being bronze, again with an orange margin, a dark centre but orange anthers. It is a jolly-looking annual, which my friends find delightful. I managed to save good seed of this zinnia last year, which was exceptional in this respect. Next year I shall have to buy again, or give it a rest, more probably.

This, the *Tagetes patula* and some orange, non-stop begonias, whose tubers I save, followed foxgloves. Following lupins, which I also treat as biennials, also means planning for a July-planted successor. *Tithonia rotundifolia* Torch is best from a May sowing , anyway, as it loathes any suggestion of cold nights. That is like a giant single zinnia with intense orange flowers. The warmth of August suited it and it grew to 5ft. If you prefer a plant with style and individuality, avoid the strain called Goldfinger, which is shorter-jointed, more compact and has smaller flowers but more densely produced. I loathe it but the breeders think they know what the public wants. In general, of course, they do not know themselves and are ready to be led. A great mistake.

Cosmos bipinnatus cultivars can be sown late, that is in May, because they develop so quickly. Next to the tithonias I planted the tall, white Purity. If a shorter, white version, but still up to 2ft tall, so no stupidly dwarf (that will come; you will see), suits you better, the recent Euroselect award winner, Sonata, is the choice.

Quite a bit of work is going on with cosmos these days, and I was pleased with Versailles Tetra, which has deep pink flowers up to 4in across, shading to near maroon at the centre. The disc itself is yellow, of course. This grows to 4ft tall and is excellent

to pick. An interesting point about cosmos is that they are naturally short-day plants which would not bud up until the autumn.
In a climate like Hong Kong's, for instance, they then hit the
cooler, winter, growing season when annuals such as we grow for
summer display are in their element. To suit our single summer
season, they have been bred for summer flowering. But there is
still a tendency to the original behaviour, and you will find, in
a mixture, that a few plants remain leafy for a long while and
become much larger than any of their earlier-flowering brethren.
When, eventually, they do flower, in September, their blooms are
particularly large and fine, and, if October is kind, you get your
money's worth. So it was with my Versailles Tetra.

In my largest bedding area, in front of the house, where the
background is white Japanese anemones and two groups of the
green-and-white variegated dogwood, *Cornus alba* Elegantissima,
I had yellow and white last year. It was the typical mixed colours
of China asters in a strain called Matador. This is tall, with a
narrow, up-swept habit which I do not much care for, but we had
plenty of plants. However, after they had been flowering for 10
days or so in early September, a shower of rain proved too much
for their balance and they lurched around like drunks.

You cannot really be expected to support all your asters, so
that is the last of Matador for me, although its colour range is
outstanding and the flower shape good. Another time I will grow
the single-flowered Madelaine mixed strain, which was such a
success in a row for picking, last year, but would bed out equally
well.

In a north-west-facing border at one side of our topiary lawn,
and therefore viewed at a distance from Lutyen's seat on the
opposite side, I planted nothing but mulleins, *Verbascum olympicum*, at the back, Arctic Summer at the front. Both had been sown
in the spring of last year. My hope was that Arctic Summer, which
had not made large plants, would remain a vegetative rosette

throughout the summer, which was Graham Rice's experience with another seed strain of *V. bombyciferum* called Silver Spire. Not a bit of it. Every man jack flowered, and as the wind blew their stems this way and that, they took on a most comical appearance. No dignity there. Those of *V. olympicum* that flowered remained stiff as ramrods, but about a third did not flower.

– February 6, 1992 –

PERENNIALS PAST AND PRESENT

A general increase in the popularity of hardy perennials, particularly of those requiring little fussing over, has been notable of recent years. Alan Bloom was their great protagonist in the early days, and the Hardy Plant Society, founded in 1957, was largely his brainchild. It limped along for a while, uncertain of its direction, but recently has taken off in a big way.

Most popular have been the low-growing, weed-suppressing perennials, designated as ground cover. Big returns for little effort is the message those promoting them have conveyed, the assumption being that most of us would far prefer to be occupying ourselves in some cleaner and less effortful way than gardening.

But ground-cover plants, such as hostas and pulmonarias, say, benefit enormously from division and replanting after five or six years, from regular mulching and, in time of stress, from irrigation. The pulmonaria has increased its range of colour and beauty in flowers and foliage, largely as a result of breeding programmes in Germany, while the same may be said of hostas, on which most work has taken place in America. Britain has always taken the sometimes smug view that it is the hub of everything new and good in the way of garden plants and their uses. Other countries are increasingly a challenge to this concept.

236

This is notably so in the development of ornamental grasses. Apart from the pampas, these scarcely featured at all in our gardens of 40 years ago. Now they even take a place among heathers and dwarf conifers and the impetus is nearly all from abroad. Ferns are a different case. There have always been fern fanatics, but following their heyday in Victorian times, they suffered a long eclipse. Now there is great excitement about ferns again, a fact which I wholeheartedly welcome while finding it a little hard to explain. In part I think we must seek the cause in a swing of fashion. Items of Victoriana are in vogue that made people wince in the 1950s.

We have seen big changes in the main categories of florist's flowers. Take the Michaelmas daisies, for instance; that is, the forms of *Aster novi-belgii*. Bloom's listed 100 different named cultivars in the 1950s; now fewer than a dozen. Specialisation is not always good for a group of plants. Mildew and a microscopic mite whose feeding habits substitute a leafy rosette for the desired flowers in these daisies, has, in addition to the verticillium wilt disease already familiar in this group, made them a bore to grow well. There are many other asters not suffering from the same debilities and we have turned to them.

In bearded irises, the breeders, concentrating on large blooms having particular qualities (ruffled margins seems to be a current obsession), have neglected the attributes of a strong constitution as a practical garden plant. Most modern, tall bearded irises require a stake to every stem. Hence the development of a race of smaller-flowered, dwarf varieties.

In the 1950s, lupins and delphiniums were mostly named varieties, raised true to name from cuttings. Nearly all lupins and a large proportion of delphiniums are now from seed strains, some quite dwarf, to minimise the necessity for staking.

Island beds became a special concept for a more all-round view of plants. Then there are the colour themes: silver and grey; yellow and white; all blue, and so forth, depending on the individual's predilections and channelling the bewildering range of choice. But the complete gardener, in any age, prefers not to be bound by rules.

– April 23, 1992 –

ADVENTUROUS SALADS

Salads are for year-round enjoyment; no less in spring than at any other season. If you use a lot of ingredients, they do not cancel each other out, but most of the more astringent elements become absorbed, and the more so if your dressing is generous with a good olive oil and not too heavy on the vinegar (balsamic vinegar gives a particularly good flavour and is now offered by Sainsbury's, I am delighted to find). The one home-grown salading that I find boorishly hot and without compensating flavour is land cress. That is a pity, because it is hardy, prolific and pleasing to the eye.

The majority of salad ingredients belong to one of three families: *Umbelliferae, Cruciferae, Compositae.* Umbellifers include parsley, celery and fennel. Lettuce, chicory, tarragon and salsify are composites, of the daisy family. The mustard-oil flavours of mustard and cress, and also rocket, lamb's lettuce (corn salad) and every sort of cabbage, all belong to crucifers. They have their special and familiar pests: cabbage-white butterfly caterpillars and flea beetles. These are a particular nuisance throughout the summer months, and I tend to sow my cruciferous saladings in late summer and autumn so that I can cut them without too much competition between September and April. However, I cannot abstain from the inestimable flavour of rocket in summer, so a sowing of that will go in any day now and I shall eat the spaces between the holes which are the flea beetles' share. We do apply a flea-beetle dust to the seedlings in their early stages, otherwise there would be no crop.

Every salad needs to have a crunchy element. In spring I buy that in, using Iceberg lettuce (little flavour in that), Florence fennel and mooli radish. Of my own growing I still have Witloof chicory from the cellar (although a light carelessly left on can spoil this). And there are green-and red-leaf chicories from the garden. They are ingredients of Thompson & Morgan's Saladisi mixture, sown in early July and still giving me chicory, chervil and rocket. Sugar-loaf chicory was sown at the same time and its main season of solid, pale green heads was in the tail end of the year. When frosted, the outer leaves go mushy and rot, but the inner core is so well-protected that I am normally able to go on eating them throughout the winter months, always cutting rather than pulling the plants. From these cuts, fresh green shoots arise in spring and these are good in a salad, although it must always be recognised that there is a greater or lesser element of bitterness in any chicory, which you just have to learn to like.

When I wrote 'normally', just now, it referred to the unfortunate taste my dachshunds have developed for crunchy salad ingredients. They ate the hearts out from all my sugar loafs, during the winter, and there was nothing I could do to prevent them.

I mentioned chervil, in passing, but this has a pungent aniseed flavour that helps a salad mixture no end, without being as aggressive or domineering as dill or leaf fennel. I was most grateful for its availability when making a béarnaise sauce, last weekend, to go with Dover sole Saint-Germain (Dovers are currently in their prime). Tarragon, the other necessary herb, is just in and I grow the stronger-flavoured French strain rather than the Russian. Not having enough of the fresh (I used most of it for tarragon chicken, a few days earlier) I was glad to have some in the deep freeze to fall back on. It keeps its aroma splendidly, this

239

way. A tarragon colony needs rejuvenating, every few years, and this is the best time to replant it in improved soil.

I always include a few sorrel leaves in my salads and I am mad on sorrel soup, blending the sorrel into it at the last moment so that it retains its bright colour and is not cooked. This entails using a fibreless sorrel, *Rumex scutatus*, with a big, soft, shield-shaped leaf, rather than *R. acetosa* from the meadow, which has a good flavour but is tough even in earliest youth.

Saladini seed mixtures should not be confused with Saladisi. A packet of the latter was given me by Joy Larkcom (whose book, *The Salad Garden,* published by Frances Lincoln, is immensely helpful) last summer. It was mainly, if not entirely, cruciferous and suffered a lot from pests, in its early months, but gave me young leaves and shoots to pick from all through the winter. Best of all was the lacy foliage of Mizuna, a Japanese mustard, which was new to me. I cannot recommend it too highly.

Another hardy mustard which I have recommended before is now offered again by T & M (having not been available for two years) as Cress Mega. In other catalogues you may find it as Salad Rape. These names need standardising. It is flavoury and not too hot. Lamb's lettuce, otherwise known as corn salad or mâché, we sowed on August 28. It is a slow developer and was ready (unprotected) for cutting from the end of February. I slash bunches of foliage with a kitchen knife and then leave it to grow again. The flavour is surprisingly mild yet tasty, so it is a good bulk salad ingredient.

For a celery flavour without the bother of growing celery itself (hopelessly popular with my slugs), I have been growing two-leaf strains. Cutting Celery is the tougher; Parcel, which is curly leaved, is my preferred choice. The stalks of both also come in useful for flavouring chicken stock.

After a salad has been dressed, I like to decorate it with flowers, straight from the garden, unwashed and undressed, so as

240

not to spoil them. Primroses and sweet-scented violets are the early spring standby. The violets grow in a range of colours – pink, white mauve and violet itself. Pansies should take over from them, but I did not grow any last year. I shall have anchusa flowers in May, as I have grown a batch of that. Borage is related, and extremely pretty, as are the blue flowers of chicory for a lunchtime salad. As they close in the afternoon, they are no use for evening salads. But in any case blue is not a colour to be seen in electric or candle light. Nasturtium flowers come in varied colours but pollen beetles can, in high summer, be impossibly numerous.

– May 28, 1992 –

IN NO MAN'S LAND

Had you ever considered allowing something positive to happen in the gap that invariably develops between hedge bottom and lawn? It has a dismal, negative air about it. Often its very presence is owed to that wicked tool (banned at Dixter), the half-moon edge cutter, with which gardeners love to show that they have been busy. But once removed, those slivers of turf never return.

Gardeners then most frequently resort to hoeing. That removes a whole lot of soil as well as the weeds. You are down to the hedge roots in no time and have to top up with soil brought in from elsewhere or with old potting compost. Another, preferable, treatment is with pre-emergence herbicide. I use that myself, and also around young trees growing in meadow. But it is steadily being withdrawn from circulation because of its residual qualities.

In the meantime, I find that certain plants introduce themselves and that, once established, the pre-emergence killers do

241

them no harm. This spring I have had a magnificent self-sown wallflower against the hedge in front of our house. And there are grape hyacinths next to it. It is the extra handsome form of *Muscari armeniacum* called Blue Spike, so I suppose I must have planted it in a moment of absentmindedness, because I have no recollection of doing so.

Allium moly was definitely planted with intent, and that was in the 1930s. It has never required attention and is regular with its fairly brief display of yellow blossom starry flowers in domed umbels.

Before going further I should, perhaps, define what makes a suitable plant for such a situation. It must not spread onto the lawn and it must not endanger the health of the hedge bottom by shading it out. *Campanula persicifolia* is all right because its mat of rosette-forming foliage keeps close to the soil. The flowering stems rise to 3ft and often poke out of the hedge itself, but they do no harm. It is the same with *C. latiloba*, whose showy blue flowers are saucer shaped rather than campanulate.

Honesty, *Lunaria annua*, is a great self-sower but unsuitable because its broad leaves rise for some distance up the flowering stem and shade the hedge. Jack-by-the-Hedge is a weed that behaves like honesty. Thistledown tends, in its flight, to land against a hedge, so you will find the creeping field thistle establishing. That must be tackled with a stroked-on dose of glyphosate (TumbleWeed). Suckers from nearby, grafted fruit trees can be similarly treated. Common toadflax, which spreads by suckering, is another such.

Then there are the infiltrators, such as certain species of oxalis (I am not sure which, but I know how they behave). To them a hedge is a challenge and they will climb into it. So will snow-in-summer, *Cerastium tomentosum*, and aubrieta. You must grab them out by handfuls before their damage has been done. Once a year will often be frequent enough.

242

But there are welcome infiltrators, which is not to say they are not harmful, but that they are so beautiful at their nefarious climax that a spot of hedge health is gladly sacrificed. Such is the flame nasturtium, *Tropaeolum speciosum*, but my hedges are far too dry for it. There is a nice example at Hidcote but the cool of Scotland suits this plant best. At Ardullie, in Easter Ross, there was – and probably still is – a long yew hedge invested with flame nasturtiums which look wonderful on a hedge and they are as happy on a north aspect as in sun, but they, again are unhappy if drought develops. There is no drier spot in a garden than underneath a hedge, unless it is the foot of a sunny brick wall.

Violets are excellent, both the scented and the dog varieties, including the purple-leaved one we have for years been ascribing to Labrador, *Viola labradorica* Purpurea. It is a form of our native wood violet. Violets are unusually resistant to the pre-emergence herbicides and thus the easier to colonise.

Primroses are good, and snowdrops; crocuses, also, especially *Crocus tommasinianus* in February and *C. speciosus* in autumn. The hardy *Cyclamen hederifolium* can build up dinner-plate-sized tubers in a hedge bottom, although some topping up with soil may occasionally be needed. The only snag, I find, is that a hedge tends to increase in thickness over the years and to engulf the cyclamen. This is happening to a white one that my mother planted quite 40 years ago. One could take the drastic step of halving the hedge, by cutting it back to the centre on one side. Yew, which this is, responds so very well to this treatment.

Euphorbia amygdaloides var. *robbiae* has sown itself at the foot of one yew hedge, here, and then spread along the channel. It does no harm at all and is charming for a large part of the year. It is as happy in sun as in shade. Small, creeping ferns will be particularly suitable in shady situations. You can see the oak fern, *Gymnocarpium dryopteris*, at Sissinghurst Castle, although it is there fronted by a hard path. A turf frontage would make no difference. Among this fern, they also have the bulbous *Ornitho-galum nutans*, with spikes of green stars in spring. By the time its leaves have become lanky and tiresome, they can be ripped off.

Celandines are excellent colonisers and there are many different named varieties. It will not matter if they get mixed up. By late spring their foliage will be dying away and the whole area can be cleaned up. If they seed into the lawn, it is a comfort to know that they are extremely sensitive to selective weedkillers. The fully double kinds do not make seed, so these might be preferred.

Celandines are equally good in sun and in shade but open more readily in sun, remaining open longer, which is an important factor with the single-flowered kinds. The purple foliage of Brazen Hussy is more intense in sunshine and makes the sharpest contrasting background to its brassy blossom.

– July 16, 1992 –

STAMPEDE INTO AUTUMN

It has felt like July for a long while, although I am writing on only its first day. Autumn flowers are already blooming. A dahlia that I have left in the ground for years is out, and an early double, bronze chrysanthemum. I hate all-the-year-round chrysanthemums, as raised for florists, but if they are flowering a bit early, yet naturally, in my own garden, I do not resent them at all. In fact, if I remove their spent blooms individually, they produce a later crop of buds and are really good value.

It is the same with many of the early flowering forms of *Phlox paniculata*. I have a very early, unnamed purple one with a pale eye which flowers almost continuously from late June to October.

244

That is, if I feed and water it well; but water is a problem. I had to compare my phloxes unfavourably with all those I saw north of the border last month, where they are taller and infinitely lusher but, of course, considerably later flowering.

Does the early season mean there will be nothing left to enjoy when calendar autumn arrives? I think not, so long as we grow plenty of those continuously flowering plants, such as fuchsias and many hydrangeas, which give up only when the frosts arrive.

The hardy plumbago, *Ceratostigma willmottianum*, is another such. In an unprotected front-of-border position, this had opened the first of its pure blue flowers before the end of June – thanks to its having successfully brought its old growth through the winter unscathed. That makes a couple of months' difference to the onset of flowering and it always looks its best in the warmer weather. As soon as it turns a bit chilly, the colouring becomes wan and the flowers look pinched.

Cestrum parqui is another shrub which, even against a wall, can easily get cut to the ground by winter frost but kept all its old growth this year and was beginning to flower quite early last month. It will shortly reach a first peak, with others to follow on the young growth. It does not relish the heat of midday, when its star flowers are semi-closed. They become radiant again (albeit demurely lime green) as evening approaches, not unleashing their powerfully sweet, nutty aroma until as late as nine or ten o'clock. A sprig brought indoors will oblige a little earlier and be easier to enjoy with your decaffeinated coffee (none of that at Dixter) after dinner.

Solanum jasminoides Album was another beneficiary of the mild winter. In full bloom as I write, it should continue well into November or even later. I wish I could say the same of its name-sake, the summer jasmine, at its best now but soon tailing off. I feel like putting in a good word for *Jasminum* × *stephanense* at this point, which I may possibly not have mentioned in the many years I have possessed it. It carries a huge crop of charming pink flowers in June, and a little way into July, richly scented at night and into the next morning. There is no follow on, but as much could be said of most shrubs.

The first flower on my white Japanese anemones has opened today. I have masses of them, and their strength will build up steadily over the next six weeks, lasting in full glory until the middle of October. Few hardy perennials are so generously rewarding. I far prefer the single kinds, whether pink or white, to the doubles, as the petals in the singles are broad and relaxed, whereas those in the doubles are narrow and fidgety. Alba, the single white that has been in my garden since before I was born, grows 4ft tall and will set off annuals or perennials of any colour, which is why I use them to back up my bedding-out area. They would also look super with red dahlias of roughly the same height, or with red crocosmias, although these are mostly a little early for the anemone's climax.

Crocosmia Lucifer was out well before the end of June this year, and will be finished by the end of July, apart from its foliage and seed heads, which are not negligible. But I have a Lucifer seeding which, to all appearances, is identical but starts flowering a good two weeks later. This is useful and something the breeders might work on.

The Mount Etna broom, *Genista aetnensis*, is flowering two weeks early. I love its diaphanous airiness and should like to have a considerable planting of it, widely spaced but nevertheless forming a grove within an area of meadow. The broom casts so little shade that the vegetation beneath it is scarcely affected. I know just where I want my grove, but the young seedlings will need good places making for them in order to compete with the turf in their early years, and this will take time. That is what I am waiting for.

Not only does this broom make a fountain of yellow in July,

but it is sweetly scented on the air, and at all times of the year its silhouette is pleasing at a distance. It is a long-lived species of 30 to 40 years but takes time to make its mark; you will need a little patience in the first 10 years.

One of the things I enjoy about high summer is the intimacy of the acoustic which the wealth of vegetation creates. It is like being in a well-furnished room yet with the pleasure of being outside. The best time is early morning, before extraneous noises and interruptions have built up and you just have the place to yourself.

Lawns and wide open spaces are no part of such a set up. You need a sense of enclosure but without feeling in any way shut in. The close proximity of ebullient plants will provide this perfectly. But they do not want to be too tall, otherwise you are down among their stems and the exciting, luxuriant part is way above your head. That is more claustrophobic than intimate. The feeling of space must never be lost. There is delicate balance, and it is up to us to maintain it.

– September 17, 1992 –

RESPONDING TO RAIN

Late August gales made it feel autumnal in the nastiest sense, and did not help the looks of the garden one little bit. I know from experience, however, that when the weather becomes settled again, as it is odds-on it will, plants will show remarkable powers of recuperation. Even with equinoxial gales late this month, all can be smiling again by mid-October. No need, therefore, to throw up our hands in despair and depart hastily for the Antipodes, yet awhile.

Rains have done a great deal of good. For one thing, I have

been able to pull tenacious weeds from the paving cracks on our sitting-out terrace. I do not use herbicides, here, as I like to leave all the moon daisies. They make a spectacular, if surprising, display at the turn of May and June, after which one grabs everything within sight and tugs. That leaves the area clear for tables and chairs from late June on, and the daisies, which have been checked and tidied, but not removed, gradually refoliate. But plantains, grasses and over-prolific seedlings of dieramas and *Carex buchananii* (a typical New Zealander, with brown-bronze leaves that make idiots say it looks dead) need to be dealt with by hand, and they will come out quite sweetly after heavy rains.

The lawns have greened up nicely and so have recently mown meadow areas. Another rain advantage is that it has started autumn-flowering bulbs into renewed activity. Buds of *Nerine* × *bowdenii* are well forward among *Aster amellus* Violet Queen, the two making a striking contrast. But if the ground is too dry, the nerines do not get going until the aster is already fading.

Most kniphofias have a limited season of a couple of weeks or so, and my best as I write on September 1, is Torchbearer, which makes dense clumps and carries sulphur yellow pokers. For contrast both in colour and form, this looks excellent against a well-flowering shrub of *Hydrangea* × *macrophylla* Ayesha, which is pink with me, but the effect would be as good if my soil was acid and it came blue.

For value where space is limited, the hydrangea knocks spots off the poker. Its season started in early July and will continue until the first frost, which is not usually until November, in my garden. It has the normal hortensia's bun heads. They start green and change gradually through palest pink to a deep shade with a touch of mauve in it. Gradations of colour within the same inflorescence are an enlivening touch, as are the shiny, porcelain-like finish on the flowers' surface and their incurved margins, so that each segment is like a little ladle. Here, it is against a north-east

248

wall and requires protection if it is to flower freely, otherwise too much of its older wood will be frosted during the winter.

White flowers look all the more striking when set off by purple stems and foliage, and so it is with the long spikes of *Cimicifuga racemosa* Atropurpurea, which is flowering in front of a deep blue monkshood, *Aconitum* Kelmscott. They are in heavy soil which is normally damp, but matters can become serious for the bugbane in prolonged drought, when its leaves will scorch. This year it is all right. It needs an open situation for the leaf colouring to be its intensest.

My *Gaura lindheimeri* are flowering well this year, and they started early; but they now look stringy, as their ever-extending spikes have a great length of stalk behind them. I should have shorn them earlier on and they would have bushed out. But, given our climate, it is too late now. This delightful plant is really more rewarding where the summers are warmer, but it is pretty good, even so. Its four white petals are arranged, with gaps between, on the top half of each flower. They have a kind of dancing quality, like gnats. June-flowering *Gillenia trifoliata* has it, too.

Gauras are not long-lived perennials, so it is a good plan to save some of their seed, which will germinate freely from a spring sowing. If your plants still have plenty of fresh young growth, they will root easily from cuttings taken now. The red spotting on gaura leaves worries some gardeners, but it is perfectly natural to this plant.

Yet another plant that had benefited from rain is the South African bulb *Eucomis*, of which most of us are growing hybrids. Some of them have purple tinting in their leaves and flowers, which is a handsome feature. They are readily grown from seed and that is the way I raised my *E. bicolor*, on which the flowers, borne in thick spikes with the usual pineapple tuft of green bracts on top, are green, margined with purple. They looked good beneath the apricot turkscaps of a group of *Lilium henryi*, which were planted

249

behind but leaning forwards. This is another case where the flowering of one member of a partnership is quite brief, whereas the other, the eucomis, continues for a couple of months. In fact, it is hard to say exactly when flowering stops and seeding starts.

I noticed at Wisley, in August, that the second flowering of *Bergenia* Morgenrote was very prolific. I may be hard to please, but that did not make me like the plant any better. Its flowers were rain-spotted. And it is a coarse-leaved hybrid. But two helpful friends have just made me a bed of *B. stracheyi* (from where they were growing in a row), which is one of my favourites, with its tuffs of neat leaves. Up to half of them will die in the autumn, changing to crimson on the way. Next year, the plants will be flowering in March, and they have been interplanted with blue *Scilla siberica*.

With the early-May flowering *B. purpurascens*, another neat species and very free, you might interplant *Narcissus triandrus* Hawera, pale yellow with heads of blossom on 10in stems.

— November 26, 1992 —

RETURN OF THE DAHLIA

In the 1950s I grew a lot of dahlias. I love the shapeliness of their flowers and their bright, clean colours. Furthermore, their grand display comes, together with chrysanthemums, at a welcome time of the year.

One of the country's best-known dahlia breeders, Harry Stredwick, had his nursery quite near to us, on the outskirts of Hastings. He was a great character and my mother and I used to enjoy visiting him. Giant Decoratives were his favourites and he named a bronze one Daisy Lloyd, after my mother. She was proud to be photographed by its side when it featured in the

250

dahlia trial at Wisley, which at that time was located where the double herbaceous borders are now. Although he grew a plant of it, Mr Stredwick disapproved of Bishop of Llandaff, with its purple, cut leaves, saying that it was not a proper dahlia at all and must have some fern blood in it.

Gradually, over the decades and more by default than intention, I gave up dahlias, but without ever losing my fondness for them. They do require a bit of attention and any accident with overwintering stock can result in serious losses. Bedding dahlias seemed easier. I had binfuls of Coltness hybrid tubers in our cellar, which provided ideal winter quarters. But then the dwarf bedding seed strains arrived. It seemed simpler to start from scratch each spring. Routines are undemanding; I sow in late April or early May, and seedlings, potted individually, are just right as a follow-on to biennials such as sweet Williams. There is no tyranny, at the end of the season, of needing to save the tubers, nor, in the next year, of being obliged to bed with dahlias somewhere, so as to keep stock going.

But I do rather yearn to be growing some of the taller, named varieties, and, with the stimulus of Fergus Garrett, who will be my head gardener from February, and an inspection with him in September of the RHS dahlia trial, at Wisley, I intend to get back into dahlias in a small way.

I am aware of the demands that they impose. Guy Barter, who runs the Wisley trials, tells me that some 80 per cent of modern dahlia cultivars are poor makers of tubers at the end of the season, wherewith to carry stock over until the next year. Before you lift after the first killer frost (on October 13, this year), you need to wait until all storage supplies have been withdrawn from the plant's leaves and stems and been converted into inulin as storage material in the roots — unless this endangers your stock from a frost severe enough to penetrate the ground and inflict direct damage to the roots.

251

To prevent the tubers drying out and shrivelling to nothing during storage, they need to be kept in moist, but not wet, peat or coir. They can be set in plastic trays under the bench of a frost-free greenhouse. Best plants are obtained by taking cuttings from sprouting tubers, in spring. When these have rooted, which they do readily, they are potted individually, and it is a wise precaution to keep a proportion of your stock growing in the confined space of these small pots, right through the growing season, in your back-up area. This treatment encourages tuber formation, so that if your display plants fail to make decent tubers, you will have a reserve to fall back on, the year after.

It has often been stated that dahlias, other than bedding types, do not take kindly to inclusion in mixed or herbaceous borders. They are more vulnerable to pests, such as earwigs and capsids, in such circumstances and less easy to protect. The trial ground at Wisely is so open and segregated, that these two pests, which thrive on shelter and a mixed community, are no problem, although aphids and mildew still are, and protection has to be given against them.

I think dahlias look their best in a garden (and as you do not see them at Wisley), in a border association with other late-flowering perennials, such as chrysanthemums, Michaelmas daisies and Japanese anemones. The clear, light blue of *Salvia uliginosa*, which grows 5–6ft tall with ease, will look excellent if I give it the company of one of the red, orange or pink dahlias I have noted at Wisley. (For those new varieties grown anonymously under a trial number, I am applying to the RHS for the name after awards have been voted and confirmed.)

The magenta-purple medium cactus, Hillcrest Royal, one of the best we saw, would look good in such company, as would Indian Summer, a small cactus, clear red with dark stems held proudly clear of the foliage. Pearl of Heemstede, a small waterlily decorative with mauve tips to white petals, would look better with pink anemones or perhaps with the cool, pale yellow *Patrinia scabiosifolia*, of which I am building up stock. This has the height and habit of *Verbena bonariensis* (another candidate for the late-season border) but not the colour.

Flowering grasses – some of the new, early-flowering cultivars of *Miscanthus sinensis* – would also mix well in the sort of border I have in mind. At Sissinghurst, they manage dahlias excellently, both in the purple border of the first courtyard and in the cottage garden, where all is orange and yellow. But that is to harp on harmonies and I am as keen on contrasts. The light blue of the salvia would associate so happily with the acid, greeny yellow of the waterlily flowered decorative Glorie van Heemstede – a dahlia that has been with us for many, many years.

How these old timers survive despite virus diseases, I do not quite know, but they do. From time to time, when virus troubles become too insistently debilitating, one has to discard a dahlia. I do not think, in this imperfect world, that it is practicable to insist on virus-free stock. If it looks reasonably free and the plant is growing well, that should give satisfaction enough.

That dahlias do not necessarily need shelter from strong winds is demonstrated convincingly enough on the Wisley trial, but they do receive and are always worth giving the strongest support. Stakes painted a bright, unnatural green should be avoided, remembering that it is from the plant we need colour, not from equipment.

– December 3, 1992 –

MY BORDERS IN WINTER

I do not find my borders in the least depressing in winter and being mixed, which means that they include a number of structural shrubs, they remain reasonably well furnished. To cut everything possible down in autumn seems to me to take a negative attitude. Like sweeping the dust under the carpet, it is a cosmetic exercise that solves nothing. Indeed, it obscures. Having removed the visible remains, it becomes quite difficult to recollect what was where, what needed dividing and replanting and what did not.

Most border work will wait until spring, by which time I can see evidence of where the permanently situated tulips, alliums, camassias and bulbous irises are. Other tulips are treated as bedders, so, areas of bare earth are where they replaced summer bedding.

Of the hardy perennials, the remains of some are good, of others, pretty insufferable (although I am quite adept at looking the other way when a reminder is unwelcome), while in between there are grasses, in particular which are excellent as they gradually die off but then go into such a messy moult, around the New Year, that it becomes a relief to clear away their debris. Such, in particular, are miscanthus; also, the giant reed grass, *Arundo donax*, and the delightful, low-growing *Hakonechloa macra* Aureola. It is my friend from its first appearance in April, right through to now, but for the next three months it deserves to be out of sight.

Calamagrostis acutiflora Karl Foerster, on the other hand, remains a telling feature right through to spring, with its thin, pale straw-coloured rods. *Stipa splendens* and *S. arundinacea* look good throughout the winter. You may be tempted to cut *S. gigantea* hard back, as its foliage is so grotty. Profit from my experience and do not, or you will get scarcely any flower next summer. The best you can do is to remove flowered stems and tease out the dead foliage with your fingers. That will need doing again in the spring as also for the glaucous-leaved fescues and the porcupine-like *Helictotrichon sempervirens*. If the clumps are beginning to degenerate, especially in the centre, bide your time but split and replant some good chunks in the spring. That needs doing quite frequently.

Pampas grasses are curious inasmuch as you can raze a colony absolutely to ground level, which has a totally rejuvenating effect. So I do that every year, but not until March. It needs its foliage, yet, if gales batter and break the flowered stems, we remove them.

The fronds of deciduous ferns can be removed as they wither. The common male fern, *Dryopteris filix-mas*, takes on beautiful russet colouring around Christmas and only needs cutting down when heavily frosted. Its fronds serve to protect the crowns or lower branches of rather tender shrubs, such as certain hydrangeas, *Melianthus major*, myrtles and the yellow shrub poppy, dendromecon. You will think of others.

Evergreen ferns are a handsome winter standby, especially the hart's tongues. They have sown themselves along the entire length of an old wall that was here before my family came to Dixter. In summer, you hardly see them behind the hostas, veratrums and other summer growth in the border. But all that is worth tidying away so as to reveal the ferns in their full, winter glory – such a warm and friendly bay green. Polypodies, especially the bright green Cornubia, are winter standbys, and so are the shield ferns, polystichum, but where these are interplanted with snowdrops, I cut them back in January, and they do not seem to mind.

The quality and mood of evergreens varies a great deal in winter. Some become quite glum; for instance, those conifers which, from being sea green in summer, turn purple as colder weather sets in. I have a pair of cone-shaped, soft-textured *Chamaecyparis thyoides* Ericoides, which do it. So do many of the forms of *Juniperus horizontalis* and, on a larger scale, *Cryptomeria japonica* Elegans. I think I prefer that to the behaviour of *Thuja occidentalis* Rheingold, which turns such a deep, withered bronze as to look dead. But it makes up for that at other seasons.

Mahonia undulata is a favourite with me in my Long Border in winter. Any solemnity in the purple colouring assumed by its leaves is offset by their light reflecting glossiness. They can be damaged by cold, desiccating winds, but my border is protected from them.

Cistus × *corbariensis* is one of the best of its tribe in winter. Its neat leaves, with undulating margins, turn purple, especially at the margins. The bush itself is solid and well furnished. *C.* × *cyprius*, by contrast, has an open habit and turns a pale, oxidised lead colour – admittedly not cheerful, but I have to admire it. Grey-leaved shrubs are, by and large, dismal in winter. One just has to put up with them.

Ivies are excellent, especially the shrubby kinds, which make good mixed-border ingredients. The adult, shrubby form of poet's ivy, *Hedera* Poetica Arborea, is smashing through early winter, not only with bright green, glossy foliage but with prolific clusters of developing berries. They start to ripen yellow in February and are then greedily devoured by wood-pigeons. Various variegated evergreens hold me in good stead, most cheerful being the green and white *Euonymus* × *fortunei* Silver Queen and the much faster growing Emerald Gaiety.

Teazels, in moderation, are valued herbaceous skeletons. Too many of their dark presences can be overpowering, so about half of them (and 99 per cent of next year's seedlings) are rooted out in autumn. Cardoons look grotesquely interesting, especially when capped with snow. That is also the best moment for the flat-headed sedums, *Sedum spectabile* and Autumn Joy. Of the Michaelmas daisies, by far the most imposing structurally is *Aster lateriflorus* Horizontalis. I do not cut my hedges of these down until March, and their dead flowerheads are entrancing when encrusted with hoar frost.

HOW TO BREAK UP A LAWN

An expanse of lawn often demands a solid interruption. It does not necessarily want peopling with plants like gnome-land, but even if there is much of interest on its perimeter, some sort of interruption to that featurelessness may seem desirable.

A blue cedar is a popular choice. Even in a small front garden this seems to exert great magnetism to some owners. Two cedars are even better – then you can call your villa The Cedars (The Cedar would sound odd). I will pass that one up.

Whatever your choice, do remember that turf is greedy and thirsty. Your specimen may require special treatment to keep it happy for quite a few years; perhaps, with a smaller feature, for all its life. A tree will eventually be able to fend for itself and will look the better for allowing the turf to grow right up to its bole. You must be conscientious about keeping this trimmed, even though the lawnmower cannot manage the last bit. Hired labour will nearly always remain blind to the tuft of long grass that has been allowed to develop around a tree trunk, because it requires separate treatment and is a nuisance to think about. Beneath a shrub, large perennial or bamboo, it is usually best to keep a circular area clear, so that top dressings and mulches can be applied.

There is one kind of plant that may be suitable in a lawn and nowhere else: the kind that is prone to suckering. Any young suckers that develop between one mowing and the next will automatically be beheaded. (This does rather preclude going away on a world tour, however.) Bamboos are especially handsome lawn features, although I should avoid one with such flexible canes that they constantly bend to the ground. The Chilean *Chusquea culeou* is ideal on a moderate-sized lawn, keeping itself to itself, arching outwards but not over much. Its canes are densely tufted with dark foliage along their length, and it has a presence. You notice it. Mine is about 8ft tall, but it can reach twice that height, according to climate (taller where moister) and clone. It is a variable species. Perhaps several species are sheltering under the same umbrella, *C. culeou.*

Other bamboos that I should recommend for the purpose are *Arundinaria murielae*, *A. tessellata* and *Phyllostachys nigra* in one of its varieties, *henonis* being one of the best.

I enjoy the larger polygonums, when I am not in terror of their suckering proclivities. *Polygonum cuspidatum* has bold heart leaves, is smothered in sprays of white blossom in autumn, and remains sightly, with its bright brown stems, after leaf fall. But your mowing round this one will need to be regular.

The false acacia, *Robinia pseudoacacia*, is never seen to greater advantage than in a lawn, its trunk and branches becoming deeply furrowed with age. Its canopy is light and remains bright green, even in late summer, and its white blossom, at the turn of May and June, is deliciously scented. This is generally borne in alternate years. However, its disadvantage should be stated. The wood is brittle and unsuited to an exposed site. The spines can be painful on fallen twigs. It suckers – a bit.

I grow the elegant form called rosynskiana (there is a much more impressive specimen at Knightshayes, in Devon), in which the drooping leaves are particularly long, with wide gaps between the pairs of leaflets. It flowers well, which is more than can be said of some of the false acacia's variants. It has to be grafted onto seedlings of common robinia, and this is too much trouble for most nurseries, nowadays.

A suckering shrub that makes a good lawn feature is the dwarf buckeye, *Aesculus parviflora.* It makes a colony of stems, 7ft high or so, and deserves to be given increasing lateral space as it develops. The leaves are of the usual horse-chestnut design, as are its white candles of blossom, but these expand in July–August, which is a most welcome time to have a shrub looking its best. Flowering is not long-lasting but the young foliage is pleasing in spring, and earlier still it can play host to bulbs such as scillas, winter aconites and snowdrops. *A. parviflora* may go down to the coral spot fungus. Mine did, but there is no special reason why yours should.

A catalpa in bloom looks splendid on a lawn, especially if its branches can be allowed to sweep the ground. Then you can most fully enjoy its panicles of white blossom, about now. But I must say that I find the tree, as a structure, rather clumsy and boring, especially in winter. Better under confined condition, to grow the golden catalpa, treating it purely as a foliage plant by pruning it hard back every winter. Given a dark background, this is wonderfully luminous when the sun strikes it from any direction. It is easily kept to a height of 6ft or more. The leaves are heart-shaped and grow all the larger for the pruning treatment.

Now a black mulberry, *Morus nigra*, is as beautiful when naked in winter as when fully clothed. It grows quite quickly and, thanks to a rugged trunk and the formation of burrs, it gains a spurious appearance of antiquity at quite an early age. This is often reinforced, when its horizontal branches become heavy, by propping them up on stout, wooden supports. But if you have occasion to saw off the branches, they sprout vigorously from below the wound, so it is a tree that can be readily rejuvenated. For crops of its delicious (though messy) fruit, be sure to acquire a female and do not on any account allow yourself to be palmed off with the greatly inferior white mulberry, *M. alba*, which can happen if you simply order 'a mulberry'. I should apply to Reads Nursery, Hales Hall, Loddon, Norfolk, which also has a marvellous selection of figs. They make super lawn specimens – witness the ones near the footbridge in St James's Park.

Plants with good foliage are your best bet, in a lawn situation. Sumachs, for instance (*Rhus* and *Cotinus*), or the herbaceous *Aralia cachemirica*, which has large, pinnate leaves but hates to be dry. *Inula magnifica* would be a handsome summer choice, as would a bold grass, such as *Arundo donax*.

– November 4, 1993 –

GRASS AS ORNAMENT

Many ornamental grasses are looking their best in autumn. Some are in flower and all are constantly changing colour as moisture is gradually withdrawn from their aerial parts. Slowly they become sere and bleached, yet continue to make lively features, some right into spring. Others will tend to moult excessively and be better cut down at the turn of the year.

The autumn-flowering kinds will give of their best in the south of our country. In the North, the growing season starts later and ends earlier, so late flowerers never quite make it. Even in the South, there are grasses that will not flower successfully as they do in the eastern states of America, where summers are so much warmer.

That is the case with many of the genus Miscanthus. *M. sinensis* Gracillimus sometimes makes a half-hearted attempt at flowering in my garden, but in the Washington, DC area, where it has been used liberally in the public plantings of Oehme and van Sweden, its flowering is spectacular. I still grow Gracillimus for the elegance of its habit and the shimmer of its narrow leaves with their pale median stripe.

It is the same story with the two cross-banded, zebra clones. Zebrinus is the name often given to both these, but it belongs rightly only to the one with graceful, arching foliage. The yellowish banding appears well into its growing season, but not at all distinctly if the site is shaded. Customers who have newly purchased it often think they have been sold the wrong plant. Strictus, however, is of a narrow, upright habit; the banding is brighter and more frequent and it is looking good, as I write, grouped for contrast among slightly lower-growing hydrangeas. But both of these, in Britain, have to be considered as foliage plants.

However, in north Germany, where the climate, in respect of cool summers, is much like ours, the revered nurseryman Ernst Pagels has been breeding a race of *M. sinensis* with a reliably early-flowering habit. The Beth Chatto nursery is now offering a wide selection of these. They vary considerably in stature from 2ft to 8ft and should really be seen at the height of their September to November season before a decision is made on which to plant in your own garden. The flowers are arranged in a cat-o-nine-tails spray, each tail crimped along its length in a newly set, permanent wave. There is a glittering sheen on them in the early weeks, and the colour is some shade between bronze and purple. Gradually this pales and the panicle becomes fluffy. A row of flowering miscanthus makes a fascinating background to broad-leaved foliage plants.

The 9ft *Miscanthus floridulus* rarely flowers with us, although I grow it for the fountain effect of its foliage. Neither does the giant reed grass, *Arundo donax*, but that anyway looks far better as a foliage plant, pure and simple. You should make a practice of cutting an entire colony to the ground as soon as it becomes unsightly, in midwinter. Often it will bring its old growth through to spring, flowering in its second year, but it is a disheveled object. On the young shoots it rises proudly to about 12ft, or even more if well fed and watered, the leaves being of a rich, glaucous hue.

The giant reed grass does need sympathetic placing. There are large groups of it in the ill-fated double herbaceous borders

at Wisley, where they rise so high above the surrounding plantings as to be totally unsupported, which gives them a strangely
beleaguered look. They would appear to far greater advantage if
planted among shrubs – rhododendrons, azaleas, hydrangeas and
the like – farther up the hill.

The Royal Horticultural Society Gardens' concern for educa-
tion is notably weak when it comes to the placing of plants in a
good context. Flowering through most of last month, they had
a grand colony of the late, orange-hot-poker, *Kniphofia rooperi.*
It could be seen from the restaurant, but there was nothing
whatsoever to set the plant off. Were they backed by the white
plumes or brushes of pampas grass, the juxtaposition would look
dramatic, but the cortaderias are jostled in among a whole lot
of other grasses in a bed of their own. Ornamental grasses generally look much better if contrasted with plants of a different
habit.

There is one such example of an effective contrast at Wisley,
in the narrow double borders (an old feature), near the alpine
houses. A big clump of *Cortaderia selloana* Aureolineata (better
known as Gold Band) grows next to a powerful yucca, with a
rosette of stiff, sharp, spear leaves on a short sturdy trunk. This
is *Yucca treculeana*. The pampas grass has a reputation for shy-
flowering, but an established colony, as here, flowers well enough,
and anyway its mound of arching, gold-and-green-striped foliage
is a feast in itself.

By the nature of their stylish and individual habit, some grasses look best as individual specimens, and they should not be
towered over by their neighbours. Such is *Molinia caerulea* subsp.
arundinacea Transparent. From a low clump of fairly ordinary
grass leaves, its flowering stems rise to 6ft or so, with a tendency
to obliqueness so that the plant describes a semicircle. The flowering panicles are widely spaced in their parts, so Transparent is
a well-chosen name. The sum effect is shimmering and glinting,

reaching a peak in October but on the way up for three months before that.

Calamagrostis acutiflora Karl Foerster is another that stands well solo, although it also makes an excellent inner-garden screen when planted in a row, whether curved or straight. By now it stands stiff as stair rods and will so continue until spring, when it needs to be cut down. The colour is pale straw, but at flowering, in late June, it is dove purple, soft and fluffy. An amazing, although gradual, transformation.

Any of the selections of *Panicum virgatum* (I have Hänse Herms) are beautiful in the autumn garden, light and airy. Usually some 3ft tall, the leaves take on various bronze, purple and biscuit tones, and the flowering panicles are of gossamer lightness.

– July 23, 1994 –

THE RIGHT PLANT FOR THE CLIMATE

There is increasing interest in and reliance on hardiness rating throughout the gardening world. The idea, of course, is to help gardeners decide which plants are likely to succeed with them. If it deters them from attempting to treat a date palm as a hardy tree in Norfolk, you might say 'well and good'. It might encourage them to try a Scots pine instead. There are, however, so many exceptions and caveats to the rules that they often do more harm than good.

The Zoning system was devised by the Americans and has been widely adopted in the last few years. It is based on minimum temperatures, zone 1 catering for plants that will endure Arctic conditions; zone 10 restricting you to plants that will stand no frost at all. The Royal Horticultural Society, demonstrating Britain's rugged independence, has adopted hardiness ratings, which run in the opposite direction to American Zoning. Thus, H1 designates the tenderest plants, H4 the hardiest, under conditions obtaining in this country.

What is meant by hardy? The equivalent word used among French gardeners is *rustique*, which suggests a general resistance to inclement conditions, of which cold is only one.

All of Australia lies between zones 9 and 10. 'Hardy', as used there, has nothing to do with frost, and just means tough. Yet nurserymen in Australia use the northern-hemisphere hardiness zones, quite inappropriate to their country. 'Consequently people fail to grow lots of good plants which they could grow perfectly well – all because English and American books say they are not hardy.' I quote from a letter from Tommy Garnett (one-time headmaster of Marlborough College), whose garden is in east Victoria. Rainfall, when it falls, and sun, especially winter sun, are much more important there, he says, giving a lemon tree as an example.

It has taken him nine years to get one going, whereas north of the Divide, where they have it much colder, citrus can be grown without difficulty near to the Victoria border. So Garnett has devised a horticultural zoning map for Victoria, taking into account these other factors militating to a plant's success or failure.

They apply no less with us, although we tend to ignore them. A hot, ripening summer followed by a freezing winter will see fewer casualties than a wet, mild run-up to winter that has encouraged soft, late growth. *Gleditsia triacanthos* Sunburst is an easy tree in south-east England, but in the North, although it will grow well enough in summer, this growth is so soft and unripe that, cold or not, it will die back in winter. The plant will make no progress.

The amount of flowering is also greatly affected by summer warmth and sunshine, although the plant itself may flourish without flowers. That may be of little use to us. Take *Daphne odora* as an instance. With us, in Sussex, it is excellent in shade, where it will flower well and not suffer the yellowing of its foliage that full sunlight is liable to induce. Yet even as far north as the Midlands, it will need all the sun and radiant heat that is going if it is to flower at all.

I remember Percy Picton, of Old Court Nurseries near Malvern, Worcestershire, telling me that, to flower it well, he treated it as a pot plant under glass. In the open, he got virtually nothing.

Forsythias in Scotland need the warmth (not the protection) of a south-facing wall if they are to flower really freely, and they will not respond to the hard, post-flowering pruning that usually works well in the South, where the subsequent growth made in summer will bud up and flower the next spring. None of this has anything to do with H4 hardiness or to zoning as understood in respect of minimum temperatures. Yet a flowering plant must flower if it is to earn its keep. At Inverewe, in north-west Scotland, most evergreen azaleas flower only fitfully or at half-cock. (On reflection, perhaps that is an advantage, when the numbing explosions of colour that are achieved in the south-east are considered.

It is not only of shrubby plants that we are talking. Herbaceous perennials, especially bulbs, need ripening, too. Bergenias flower much more freely in the South-East, although the plant be as tough as old boots. What of *Amryllis belladonna*, the South African bulb, whose dense ranks of purple-flowering stems, crowned by pink trumpet flowers before a leaf has appeared, can make a stunning display in the September garden? But even in the South, to be successful as a flowering plant, it must be given a basking position, preferably backed by a heat-retaining, south-facing brick wall. Even then, it may flower fitfully if the soil is heavy.

I wonder if soil is a factor that Tommy Garnett has taken into consideration. Whether light or heavy, this makes such a difference to a plant's performance.

Performance: there's a word that applies as much to foliage as to flowers. They can grow our deciduous trees well in Victoria. Their streets and parks are crammed with wych elms, but do they take on that wonderful, luminous lemon yellow colouring in autumn that is promoted and triggered off by an early frost?

But to return to the hardiness question. I believe that ratings and the sound advice from nervous and twitchy professionals puts many amateurs off the growing of many plants which could give them immense pleasure – perhaps not for ever, but for long enough to set the adrenalin coursing on frequent occasions. To garden a little dangerously is much more exciting and rewarding than stolidly playing safe.

No matter where we live, the adventurous gardener will always be operating on the borderlines of what is safe and sensible and what is downright rash (and there is a date palm flourishing in a Norfolk garden – at the Old Vicarage, East Ruston). If you lose all your evergreen ceanothus and hebes and much else in a stinking winter, do not be one of those whose nerves will need another four or five years missed out of your life. Do not weep over the consequences when a cherished favourite is lost. It is not to be taken as personal insult.

– November 3, 1994 –

LEAVING THE LEAVES

Given the slightest encouragement from the weather, there is a tremendous lot we can get done in November, and the work is of a kind that leaves us with a feeling of accomplishment. It is a great shame that, more and more, planting emphasis has turned from autumn to spring, although the weather is often a lot more comfortable for working now than then.

266

Garden centre purchases lean heavily on the appearance of the goods at point of sale. A bare root shrub or tree may not look much at this season but, most often, it is in just the right state to get established with the minimum of distress.

If there are still some leaves on it, albeit deciduous (this is common in roses), so much the better. Before becoming fully dormant (or as dormant as plants are in winter which is never completely), it will have the chance to settle in; that is to say, to form a callus over wounds. Such wounds should be cleanly pared before planting, since a clean wound heals the most easily. Generally (unless to do so would be a bad joke), it is a good plan to water in after planting, so as to settle the soil round roots and to eliminate large air space. But the wetter the ground, the less firming a plant should receive when being tucked up; you do not want to squeeze all the air out of the soil.

If staking is necessary to prevent wind rock, tie loosely, so that there is some play when the wind blows, not complete rigidity. In this way, the shrub or tree will be encouraged to learn to stand on its own leg(s). It will react by broadening at the base, like an inverted carrot. That way it will soon not require a stake any longer.

Pruning at planting is another solution to the wind-rock problem. If there is a lot of top-hamper and little root at planting time, a balance between roots and branches needs to be restored by pruning. This additionally puts less strain on the root system to supply the top growth with moisture and nutrients.

Most amateurs are impressed by a generous exhibition of branches when buying a bare-root tree/shrub, so that is the way it is sold them. But you would do well to get busy with knife or secateurs in a shortening operation, even before planting.

Wind rock is often a problem even in established shrubs. Repeat flowering rose bushes are often the better for having their branch system reduced by half in autumn. Pruning can be completed at a later stage (winter or spring, according to your climate or preference). A hard pruning in autumn of some of the less robust buddleias can be lethal, but reducing the branches by half will do no harm and still leaves quite a bit of foliage on the shrub.

Do not feel that none of your clematis can be laid hands on now, but do be selective and use a spot of intelligence about which you treat. Leave the spring-flowering montanas, macropetalas, alpines and the like strictly alone. Every strand of young wood removed will lose you a dozen or more flowers. Tidying them up because they are blocking the light from windows may be important, but leave it until the end of May, when they have flowered, if you can possibly restrain yourself (or if you can restrain your husband – more difficult).

But the hideous scarecrow of blackened leaves that summer-flowerers such as *Clematis* × *jackmanii, C. viticella* and all their derivatives currently present need not be tolerated. Cutting them to the ground right now would do no harm as their next year's flowering will be on young shoots made next year.

Give your meadow areas their last cut and make it as tight as you can. The autumn crocuses and colchicums have finished, the daffodil snouts are not yet through, but soon will be. Now, before the ground becomes too soggy, is your chance. We have only just given our 'prairie' area its one and only annual cut (prairie perennials tend to flower, and hence to scatter their seed, late), so it was pretty rough.

A BCS (walk behind) Power Scythe has coped with the job admirably. You do not even need to have someone raking the cut grass out of your way when returning to cut the next parallel strip.

We have bought the lowest-priced in the range, the only alternative adjustment for which is a rotovator attachment. More expensive models can have attachments to do all sorts of other work, but in my experience the simpler and more directly purpose-made the machine, the less there is to go wrong. This one has a front-mounted cutting bar and direct drive (no belts to loosen or break or to cause loss of power).

But we want the meadow grass to be as a lawn at this stage, both to reduce its vigour (to which end, all clippings are removed to a compost heap – and in any case I hate picking them up on my feet and clothes) and to allow the small, winter-flowering bulbs – snowdrops, crocuses – to be seen to best advantage. The Kubota ride-on mower is well spoken of. Again it has direct drive, and there is a fan blower to get clippings into removable bags. If the clippings are too heavy and wet for this to operate well, they will have to be raked by hand.

When the turf is at its shortest, it is easiest to plant bulbs. Thank goodness there is now a sensible, foot-operated, long-shafted bulb planter available again (ours is pre-First World War and still in its prime). You can use it for plants other than bulbs, of course, nibbling with it round the edge of the original hole if the plant's bulk requires this. We have a number of pot-grown primrose seedlings to go out, and a good batch, also from seed and subsequently lined out, of *Dianthus carthusianorum*. This is a species that you see in meadows throughout central and eastern Europe; heads of magenta flowers are held on long stems. Whether it will thrive in my sort of meadow remains to be seen. One has to experiment where books are no help.

As to fallen leaves, why not let them be (there are far more important tasks) until the wind has driven them into drifts and they can be gathered together for mulches round the rhododendrons or to make leaf mould? People get so neurotic when they see leaves lying about.

THE POINSETTIA

The surge of interest in poinsettias as house plants has been loudly expressed, of recent weeks, by their plentiful supply notably in superstores. It is a plant in which I have hitherto taken only a passing interest. This is because you see in homes and offices so many debilitated specimens that have long outlasted any claims to beauty, but which still cling on to their coloured bracts. Reason proclaims that their time has come, yet their owners are reluctant to throw them away. It is not so much that they continue to admire their jaded possession, but that they have virtually ceased to see it. To me, this gives the poinsettia a bad name.

But there is currently a trial of this plant in the Conservatory at Wisley, the RHS Garden, where it is grown as well as it is likely to be grown, and clearly demonstrating great progress in its breeding development of recent years. Having closely examined this trial, next morning I took a look, instead of a passing gaze, at the poinsettias on offer at Sainsbury's. Those in small pots seemed puny objects, but the well branched specimens selling at £4.99 struck me as definitely worth the price. I meant to buy one, but they were near to the entrance and, by the time my shopping was completed, I had forgotten my intention. They should have been near to the checkout.

Poinsettias were named, in 1836, after their discoverer, J. R. Poinsett, American Minister to Mexico, which is their native land. Kingsley wrote of them in 1871: 'What is this that hangs over into the road, some 15ft in height? What but the poinsettia, paltry scions of which adorn our hothouses and dinner-tables.' They are nowadays seen in their tall, wayside manifestation in many sub-tropical countries.

When I was a student, we displayed them in the conservatory at Wye College. Old plants were headed back and cuttings taken of the resultant growth in late spring. Their naturally tall habit would send them up to 6ft or more in a single growing season, to some extent catered for by stopping the young plants once, which made them branch a little.

Smaller and No Longer Taken as Red

The inconvenience of a tall plant in most homes was at first controlled by the use, while on the nursery, of growth regulators. Had the plants been retained in private hands for more than one season, the owner would have been somewhat disgusted by their return to an unmanageable height. Now, however, breeding work has resulted in strains which are naturally dwarf and retain their dwarfness. One less artificial control is needed.

There have also been outstanding developments in colour. Poinsettia is, botanically, *Euphorbia pulcherrima*, and the colourful plant part are the bracts, handsomely surrounding a tiny, insignificant inflorescence. Red is their natural colour and still the most popular, as blue is in delphiniums. But there are now pink-flowered varieties, cream and white.

There is a fashion tendency for red poinsettias to have very dark green leaves. I see no advantage in this. And in some varieties, such as the red Freedom, it seems to me that the plant's overall appearance would have been improved had the red bracts been framed below them by a ring of larger leaves. But the leaves were quite small. This may be an advantage when the plant has to be wrapped for sale. Indeed, the supermarkets exercise a powerful influence on the direction that breeding work takes. Colour under the store's lighting is considered.

The plants bought in time for Christmas were raised from cuttings rooted in early July. This is how they arrived for trial at

Wisley on July 20, when they received their first potting. They were potted on on August 14, and went into their final pots only a week later, so rapid was growth during favourable weather (and weather exerts as great an influence under glass as outside).

You could keep your poinsettia and develop it into a larger, handsomer plant in its second year, if you treat it kindly in a greenhouse. Or you could head it back in early spring and take cuttings from the resultant young shoots.

— June 22, 1995 —

CLIMBERS

Climbing plants do not necessarily need anything to hang on to. As a feature on flat ground, they will often mound themselves into a shrub, or else lie on the ground staring (or smiling) up at you. They may cover quite an area, which is sometimes what you need. And it is a way to fit in another climber when you have run out of walls and fences.

Sometimes a climber is required to do the reverse of climbing, and to hang down a wall face from above. That may not be too easily organised. For one thing, the soil at the top of a retaining wall is apt to be far too dry for the happiness of the plant behind it.

Such has been my experience with *Tropaeolum polyphyllum*, which is more of a trailer than a climber, anyway. Its gloriously glaucous, palmate leaves make twisted ropes of luxuriant growth in late spring and early summer, soon to be joined by clear yellow nasturtium flowers. And its questing rootstock will discover every crevice in a retaining wall. Planted at the top, it will soon have made a three-dimensional curtain of growth all through the available surface.

But the 'big if' is whether there is moisture enough to keep it happy. In Scotland, even if rainfall is low, as on the east side, there is a coolness which admirably suits this tropaeolum. But in my Sussex garden, no. I have not yet given up, however.

The other possible snag about trying to drape a wall from above is that the plant may prefer what is sees in the opposite direction – and that may not be where you want it. A Virginia creeper would be the plant that I should choose for the purpose. *Parthenocissus quinquefolia* has the greatest vigour; alternatives are *P. henryana* and *P. inserta.*

Leaving aside the vertical, *Vitis coignetiae* looks splendid on the horizontal, especially if it can hoist itself a little over some workaday berberis or cotoneaster that you haven't bothered to get rid of. The vine can be cut back to base after its autumn conflagration, so it needn't take over the whole garden.

I know that ivies are used a lot as ground cover, but I still find most of them rather negative in this role. *Hedera helix* Buttercup would be good, however, given an open situation where its yellow colouring can develop brightly. In shade it reverts to green. Some of the boldly variegated ivies do retain their patterning in shade, and when the variegation is white, they help to lighten a dark spot.

Of clematis on the level, *Clematis* × *jouiniana* will do an excellent job over a large area. You may have to check its tendency to root itself. It is a non-climber, has large leaves, which shade out weeds, and foams with countless smallish, cruciform flowers in skimmed-milk blue. The type plant does not flower before September, in our climate. Preferable, in most situations, is Praecox, which flowers non-stop from July to late September. This can be pruned hard, in the dormant season.

C. flammula is good, and this is the way you see it in its native habitats – not generally climbing at all – although it can when it needs to. I like the gloss on its deep green foliage, but the foam of

273

scented white blossom is the thing. It is a purer white than most clematis, with small cruciform flowers.

Large-flowered clematis of the kind that, against a wall, all too often rush up to the top, where they are out of sight except from upstairs windows (generally belonging to the flat above you or to the next-door neighbour) are particularly successful, at ground level. A wide-opening flower will be most suitable. It might be the bright pinky mauve Comtesse de Bouchaud, which looks good against lawn grass. You can stop mowing the lawn, just there, while the clematis is doing its stuff. It won't mind being cut right back to base immediately flowering is over.

There is plenty of choice among so-called climbing roses, which are really scramblers, hooking their way upwards with their curved prickles when given the chance. As a huge mound of blossom in an open situation – it might be a woodland clearing – they look most impressive. But when acquiring a ground-cover rose, do make sure that it is on its own roots. The need to plunge into the centre of a hostile thicket, as I have seen with grafted Max Graf, in order to remove suckers of the stock, could make you want to give up growing roses.

I have written on occasions of the pleasing habit assumed by the climbing hydrangea, *H. petiolaris*, when treated as a shrub. It will make a frame some 4ft high and as spreading as you allow, for it self-layers, but this is easily checked. The twigs of young growth are warm brown in winter, showing up best in sunshine, as does the yellow autumn colouring of the foliage. The only possible snag in an open situation is that late spring frost may catch the young flower buds and reduce their flowering the following June.

Frost damage on its young foliage is almost endemic with *Actinidia kolomikta*, but it always pulls itself out of that within a few weeks, and the shrub is really hardy. Its best performance as a free-standing shrub that I have ever seen was in south Sweden.

The point of this species, as a garden feature, is the curious variegation that its leaves assume in late spring and early summer. From being green at first, the tip to some (not all) leaves changes to white; then the tip of that to pink. In all there are bands of green, white and pink – all on the same leaf, but only on the upper surface. The underside remains green.

Be warned that cats can become enamoured of *A. kolomikta*; we all know the destructive power of love.

Whether *Solanum crispum* should be described as a climber is doubtful, but it is usually trained against a wall. A waste of precious wall space, in my view. Out in the open, it makes a large, loose shrub, effective in its early summer season, with masses of mauve potato flowers. I should like to see it teamed up with *Cytisus battandieri*, which is equally vigorous and no more in need of wall protection.

– February 15, 1996 –

CHEERFUL FEBRUARY

If January was cold, February is often no better than an extension of winter, rather than a harbinger of spring. I remember that, according to where they measure these things in London, February 1947 produced only 17 hours of sunshine, and there was a great shortage of fuel, at that time.

Still, I find February a cheering month. Seen from my bathroom, the sun now rises to the left of my neighbours, instead of to the right; and, in the dining room, it no longer shines in my eyes at lunchtime. Good signs. We also tell ourselves that, if spring is not early as it has been of recent years, there will be less chance of damage by late frosts on prematurely expanded young foliage and magnolia buds, not to mention *Rhododendron*

275

× Cilpinense, which is a predestined week from the day it opens its flower buds.

Nowadays – for the past 10 years or so – we have to cope not only with global warming when we are experiencing a summer drought, but with a wind-chill factor at this time of year. Canna, my dachshund puppy, is horribly hardy, and seems to enjoy keeping me waiting in the wind chill for her to do what she should. But there are a great many other distractions that amuse her more.

My plants do not seem to have suffered much. I got nervous over the astelias, so Fergus has packed them around with fern fronds. These are hard to come by now. We don't live in a bracken area, so he had to cut down our *Polystichum setiferum* Pulcherrimum Bevis, which was still looking handsome, in a slightly bronzed condition.

How to tidy your garden without really meaning to, might be quite a good subject. We are cutting down the clumps of pampas rather early, and without noticeable regrets. Their ghostly, grey pallor has a certain lugubrious attraction, but it is understandable that W. H. Hudson, the field naturalist, who was brought up near the Argentinian pampas in the mid-19th century and loved this grass in the wild, was disparaging of it in cultivation, writing of its 'sadly decaying, draggled look at all times'.

'To my mind, it is often positively ugly with its dense withering mass of coarse leaves, drooping on the ground, and bundle of spikes, always of the same dead white or dirty cream colour.' He compares that to 'the various ethereal tints that give a blush to its cloud-like purity' in the wild, and continues with one of his most eloquent descriptive passages (*The Naturalist in La Plata*, 1892).

Pampas grass can be fresh and glistening in cultivation when it first comes into bloom in the autumn, but this condition is not retained, and a depressed appearance gradually takes over, although considerable dignity remains. You can go over colonies with a strimmer any time now. A blade attachment will be needed. Alternatively, use your second best hedge trimmer. Strim over the epimediums, also, to get their scarred old foliage out of the way and to leave the field clear for flowers and coppery young foliage. The flower buds could be damaged if you left this job until much later. Every other year, we strim over our periwinkle colony (*Vinca minor*). That gets rid of the tangle of old stems and reveals the flowers in a clean setting.

Fergus has given the old Souvenir de Louis Spaeth lilac (the most popular single purple variety) its quinquennial pruning. Stems or branches terminating in buds that are fat enough to contain embryo flowers are left intact. You can test this by cutting one or two of them in half, transversely, when the purple buds will be revealed, if present. Those branches that are too weak to flower are removed. Like most pruning, the job develops its own rhythm. At the end, the tree/shrub has been opened up and will, with the assistance of a good organic surface mulch, be encouraged to make strong new growths. A lilac should live for ever. I write of the common *Syringa vulgaris*, which has the best scent of all.

Next to this lilac grows *Mahonia japonica* (of the lily-of-the-valley scent), which, in a long season, should be at its best now. Fergus said its looked pretty good from the top of his stepladder, but the flowers were a mush, seen at close range, and there was no scent. But it has plenty of buds yet to open.

Sarcococca confusa is flowering, but neither of us could get a whiff of scent from it. So I picked a sprig and, within 10 minutes of taking it indoors, the fragrance was overpowering. Yet *Olearia solandri* was as strong on the air outside, with its heliotrope scent, as at any temperature or time of year. Other good scents of this kind which seem not to depend on the weather, are the cedar smell of *Hebe cupressoides*, including Boughton Dome, and gummy cistuses, such as *Cistus* × *cyprius*.

I fear for the health of plants which insist on making young growth throughout the winter. *Gladiolus tristis* seems undeterred and will, I believe, start flowering in April as usual. It self-sows freely, often in the most endearingly inappropriate places. One such is in the middle of a grey cushion of *Rhodanthemum hosmariense.* That will be covered with its white, yellow-centred daisies at the same time as the gladiolus is flowering. Only two months to go.

Narcissus tazetta is from south Europe and on the tender side, its rich, dark green foliage (without a trace of glaucous) prominent from early in the year. I have that close to a warm wall and it hasn't turned a hair. Neither have the dormant flower-bud clusters on *Grevillea* Canberra Gem, which we eventually had the courage to plant out last summer. Bright pink in colour, it is one of those southern hemisphere members of proteaceae which always need to be treated as a gamble.

My favourite, and one that remained hardy for me through many winters before succumbing in the early 1980s, is *Grevillea juniperina f. sulphurea.* Its needle leaves are a particularly bright and cheerful shade of green. The pale yellow flowers, in late spring, put on a good display. I must get it back.

– April 18, 1996 –

A SLOW SPRING

It is a maddeningly slow spring. Instead of daily new excitements by the dozen, I peer for any sign of change.

Frosts in early April are nothing new – it went down to – 3 deg. C in my porch last night – but they still cause anxiety. The apricot against my bathroom wall is smothered in blossom, but can it possibly set any? As the bathroom is noticeably warmed at the end of a sunny day, even as early as March, I hope that the reverse will apply, and that the apricot is benefiting from the warmth from the bathroom at night.

Hoar frost is beautiful, of course. On the broad leaves of the Fosteriana tulip Purissima, it makes a criss-cross mosaic of needle-fine ice crystals. Other, hairier leaves are fringed in white whiskers.

Soft stems, such as the daffodils' and hellebores', keel over in abject positions, but they bob up again, thank goodness. The lance leaves of *Tulipa orphanidea* show up with particular clarity when there is frost on them, although they are in meadow turf, and I am reminded that the few bulbs I planted in the thirties have now colonised a big area, this being a stoloniferous species. One year, I had a couple of blooms; never before or since. Wouldn't you think that after a summer like the last one, they would be encouraged to flower? I still live in hope.

The yellow *T. sylvestris*, with its delicious scent, is another species with the same habits, although that does occasionally flower where it has colonised, and I believe there are some strains more floriferous in our climate than the familiar, costive non-performers.

When the daffodils eventually perform, it looks as though they will make an exceptionally bountiful display. Certainly, the Lent lilies, *Narcissus pseudonarcissus*, will be spectacular at their level of modesty. Dog's-tooth violets, *Erythronium dens-canis*, are currently at their showiest, although some clumps have few blooms, some, none. I can only put this shyness, which I have noticed before, down to congestion, although other congested clumps are flowering well.

In the Exotic Garden we planted *Chamaerops humilis* last autumn, a palm with fanshaped leaves. It scarcely had time to settle in before the winter, but has come through with flying colours. Supposedly less hardy than the familiar Chusan palm, *Trachycarpus fortunei*, *Chamaerops humilis* (a native of southern

Europe) makes a shrub, rather than a tree, so we should not worry about its size for a while.

I have tipped back my young *Acer negundo* Flamingo with a view to encouraging a plentiful supply of young, pink-flushed foliage over a long season. Also treated this way for the sake of continuously produced young leaves, is *Gleditsia triacanthos* Sunburst, on the Long Border. At first, all the leaves will be lime yellow-green. This early foliage will then darken to green and will form a background to further brightly coloured young leaves produced from the tips of the still-lengthening shoots. An un-pruned tree does not have this urge to keep on growing, and settles down to uniformly green middle age by the end of June. Many species that would naturally become trees can be retained as shrubs by annual shortening of all their branches. Eucalyptus are a classic example. *Eucalyptus globulus* has for long been used as a break to garish (or bright, if you like them) colours in sub-tropical bedding. Its glaucous, juvenile foliage is, roughly, heart-shaped and sessile against the winged stems. You sow the seed shortly and bring on the seedlings so that they are in 5in pots by the end of the season, overwintering them under glass.

Next early summer they are bedded out (contrasting well with purple canna leaves) and will make fantastic growth in the course of the season (requiring staking) to 10ft or more. They can then be discarded and replaced, if you wish, with young stock. If you leave them, they may survive the winter, although not a particu-larly hardy species. Ours all survived, last year, but I wanted to replace them with *E. gunnii*, similarly raised. Its growth is rather less gross and its leaves neater, although less glaucous. So we dug out the six or eight *E. globulus* and gave them away, in two direc-tions. Rather to my surprise, they all survived. If you retain your stock as foliage features, it needs cutting back pretty hard at this stage, say to one foot or a little more, depending on how tall you want them to be by the end of the summer. If not cut back, the leaves will quickly develop into the adult, scimitar-shaped type.

The young shoots of certain herbaceous perennials are particularly attractive in spring. Peonies are notable. Many of the *Paeonia lactiflora* hybrids are deep, rich carmine. They will usually be the pink- and red-flowered kinds, later on. But *P. mlokosewitschii*, whose pale yellow blooms will open quite early in May, has the fattest shoots, richly tinted dusky pink. We should really make more of this asset by interplanting with early-flowering bulbs that will contrast or harmonise with the peony shoots. There are hyacinths in colours to suit all tastes.

The hemerocallis that look the sleaziest in late summer after flowering are the brightest and freshest now. None more so than the variegated form of *Hemerocallis fulva.* That has a broad, pure white stripe along each leaf. However, I do not think it is easy to get the best results from it. If your attention wanders, it gets weak and starved or reverts to plain green. Still, with Fergus and his deep digging and barrow loads of mushroom compost to support me, I am tempted to have another go.

Clusters of young kniphofia shoots look good if you have stripped away the lanky, old, overwintered stuff, which can now be done with impunity; *Kniphofia linearifolia,* an October flowerer, has bright, light green leaves all through the summer. The flowers are an unaggressive shade of orange.

— August 8, 1996 —

GETTING ON WITH VEGETABLES

Our success or failure with vegetables to date this year has mainly depended on preparation of the ground, on sowing dates and on water availability. Perry, in his second year of vegetable care, has taken a great deal of trouble over sowing, thinning, weeding and, when possible in view of heavy demands elsewhere, watering.

There is a terrific crop of peas, as much for freezing as for immediate consumption. The difference between your own home-frozen peas and what you can buy is amazing. We are growing two kinds, sown on April 17 and again two or three weeks later with half the quantity. Hurst's Greenshaft has been (and continues to be) our preferred variety for several years now. It fills a fair-sized pod that is easily shucked.

But we are also growing a petits pois called Lynx and I can't quite think what made me order that. It has cropped abundantly and over a considerable period. Its flavour is excellent, although not superior to Hurst's Greenshaft, but it is a pain to shuck, the pods being so small and, once filled, quite difficult to open. In a world where small, or big, is beautiful – any size, in fact, that does not come naturally to the plant in question – petits pois command a premium price. If shucked mechanically, Lynx would present no problem, but in the home, it is painfully slow to deal with and there is no real reward.

The broad beans – of the variety Express – have been equally successful. We sprayed against black aphids on our spindle and viburnum bushes before they moved across to the beans, and then again, the moment they showed up there. As a consequence, I was able to gather almost all the tips of the bean shoots for cooking as a green vegetable. That was in late June and early July, after the crop of pods had flowered and set.

I am not sufficiently fond of runner beans to have sown any. Dwarf French beans are tricky on our cold and heavy soil if sown at all early. We took a risk with Radar on May 14. They are gappy and flowering only now (late July). The second sowing of Tendergreen (both were from Thompson & Morgan) was made on July 1 and are a beautifully even lot, but will not be cropping, I daresay, until next month.

Beet, a round variety called Monogram, can be space-sown

without further thinning. I started pulling that in mid July from an April 30 sowing, but a later sowing will come on in time for autumn and early winter.

Calabrese Green Comet, being an FI hybrid with few seeds to a packet, was sown in a pot on April 22 and subsequently lined out. That is just coming in now (July 22) and it looks well, but will doubtless receive the attentions of caterpillars when an influx of cabbage white butterflies arrives – they haven't yet.

Little Gem is the best of all lettuces and the first crop came from a late-March sowing in a cold frame, the seedlings being lined out subsequently. Unfortunately, Dahlia, my elder dachshund, has a passion for well-hearted lettuce, and she ate out the centre of every one. After that they made numerous side shoots, from which I reaped some benefit. The first outside sowing was made on Perry's birthday, May 8, and he inadvertently wrote '59 instead of '96, when dating the label. Dahlia left me some of those but there will now be a gap, as the next sowing was not made until June 28.

Purslane, sown on May 14, looked miserable for a long while but a good soaking has transformed the situation, and there are now masses of its fleshy shoots for my salads. Never imagine, as many do, that a succulent plant can always be kept short of water. At the stage of its most vigorous growth, abundant water is much appreciated.

I always feel it to be the greatest insult if I am obliged to buy parsley. Last year's plants will, unless killed by a hard winter (ours was not that hard), continue to crop into June, when they inescapably run up to flower (I keep a few plants for seed unless they are horribly in the way). By then, you must have young plants of this year's sowing ready to take over. They were – just, having been sown under cold glass in March, potted individually and planted out into well-prepared ground. A subsequent, open-ground sowing was made on May 13 and is just coming in as I write. That, without premature bolting, should last me through until May–June next year, although a killer winter is always on the cards.

We had a marvellous crop of shallots last year (I am happy to buy onions, as required), which have lasted in storage right through to now, shrivelling only a little. They provided sets for the new crop, which were planted on April 17, grew quickly and are ready to harvest now, their leaves having died off naturally. I wish I knew the variety. It has shown no tendency to bolt and flower.

Of maincrop potatoes, we saved our own 'seed' of Pink Fir Apple and that is growing strongly, having been twice watered and, to date, twice protected with a spray against blight. We are repeating this fortnightly, as also on the tomatoes. This proved to be so worthwhile last year, and Pink Fir Apple lasted through to May, unlike Ratte, which started sprouting in storage in January, shrivelling as a consequence. Don't be fobbed off with that as a substitute for Pink Fir Apple. Order in September for delivery next late winter, to avoid disappointment.

We have also grown Charlotte, as a second early, and I am sorry that we did not plant more of this, as it keeps well and its waxy texture is useful for various purposes (other than mashing); what you normally find on the market are floury kinds. None of our potatoes were set out until April 19, but Charlotte was ready for digging from the end of June.

— November 21, 1996 —

WINTER SCENES

What will the winter scene in our gardens be for the next three months? We shall salute the evergreen shrubs, until they get battered and torn. Down the scale are those lowly perennials which also retain their leaves.

Retaining one's leaves in winter is not necessarily a virtue. Those that are grey or glaucous look particularly gloomy, not to say sodden, beneath rain-laden clouds. And what shall we say of the *Helleborus orientalis* hybrids? In *Perennial Garden Plants*, Graham Thomas writes: 'The splendid evergreen foliage makes a sort of prostrate platform for the sheaf of flowering stems.' Not in my garden. I can't wait to remove the scarred old leaves on mine, and it is not too soon to do so. The flowers will then stand pristine and unalloyed.

I cannot say that I am very successful with bergenias, in winter, either, especially the large-leaved kinds like *Bergenia cordifolia* Purpurea, which has been a must since Jekyll's protagonism in so many of the gardens whose planting she planned. But what a bore it is at Hestercombe, in Somerset, for instance. I know it is valuable for making a statement, but need it be so emphatic and reiterative? When large-leaved bergenias are planted on a promontory or to mark an outline, they get the bit between their teeth and spread way out and beyond where they were planted.

What's more, they are always most exuberant at the margins, where they have found new freedom but where they were not intended to be. The result is that you soon have twice the area of them that was originally envisaged. They become boorish and you long for a touch of frivolity.

This particular bergenia is one of the most leathery. And there's another thing about a large leaf that is with you through the winter. If it has been nibbled at, not to say gobbled at, during the growing season, by vine weevils, slugs or whatever, the marks will remain for the next six months and more. I shall never forget a vast sweep of bergenias in front of the Federal Reserve building in Washington, DC, in October. Its foliage had been decimated by some pest. Probably, there was enough of the plants left not to have affected their health, but they looked awful, and such a lot of them.

Bergenias are not keen on my heavy soil. They grow all right, but they don't do wonderful things that they perform in Beth Chatto's garden in winter. Her soil is light, although enriched, and the siting is open, which promotes the wonderful winter colouring of which they are capable; every shade of crimson, toning down to silver, and with different colouring on the top and underside of each leaf.

I defy anyone to produce good colour on some of them. Silber-licht (white-flowered, fading pink) and Bressingham White – of which Beth's catalogue description tactfully comments, 'winter foliage not remarkable', could only inspire gloom, especially by the time of spring's arrival, when you must concentrate on their flowers.

My favourite of the large-leaved kinds in Ballawley. Its surface shines and the leaf's underside turns a beetroot colour in cold weather. You can't give it too exposed a situation, or the wind will tumble its leaves, as Margery Fish put it.

The small-leaved bergenias are much more fun. They are prick-eared, and even if they don't perform the efficient ground-covering job of their more butch relatives, you don't find many weeds among them. Smallest in leaf is *Bergenia stracheyi* and its white-flowered *alba*. They make fat clumps that are easily moved about and I use them for bedding, to make an early display. They should be at their best by next year's early Easter – for they flower abundantly – and we shall plant squills (*Scilla siberica*) among them. In the summer, they have a reserve area. Although evergreen, they lose a proportion of their leaves each autumn and these colour bright yellow and carmine, before dying.

Bergenia purpurascens is somewhat larger-leaved but still neat and upright and turning good shades of purple, when cold. Its reddish purple flowers, in May, are borne on stately stems and always make a generous display, Ballawley, incidentally, is often claimed to be shy-flowering, but this is only when it is congested or starved. The flowers are pure magenta.

We liked Wintermärchen, when we saw it in Beth's stock beds, last month, and brought a plant home. That had neat, shiny fresh green leaves that will (or should) become carmine on the reverse, in winter.

The saxifrage family, to which bergenias belong, is strong on winter foliage. *Saxifraga stolonifera* makes loose rosettes of scalloped, hairy leaves, almost round and with green and purple marking running down the veins and inter-veins. They lie close to the ground and the plant spreads by stolons, being excellent in shade. So is *Tellima grandiflora*, and that has purple and green patterning, although the leaves stand up more and have wavy margins. There are several named colour variants, with more of purple or red.

The evergreen ferns are a great standby. Perhaps the polypodies include some of the freshest-leaved kinds, especially *Polypodium vulgare* Cornubiense, which has quite intricately divided fronds of the brightest green – surprising, in winter.

Another good polypody is Bifidograndiceps, which is crested like a stag's antlers. Behind this I have the newly expanded foliage of *Arum italicum* subsp. *pictum*, which is in contrast and will make a great display through winter and spring. I also enjoy the sharply outlined arrow-leaves of *Arum creticum*, through the winter, although they are plain green.

– March 1, 1997 –

MEADOW SWEET – THERE'S NOTHING WILD ABOUT A FLOWER MEADOW

A copy of *Classic FM Garden Planner*, a newly-published paperback, has reached me. It contains hints on a variety of subjects,

287

but also leaves a lot of space throughout for making notes. As the binding is stitched, it is not one of those maddening paperbacks that falls to pieces the moment you bend its pages back on themselves to keep them open. It is well-behaved in that respect.

But in respect of information provided, I have bumped into a real howler, written by one of the four contributors, on the subject of having a flowering lawn, where the contents are allowed to grow to their full natural height. It always sounds simple – just let the lawn go, scatter a meadow seed mixture over it, and there you are. But you are not. 'The trick,' writes the contributor, 'is to buy or raise good plants, and actually set them into the lawn – then they'll spread naturally.' This is absolutely correct. But then, 'choose grassland species, such as field poppy or corn cockle . . .' But these are not grassland species at all; they are the weeds of arable land.

The gardener's choice, therefore, is between a meadow – which is basically grass with colourful additions of plants that grow naturally in turf – or disturbed land, which will grow you annual poppies, cornflowers, corn cockle, corn marigold, scarlet pimpernel, cannabis (only that isn't currently allowed) and suchlike. In the latter case, grass should be excluded, unless it is an annual, such as the quaking grass, *Briza maxima*. At the end of the season, when all these plants have shed their seed, everything should be cut down and the area cultivated so as to make a seed bed for the following year's crop of charming annuals.

If you like this idea, it is easily put into practice on the understanding that annuals are the name of the game. Perennials could muscle them out. One note of warning should be sounded: your cultivated ground will also be a seed bed for less welcome interlopers, which you will call weeds.

I remember a field in the south of France that had been treated in this way, sowing it with baby's blue eyes, *Nemophila menziesii*. But this situation also ideally suited that common weed of cul-

288

tivation, charlock, which grows 1m tall and has yellow flowers like rape, but is of no value and not especially pretty. Baby's blue eyes were eclipsed.

A flowering lawn is a permanent feature, and one to build on over the years. It is much easier to convert a traditional lawn into such a feature, than to start from scratch, with a bare piece of land. So let us suppose that you are converting a lawn into a meadow. Starve the ground as much as you can. Starved turf will sustain by far the most varied population of species, without any one or two taking over and killing the rest – as often happens on well-nourished turf.

Management dictates that the grass must be cut at some stage, otherwise it will become dense and tussocky, which is bad for many species. Also, it will look unsightly. The contributor suggests a cut in early spring and another after all the flowers have shed their seed. That is my current policy for certain areas of lawn among topiary that I have allowed to grow long for the past two years. In September, when we need to trim the topiary, we also cut the lawn. That way, everything looks trim for the next six months. And spring is the time to add more of the kinds of flowers you would like to establish. Last year, I grew some hair-bells – *Campanula rotundifolia* – from a commercial seed source. The seedlings were pricked out, then potted individually. Any moment now, they will be planted into the lawn.

My lawn already contained a fair number of 'weeds', which I can now gladly encourage – daisies, yarrow, ribwort plantain, common violets (not the scented kind) and dandelions. It's so nice officially to be able to grow dandelions. They are such a luminous part of the April scene.

I also always had white clover, in the lawn, which is difficult to get rid of, even with herbicides. So there it remained, green in time of drought when all the grass around it was brown. In June, it flowers abundantly and scents the air. Wild-flower lawn

289

mixtures often exclude clover because it fixes nitrogen in the soil, thus enriching it, but my lawn hadn't been fed for more than ten years. It was already so starved that clover makes no material difference.

A spring cut to your flowery lawn does preclude growing spring bulbs in it. So, in most of our areas of meadow (and we have been working on this form of gardening for many years), we adopt a different technique. The first cut of the year is not till August, when the grass is removed and composted. We cut it almost as tight as a lawn. Autumn crocuses and colchicums flower in the turf in September and October. After they have finished, the areas receive a second cut. Again, the mowings are removed and composted. If they are left, not only are they a nuisance – you pick them up on your shoes and you can't enjoy lying on the turf – but they return nutrients to the soil, which is not what we want.

Grass cutting is finally completed by late November, and up come the bulbs – snowdrops, crocuses, narcissus, camassias, bluebells, star of Bethlehem and snakeshead fritillaries.

The trouble with starting a meadow from scratch, on a cleared area, is that the soil is always too well nourished and coarse plants will take over.

– January 22, 1998 –

TIME TO THINK

Before spring's arrival and while there is still time to think, here are a few leads. If we love plants, it is obviously impossible to grow all those we should like to. Because a plant has always been there, it doesn't mean it has to remain there for ever. But you must give new introductions time to settle and show what they can do before deciding whether they are for you or not.

Very likely you won't have the right or final place for them first go. That doesn't matter a bit if the plant is a readily movable object. It must be made to fit into its surroundings, which are as important as itself. Borders do need constant change, but we mustn't be excessively fidgety.

This is partly a question of temperament. You need to feel comfortable in your garden and to have a distinct sensation of enjoyment simply to be in it. You may not, at first, have great self-confidence about what you are doing, but you need confidence that this will come with experience. Don't let know-all friends disturb you or take too much notice of their opinions. We need opinions but not all of us need the same ones.

You will receive a great deal of advice about colour, currently one of the most fashionable subjects, even to the extent of ignoring most other considerations. It has become okay to allow bright colours into the garden but their handling brings on a state of nerves, which results in their all being herded into one area. 'This is my red area', you will be told, or 'my red, orange and yellow' border. Let's get it over with, is the message, like children having mumps. Then we can concentrate on soft harmonies elsewhere, and feel safe.

In my opinion – here we go – it is easy to be too self-conscious about colour. Given the right circumstances, any colour can be fitted into any part of the garden and in juxtaposition with almost any other colour. Strong colours don't have to be hived off. That's the easy way.

A feeling for form needs to be developed. Strong shapes will tend to be lacking in the all-herbaceous border, so we run for salvation to the ever-reliable bergenias, yuccas, acanthus, onopordum, *Euphorbia characias* subsp. *Wulfenii*, perhaps a few agaves bedded out for the summer. These are pegs on which to hang the flimsier elements. Don't be content with just these; there are plenty more waiting in the wings for our attention.

Form will sometimes come from quite ephemeral ingredients, such as the annual, purple-leaved orach, *Atriplex hortensis.* Or from biennial mulliens. I could use the branching candelabra of *Verbasum olympicum* anywhere, front, centre or back. Although its flowers are yellow, they will combine happily with pink.

Include some mauve and purple while you are about it – cardoons: *Buddleja* Lochinch, *Clematis* Jackmaii; creamy plumes of *Artemisia lactiflora*, if your soil is heavy; big, pale grey bushes of *Artemisia arborescens*, if it is light.

Do not take any plant for granted. Look at it critically at different times of the year. It may, like *Arum creticum*, be so exciting for the few days that it flowers as to deserve a place in the garden, but then, with such a plant, which disappears from sight in early summer, neighbours can mask its presence thereafter.

But what about peonies: not so easily masked; maybe the price that one has to pay for brief excitement is too high. Or maybe it isn't, but do at least give thought to such matters.

And never forget that to do themselves justice, plants must be grown well. Give them the space they need, feed and mulch them and give them moisture when stressed for it.

– February 12, 1998 –

ARRIVAL OF A BOUQUET

Finding myself in hospital with some serious heart trouble, I was truly delighted when a large and handsome bouquet arrived, per Harrods, from my vet and his wife. Nick is one of those omni-competent people who will turn his hand to anything from drawing an elephant's tooth in the Kiev zoo to removing stitches from my scalp when I've given it a bang.

Speaking to the man at the other end of the line, Nick told him: 'We are talking about a man whom it is difficult to send flowers to . . .' 'Will you leave it to us, sir?' came an understanding voice from the other end.

The most ghastly flowers to be given are those glitteringly Cellophane-wrapped bouquets with roses (no scent), carnations (no scent), gypsophila, iris – nothing with a shred of personality. I, on the contrary, received a black, five-litre bucket containing a bold assortment of seven different ingredients.

There are the flashy ones; a stem of red amaryllis, alias hippeastrums, which have large bulbs, rest in the summer but return to life by flowering even before they show a leaf. They are generally best seen as cut flowers, because a single bulb with one flowering stem looks odd. On the other hand, if you are clever with them, hippeastrums can be kept for many years; the bulbs will increase in number and you will have lots of flowering stems of varying sizes, which looks natural and relaxed. Then, an anthurium. This belongs to the fascinating family of arums, and the disc, or spathe, is flat and rounded in outline, like a painter's palette, and it is coated with a metallic sheen. Above this spathe is a prominent spadix, raised like Merlin's arm when he received the sword, Excalibur, from King Arthur.

Anthuriums have never formed a part of my horticultural life, but I believe them to be quite easily grown, as they are popular house plants in the Netherlands. They include a good range of oranges, pinks and reds and I always enjoy them in displays at the Chelsea Flower Show.

An extremely handsome orchid is a high spot, about 12 blooms to its one stem, pure white but with a ring of purple flecks on the labellum. It is a far more beautiful and generous shape than a cymbidium, a type of orchid that I rather dislike, with particularly disagreeable coarse leaves. I have a feeling that this may be a lycaste, which is a classical-sounding name for a classical-looking flower.

Then a pair of bronze red gerberas. I adore gerberas. They are exotic-looking daisies with several rows of rays composing a perfectly formed bloom. They are a triumph of the florist's art, with the stamp of artificiality which only art can provide. There is a place in this world for snowdrops, but there is also a place for gerberas.

Now we come to some imaginative touches: there is a spray of blue delphiniums – light, well spaced, single flowers, each with a spur. Nothing solid, muscular or butch; they have been taught to move tip-toe from an early age. When I pick delphiniums from my garden, nothing will stop them from suddenly shedding every petal on the third day. We are told to turn them upside down before arranging them, and fill the hollow stem with water; then to right them, keeping one finger against the base of the hollow until your tiny mitt is back into the container's water with them again, so that a column of water is now neatly suspended mid-air. All so simple; anyone can do it, but if you can somehow remove your hands without removing your finger in the process, it is a help. Of course, it doesn't work, but in this case, without any fuss, my delphiniums are as fresh on their fourth day as they were on their first.

Next surprise, dear old forsythia. Not some special kind with bloated petals; stiff, yes, but cheerily pleased with itself and deserving to be. On arrival, it was still all in bud, but is now all in flower.

There is a spray of eucalyptus, with neat, grey leaves, quite small, and then, triumphant over all (in my opinion), two sprays of ivy leaves and ripening berries. The leaves are plain, not lobed, and shiny, and the berries form plump umbels.

It will thus be seen that whoever put this bunch together was not a plant snob. If an orchid goes with an ivy, so be it; let them keep company. There is no artful colour scheme. All the colours are happy in one another's company. The bucket is plain and serviceable, generous but without undue refinement.

As I write this, my godson has brought me a spray out of his own small Hackney garden; just as welcome as hothouse blooms. A foundation with three rosettes of *Daphne odora* Aureomarginata, mostly buds but just out enough to waft as you expect; two snow-drops; a perfectly symmetrical hellebore flower, the stamens so evenly distributed that you feel a clock hand should be spelling out the seconds round them; a sprig of winter jasmine; another of mimosa. This is the one which is hardly ever out of flower – *quatres saisons*, I think they call it in France – and the vanilla scent is all that it should be. Finally, a red spike of *Schizostylis coccinea*, which has a curious way of managing its affairs. Start-ing to flower quite late in autumn, it then doesn't know when to stop.

I don't have one of those orderly minds that thinks everything should perform at the right moment and know its place in the or-dained scheme of things. It's nice to welcome flowers whenever they feel like putting in their appearance. Certainly, plenty have materialised since I've been here and I do not doubt there'll be plenty more when I get home.

– May 7, 1998 –

EARLY DAYS OF WRITING

When I was first engaged to write this column, in 1963, I had no predecessor. The editor, John Adams, produced a piece by Roy Hay, written for *The Times* on the previous Saturday, and asked if I could emulate that. It was all about lawns, lawn care and mowing machines. With embarrassment to us both, I had to confess that this was not my line. I did not emphasise that there was no side of gardening that I found more boring, but that was the fact.

However, dear Arthur Hellyer, editor of *Amateur Gardening* on the floor above, was summoned as mediator and an accommodation was arrived at. I had a half-page in very small print and no illustration but, as a result of this simplicity, I could write my copy only 11 days before its publication, so I felt really close to events.

We had then just emerged from the coldest winter ever recorded. Twenty-five degrees F of frost (-14 degrees C) is very low for us. Everyone was saddled with corpses or potential corpses, and the question was: did one suffer these hulks gladly? If so, for how long? Or did one sweep them aside, with a covert sense of relief, and use the space for some new and entirely different excitement?

Shrubs often get untowardly large. You can, if you love them, move their neighbours away as the need arises. But that is not always possible. I had a vast *Escallonia illinita* Iveyi at the back of my Long Border. It was evergreen and a handsome feature for about 10 days at the end of July, when covered with domes of white blossom among glossy foliage. But then it ran to seed and was something of an eyesore for the next eight months.

When a winter maimed it, I cut the affected branches back and waited – for a while. Then I thought, why should I go on waiting? And had it out. There was a large, dead area in the yew hedge behind it, into which we had to introduce a young seedling. My neighbour's escallonia, about the same size as mine, recovered fully. But I have never had regrets. We have to move on.

For 10 years or more I have grown, in an even more sheltered position, *Escallonia bifida*, a South American species and a parent of Iveyi, but with larger panicles of star-shaped white flowers, covered in their late August–September season with a gorgeous display of butterflies. I love it far more than its offspring.

That took the place of a red-flowered callistemon, which I mentioned in my first piece and which served me gallantly for many years, always putting on a generous display of its bottle-brush flowers. A hard winter would set it back, sometimes even to ground level, but it always returned. What an ugly shrub. In the end, the worm turned.

I think, with many shrubs, especially those which flower in spring for 10 days or so and then nothing, I am now far more inclined to take my pleasures from seeing them in other people's gardens, when at their peak, rather than be lumbered with them for all those dull months in my own.

I 'lost' four specimens of evergreen ceanothus that winter. I say I lost them but, laying down the law, I claimed that if a ceanothus looked dead it was dead. I have since met examples which, on the contrary, broke into young growth from seemingly dead wood. Yet, such pangs of loss as I sustained were soon forgotten. The one survivor was *Ceanothus rigidus*, which is one of the earliest flowering, a sort of dusky indigo and very neat-leaved. When it eventually succumbed, at a ripe old age, I did not replace it.

Ceanothus keep on improving, with flowers of an ever more intense shade of blue. There is no shrub to touch or compare with them. I have three specimens; that is quite enough. Five was too many. One of them, Skylark, has the advantage of flowering in June–July, when the others have finished. On the Pacific coast of America, where they grow wild, I was interested and disappointed to find that all were of a comparatively dirty and impure colouring. A case of the selected and cultivated plant being an undisputed improvement.

In those days, I was growing *Eucalyptus perriniana* and that was a survivor. I can't quite think why I gave it up. The juvenile foliage makes chains of almost perfectly round discs along the young shoots, giving it a strangely formal appearance. I think I was deterred by failing to raise it successfully from seed, which is the best way of rejuvenating one's stock. I must try again.

In the second week, I wrote of biennials, notably of wallflowers and *Anchusa azurea*, treated as a biennial. You raise stock from seed, line out the seedlings to grow on and when lifting them to bed out, remove lengths of young root to grow on, for the next year, as new stock from root cuttings.

I claimed, then, that there was not a really good seed strain available, and I stay by that. I am hoping that Thompson & Morgan will produce something from their own breeding programme.

I gave details of how I staked anchusas, just as they were coming into flower: one stake and a tie with fillis that takes in, with a loop, all the main stems before returning to the original clove hitch on the stake itself. I still use exactly the same method, so some things do not change.

Neither does my treatment of wallflowers, although the crop is not infrequently ruined for one reason or another. For instance, waterlogged conditions on our heavy soil or, last year, mass deaths from club-root on a piece of infected ground on their growing-on area. Dressings of lime and a rest from crucifers for three years looks after that.

I still like to mass my wallflowers, cheek by jowl, and to use tulips, not scattered among them but in groups behind them or in the middle of a wallflower planting.

— June 18, 1998 —

THE JUNE GAP

The June Gap occurs in those gardens where spring bedding has to be thrown out and summer's contribution has not yet settled in. We seem not to have suffered from that, this year. There is more bedding out than ever, despite our (feeble) efforts to cut down on it, but somehow it has been staggered.

Sweet rocket, for instance, is still in full blow, as I write, although we shall have replaced it before the end of the month. Under semi-wild conditions, as is increasingly noticeable the farther north you go in Scotland, it is truly perennial and self-sustaining, and that is the way to grow it in a wild or woodland garden. But we prefer to treat it as biennial. It is the white strain that we have, this year, and I have to say that it has a very blank, unwinking stare. This gives it a prominence that I find a bit obtrusive in full sunshine. In shade it would look more muted.

Bright, yet not too pushy, in my estimation, is a combination of poppy and buttercup. It is the very large-flowered, crimson oriental poppy, Goliath (which is not the same as Beauty of Livermere as seen in the poppy trial at Wisley), of upright habit to 4ft. This, in one place that I have it, is seen through a veil of *Ranunculus acris* Stevenii, which is a 4ft, semi-double form of the field buttercup and of a widely branching habit. The combination is bold, but the buttercup's comparatively small flowers obviate excess.

Welsh poppies are good servants, although bad masters if they seed among small plants – ferns, for instance – and muscle them out. I like them among hydrangeas that have not yet started performing and they are excellent among the stems of a suckering colony of *Clerodendrum bungei*, which comes late into leaf. The usual colour of this poppy in the wild is yellow, but orange is just as welcome and the two mix happily together.

I have never known my Dutch, bulbous irises to flower so freely. If left undisturbed, their clumps will last indefinitely. Some that my mother planted before the Second World War, under a dripping, gutterless roof – a yellow and white one – are generous as ever. Another, blue one (all have a yellow flash in the centre of the falls) whose origin was in the dim past, grows among a colony of the poached-egg flower, *Limnanthes douglasii*, and gives it body. The annual is hardy and its seedlings appear late each autumn, after I have cleared away the summer crop of nasturtiums or marigolds.

From Peter Nyssen I bought a Dutch iris last autumn called Bronze Queen, which is indeed brown, with standards of a murky sort of purple. I like it but it needs highlighting and I think would look good among a planting of the late mauve wallflower, *Erysimum linifolium*. That is an excellent late spring bedder and its seeds should be sown about the end of July.

Although the everlasting pea, *Lathyrus grandiflorus*, is quite invasive and needs to be checked under border conditions, it always gives me a thrill to see it coming into bloom. It has quite large flowers of an intense purple magenta. We give it a few pea sticks to help it up into a pollarded white willow, *Salix alba* var. *sericea*, but if you could spare it the framework of an unpruned, purple-leaved cotinus, that looks better still.

Another excellent perennial pea, flowering now, is *Lathyrus rotundifolius*. At its best, the flowers are brick red, untainted by pink, but you need to acquire a good strain. It is often raised from seed, but is not difficult from cuttings, either. That is the best way with a pure white *L. latifolius*, although a seed batch may come mostly pink. This is the pea that Miss Jekyll used in her great mixed borders, manipulating it to cover perennials that had finished flowering.

In the meadow areas, I have never had a better display of spotted orchids, *Dactylorhiza fuchsii*, and their dense spikes come in a wide range of shades, from near albino, through various mauves to near purple. Last year, they suffered badly from I knew not what, so I sent a specimen to Wisley and they said, what I could well believe, that the orchids were suffering from drought. The

300

spring had been excessively dry. Thank goodness they have fully recovered and seem to have enjoyed the wettest April since our records began, before the First World War.

This orchid is as happy under oaks as in the open but its colouring is richer in sunlight. Being a comparatively late flowerer, its seeds ripen late, too, and this is our principal reason for not starting to cut most of our many meadow areas before the beginning of August. Now that we leave grass uncut in our topiary garden from February to September, orchids have moved in from other areas – notably this one and the green-winged *Orchis morio*. This has happened in four years. Their seeds are so light that they can be blown to a distance on the air. Spotteds also appear in paving cracks, where we are not using herbicide, and in areas of border that are left undisturbed.

The horse pond is at its most attractive in early summer, the more so this year for the flowering of water violet, *Hottonia palustris*, which had remained vegetative for the previous five years. That happens when its growth is very thick underwater. Some agent thinned it last year and I even thought I had lost it. Not so, but it has been free with its whorled candelabrums of mauvey white, primula-like blossom. It belongs, in fact, to *Primulaceae*.

Its lacy green foliage, seen as great subaqueous clouds in winter, makes it, together with water soldier, *Stratiotes aloides*, my favourite oxygenator. Too many of this group of plants are over-invasive, choking the water right to its surface.

It has been interesting to see the order in which the water-lilies have started flowering. The crimson Escarboucle was first, mid-May, and will be the last to finish, in late October. Rose Magnolia and Rose Arey were next. James Brydon has far to go. It has a great burst of blossom in July–August, but a limited season.

301

COLOUR CONTRASTS

A friend, describing a planting that she found somewhat abrasive, added that of course I would have liked it because I preferred contrasts – that is, colour contrasts to colour harmonies.

I have been thinking about that and would like to believe that both uses of colour appeal to me equally. It's just that so many gardeners are more at home with their harmonies (often in soft shades) than with contrasts (which can be startling) that I feel greater need for championing the latter than the former.

Just now, we are enjoying a bold harmony very much, the boldness coming from shapes rather than colour. There is a swathe of *Phlox paniculata*, 4ft tall with domed heads of soft mauve blossom, behind *Astilbe chinensis* var. *taquetii* Superba, 3ft with narrow spires in bright rosy mauve. The chief contrast is between domes and spire-like panicles.

So, while you might talk about a harmony, in two shades of mauve, you could equally be talking about a contrast of form. I do believe that some sort of contrast is necessary, to hold the attention. Were you to put *Verbena bonariensis* with *Thalictrum delavayi* (*T. dipterocarpum*) the light purple colouring would almost match, but in both cases heights are comparable (6ft), the flowers are small and the texture thin; nowhere is there sufficient contrast to grip the attention.

With a case in my own garden, where for years I have admired the subtlety of my pairing, I have come reluctantly to the conclusion that perhaps I have not been so clever after all. Over my *Hydrangea villosa* I allow the annual growth of a *Clematis viticella* to form a mantle. The hydrangea is in warm shades of lilac mauve, and the nodding, open lanterns of the clematis, elegantly

302

presented on long purple stalks, are in muted shades of purple. But I invariably have to point out all this to any friends or visitors whom I am showing round, or they would certainly miss it.

This cannot happen with a colour contrast, the principal question here being, do we like the two colours in juxtaposition? Don't rush to the colour wheel to find out. Just think about it and get the feel of what you see, not forgetting the context.

The double mixed borders at Wisley are greatly improving under the care, during the past 18 months, of David Jewell. It is now a pleasure to look at details in them and to decide what you like, what you think might be done differently and how. There is a delightful and, so far as I know, original contrast at the back, with pale yellow, black-centred annual sunflowers and a pale blue sweet pea climbing up and through them at the front. Seeing sweet peas actually being used ornamentally, with other plants, instead of forming a monoculture, makes a pleasant change.

But they are not in flower for long, while the sunflowers should continue to be productive for a good many weeks. How could one organise an inbuilt follow-on? I thought that *Polygonum orientale* would do the trick. It is an annual, eventually reaching a height of 6–8ft, sprinkled all over with spikelets of pink blossom. It's not too assertive a pink, the flowers being individually tiny, so it would contrast nicely with the sunflower. Its seedlings could be simultaneously interplanted with the sunflower, and its peak, from a hesitant start a month or more earlier, would be reached in September.

It is great fun working out these things and then trying them. There's many a slip, but you're learning all the time and, although gardening is admittedly first a question of growing plants well, their artistic usage is the icing on the cake.

A sumptuous harmony that I can recommend is *Canna* Wyoming with small, decorative *Dahlia* David Howard (deservedly one of the most popular of all cultivars). The canna, which will soar to 7ft or more if well nourished, is rich orange in colour, above sculptural purple foliage. The dahlia, which has a fantastically long and prolific flowering season, is apricot orange above pinnate foliage, itself somewhat purple-tinted. It may be 6ft high by the end of the season.

I also fancy organising a contrast for the dahlia with the intensely blue-flowered *Salvia guaranitica* Blue Enigma as a teammate. That has healthy, glossy, deep green foliage and grows to 6ft, starting to flower in July but going on, persistently. The salvia's flowers are small, and the dahlia's, of saucer size, are comparatively bold. I haven't done this yet, but I can see it.

Another summer contrast that I have indulged in for years is with the above-described *Phlox paniculata*, behind but also intermingling at the margins (a great device in the best border planting) with *Hemerocallis* Marion Vaughn, which is a luminous, pure yet soft yellow. The phlox does need support halfway up its slender stems. Link stakes do this nicely and are discreet. In choosing hemerocallis, the day lilies, freedom of flowering should be paramount and size of flower secondary. Often, large flowers go with a clumsy, thick stemmed habit, over-large leaves, niggardly flower production and a particularly obtrusive manner of dying. Even Marion Vaughn is the better for almost daily removal of spent blooms. I'll go and do that now.

— September 10, 1998 —

THE SCENT OF AUTUMN

What causes the smells of autumn, I do not quite know; fungi, decaying fallen leaves, rotting fruit with more than a hint of fermentation. All these must play their part with other unidentified ingredients. It is a heady mix.

Butterflies flaunt. After a long lull, there suddenly seem to be a lot of them. Red Admirals on rotting pears are especially noticeable. As always, they all love *Verbena bonariensis*, which is flowering more freely than ever, following a coy start at the end of June. But the butterfly flower of the moment is *Escallonia bifida*. It is covered with domes of its pure white stars and all the butterflies (except the cabbage whites) show up to perfection on it. Counting them is quite a game.

Morning dews are heavy, revealing every cobweb in elaborate detail. Rather a shame that many of our yew hedges have been trimmed by now, although only in this one respect of losing our richest cobweb bank. In other ways, their smart outlines are immensely satisfying, especially when one reflects that they will be retained right through to the end of next May.

With the mornings now dark until quite late, I enjoy studying the constellations, especially Canis Major and Orion, that we shall be seeing at more conventional evening hours in January and February. The air may be sharp, morning mists persistent, but when the sun does break through, what glorious warmth. On many such days (in Dixter, at least), it is warmer out than in.

Autumn can so often give us long spells of beautiful weather, when it is a pleasure to dally (how different from the cruelties of April), that Fergus and I make a point of planting for it. Michaelmas daisies that have been coming on, off-stage, both in pots and in the open ground, are moved, just as they are about to bloom, into sites vacated by summer annuals. Chrysanthemums, likewise. Cannas and dahlias will continue unabated until the first frost.

We don't want that frost to spoil the fun, but it has to be admitted that there is frantic activity when it threatens, lifting and housing tender plants that many people would never move out of their conservatories. Plants such as dahlias can await our pleasure before being lifted, although we don't want to face their scarecrow garments indefinitely. Besides, there is always a mad rush, at the last, to switch over to spring bedding before the rains make everything soggy. And a rush, for the same reason, to give the meadows their last cut, so that all is trim to form a setting for snowdrops and crocuses.

February to March crocuses, that is. But first we have the pleasures of their autumn-flowering relatives, especially generous colonisers being *Crocus speciosus* – which is as near to blue as any crocus – and *C. nudiflorus*, stronger in the stem and rich purple. The timing of their flowering depends very much on moisture availability. A good, drenching rain, following drought, will start them off.

In the north of England and farther north than that, the ground is never as hard and dry as in the south-east. Many flowers may habitually bloom a month later than down south. But I have noticed that *C. nudiflorus* is often weeks earlier than with us, thanks to the moisture factor.

The flowering of *Cyclamen hederifolium* is also timed by moisture availability. We have one colony under a rooty lilac where the soil is habitually parched and the cyclamen may be at their peak in early December, whereas interplanted those coaxed into early flowering will start in late July. The onset of *Nerine bowdenii's* display may be delayed until October, under our huge bay tree. Where I want it to coincide with another, less sensitive flower's more predictably timed display, we water heavily in early September, to speed up the nerines' clock. We have interplanted their dormant bulbs with *Aster amellus* Violet Queen, which can make an excellent pairing, if we are in luck. It is a self-supporting, large-flowered Michaelmas daisy, 1ft to 18ins tall.

In a way, I hope for heavy rain and muggy weather to follow drought, as that will bring on the mushrooms, their white dots such an excitement, sprinkled over the meadow areas, their supple texture so much more delicious than the muscular, cultivated types for which we were grateful at other seasons. Usually, I have to admit, heavy rain is followed by chilly air, and the mushrooms refuse to be coaxed. In my garden, that is, Beth Chatto, in her Essex desert, never fails to gather a wonderful crop from her grassy car-parking area.

In Orkney, which I first visited one September, mushrooms were everywhere and being kicked about by sheep. Ah, it will be the chanterelle season when I'm in Scotland this year, and I have friends to stay with in Perthshire who are strongly aware of their culinary potential. Chanterelle-hunting among the birches is as exciting as mushrooming.

Perhaps the birches will be at the peak of their luminous yellow fall colouring when I'm among them in October. And the wych elms too. There are still plenty of them about despite the disease. They really need a frost to start them off.

Both frost and autumn rains have their advantages and, whatever the weather, it will be beneficial for something. But most of all I hope for calm. Mists that clear so that we can enjoy the inimitable golden light of sunshine through haze. I like, on a still day, to hear the plop of acorns into our stretch of moat that is overhung by oaks.

Thrushes, with a promise of spring to come, will already be singing again and all the birds will be smart in fresh plumage. True, it is sad to say goodbye to swallows and house martins, but one can go on searching the sky for them with spasmodic success quite late into the season.

When we have had enough of outside, the first fires of autumn can be lit for a cheerful evening and the wood, which has been hanging about all summer, will be tinder dry – all blaze and hardly any smoke. Autumn is good.

– November 26, 1998 –

NOVELTY – THE PEBBLE MOSAIC

'What's new this year?' is a question frequently put to me and my mind tends to go blank as I don't think in terms of novelty. My new electric cooker, for instance, elicits more excitement from my friends than from me, I am simply interested in the heating potential of each unit. I like to have an oven fan but I wish it didn't have to operate all the time. Rapidly moving parts are just made to go wrong and, before you know where you are, you're told that your model is obsolete and the spare part either costs a fortune or, more likely, is unobtainable. My last oven's fan went on when I turned it on (until it gave up), but not otherwise. 'They don't make them like that now.'

But in the garden there was one positive novelty, the pebble mosaic, and that has given me a lot of pleasure. Created on the spot last March, it and the surrounding paving have replaced the rectangular piece of lawn in our Wall Garden. The improvement to the appearance of the whole area is vast and the surrounding plantings have taken on an air of greatly increased importance. They have more elbow room.

The mosaic was designed by a friend, Miles Johnson, when staying at Dixter one weekend, and represents my two dachshunds lying end to end in relaxed attitudes. It is nice to have something relevant to the place and to me. Maggy Howarth, who is a mosaicist by profession, did the organising and started the work, which was then continued and completed for her by Mark Davidson during three weeks in March, just before we opened to the public. He was protected by scaffolding covered in translucent plastic and we were prepared to heat the interior, but the weather was mild and this was unnecessary.

308

Most of the pebbles we bought from a gravel works near the coast at Lydd, where they are graded with a view to this kind of work, but we were allowed to select Canna's (the younger dachshund's) nose and eye from the late Derek Jarman's amazing garden at Dungeness. Maggy brought some rather special, river-bed pebbles, shaped and coloured like mussels, down with her from Lancaster.

So much for new works. As regards plants and plantings Fergus and I have felt rather dissatisfied with ourselves in some ways. When we need a new plant or plant for a certain spot, we try to think of something that would be a change and that we should like to introduce, but too often it has not been there, to hand. Newly acquired plants frequently need to be grown on a while or increased in numbers in a back-up area, before going on display.

We both make notes, during the course of the year, of plants seen elsewhere and coveted, but are only now getting down to the rather lengthy business of actually ordering them. At the RHS Westminster show, early this month, Mallet Court nursery was showing a holly in fruit strings of bright red berries, interspersed with neat leaves which will later be shed, this being a cultivar of an American species, commonly seen in East-Coast states. It is *Ilex verticillata* Winter Red, which is female and, sensibly, Mallet Court also offers a male pollinator, Southern Gentleman.

With our native *I. aquifolium*, we seldom bother about planting a male for pollination purposes, since there are so many round us growing wild anyway, that almost automatic pollination can be taken for granted. It is probably the same with *I. verticillata* in the US. In England, *I. verticillata* has something of a reputation for being shy berrying and I had always assumed that this was because our summers weren't hot enough to ensure ripening of the wood and hence a good fruit crop. It might, I now realise, be simply because a male pollinator is not present unless deliberately planted. I intend to prove the point one way or the other.

309

Another holly shown by this nursery was *I. latifolia*, of which I bore away a young plant on the spot. It doesn't look like the ordinary man's concept of a holly at all. It has large, thick, evergreen leaves, bright green, oval, smooth and entirely without prickles. This comes from Japan and I'm not certain about its hardiness for me, but I don't mind treating it as a pot plant for a while, putting it out for the summer. If easily struck from cuttings, I can try it both as a hardy and a half-hardy plant. I'm not concerned about its berries or sex life, in this case.

So many bamboo species have been flowering of late, which is maddening, but the silver lining to that cloud is the possibility of obtaining a wealth of seedling from the flowered plant. We had to say goodbye to my Chilean bamboo, *Chusquea culeou* which had been a lawn specimen for more than 20 years, but we have seedlings of that. Meanwhile, we have acquired a small plant of the voluptuous *C. breviglumis*. I hope it won't do the dirty on me by flowering, for a while.

I managed to get a young plant of *Wisteria venusta,* which I wrote about last April and ordered from the Plant Centre at Wisley. It came with an outlandish Japanese name, but I am assured that it is the right thing. We have given it a huge wall, lots of wire and some good soil, to start it off.

On the bedding out front, with which Fergus and I love to experiment, we had one great success – in our eyes, that is; it probably horrified the soothing harmonies brigade. Mixed, single-flowered (much nicer than double or cup-and-saucer) Canterbury bells were interplanted with second-year seedlings planted out of pots) of *Lychnis* × *haageana*. This is about half the height of the bell-flowers, but asserts itself with large and brilliant pure red flowers, in June.

Most of the canterburys were purple or blue, but some were pink, and we didn't think that mattered at all. They went on flowering because I dead-headed assiduously as soon as the flowers turned brown, and new crops of buds were produced. These were finally flowering with a direct sowing of ladybird poppies, *Papaves cammutatum*. In red and black.

CHURCH FLOWERS FOR A WEDDING

To the endlessly repeated question, 'when is your garden at its best?' one of my commonest replies is: 'On the 9th of July.' And so it actually was this year. I said so to Fergus on that day and he replied: 'But there's such a lot yet to come.' But best is when there is still plenty to look forward to.

So what a blessing that Edward Flint, whom I often used to refer to eight or nine years ago, when he was closely associated with Dixter but still a student at Wye College, decided with Nicky, another ex-Wye student, to get married on the 10th and asked Fergus to do the church flowers. I insinuated myself, saying I would do a large arrangement in the font, if I was allowed to, but it turned out to be quite a lot more than that.

The last time I had done wedding flowers was in the early 1950s (the marriage subsequently broke up) and things have moved on since then, the most notable change being in the introduction of 'oasis', which in turn brought on the vogue for pedestal arrangements. I flatly refused to do pedestals, but Fergus blithely moved into that sphere and did four.

The previous Sunday's church flowers had been of three excellent pedestals, including *Lilium auratum*, which filled the church with its scent; column stock (with little scent) and carnations (with one). But we had not the slightest intention of falling back on florists' flowers in July, of all months.

We picked so heavily, on Thursday, that besides three deep

311

buckets, to give the flowers a long drink in, and several more large containers, Fergus mustered the old galvanised iron water bodge, which we normally dip cans into when planting. At the end of it, we had sheaves and sheaves of material, as the professional arrangers like to refer to it – flowers, foliage and poppy heads.

And yet when we reached the church on Friday morning, the space on which to make some impression seemed vast. The nave of Salchurst's parish church (which also serves Robertsbridge and is some 10 miles from Dixter), is inordinately long.

For boldness in my font arrangement I had teasels (not quite in flower but all the structure there) and cardoon candelabrums from the exceedingly spiny but deeply cut-leaved strain that I originally had from the Chelsea Physic Garden. So it was a question of leather gloves when handling them. I was also lucky to have some good spikes of delphinium still in flower at this rather late date.

Delphiniums, as all flower arrangers know, are tricky. I have read the recommendation that you should turn them upside down and fill the hollow stem with water; then right it, holding a finger against the stem base to prevent water loss and not releasing it until the delphinium is in position and in the container's water, which will retain the water column in the stem. Whew! And mine is not a tiny mitt. However, in my own experience, delphiniums as cut flowers will generally not let me down for the first three days, after which, suddenly, and without warning, all their petals are shed simultaneously. I only hope that didn't happen during the Sunday services, but all was well on the Saturday.

So I used a purplish blue delphinium in the font, contrasting it with the large yellow heads of *Inula magnifica*, just then at the perfect stage with flower buds all round the central expanded daisies. Good filling was provided by *Nepeta transcaucasica*, of which Thompson & Morgan offer seed, although it is a hardy perennial; 4ft tall, of stiff habit and with an uprightly branching inflorescence, nepeta 'blue' in colour.

I kept pink for my mother's large, copper Swiss milking pail, up by the (mercifully unused) lectern – an eagle on a column all in that light brown stained wood whose colouring my father used to refer to as constipated dog. Here I was able to use a pure blue delphinium and pink alstroemerias.

Meantime, Fergus was doing wonders with his pedestals, to which he brought no more experience than should I have done, but a good deal more courage. Binding your 'oasis' safely tight is not child's play. Besides this, thick-stemmed flowers and foliage are useless, as 'oasis' won't hold them. So that excludes a lot. Fergus went to town with reddish-purple dioramas and with flowering grasses, notably *Stipa splendens* and *Calamagrostis* × *acutiflora* Karl Foerster, both at their fluffiest.

He also used border phloxes, then at perfection in the garden but not too dependable as cut flowers. I came a cropper with a small vase in the porch, largely of the tree mallow, *Lavatera* Blushing Bride. The appropriateness of its name was irresistible, but some of it was drooping bride by next morning.

One of Fergus's excellent and favourite ingredients was the rosy mauve sage, *Salvia sclarea* var. *turkestanica*, with architecturally branching candelabrums. Its smell is unpleasantly pungent, but only when you are bruising it.

I had instructed Perry, who grows my vegetables, so leave the old surplus leeks to use their heads mixed in with three kinds of eryngium to form a frieze against the wall near the pulpit. Best were the ruffs of large, pale bracts of *Eryngium proteiflorum*. That was fun.

So was the wedding.

BRITTANY MAJESTY

Some planting is great; some is truly the greatest – and it doesn't have to be in Britain. I have just, for the second time, visited the most inspirational garden I have ever seen. It is on the north coast of Brittany, in France, and is extremely exposed to wind – so a spring garden is largely out of the question – although it is rarely frosty. It belongs to Timothy and Isabelle Vaughan (both of whom received training at Wisley, more than 20 years ago) and was started by them only nine years ago, but looks entirely settled.

This garden, like mine, reaches its peak in July, but was still fascinating and rich in colour and form in October, when I paid my first visit. However, it differs from my garden in certain essentials, which it is interesting to analyse. There is no back-up area, and no annuals are grown. There is a basic structure of solid shrubs, but between and among them the perennials and self-sowers spill ebulliently, as they do also on to the adjacent paths, which are all of local granite and 2m wide. Such a width seems enormous at first glance, but it allows for plant overspill from both sides without losing space for humans to pass. Tim likes topiary, but it would be inappropriate in this garden, so he shapes and moulds his shrubs into rounded forms, twice a year – usually with secateurs, although with shears when appropriate. He enjoys doing this. 'I find it therapeutic,' he says. The most-used shrub is box, of varying kinds for vigour, leaf-size and leaf-tone or colour. Much of this is clipped into balls. They act as points of resolution and of rest, amid the fuss of colourful flowers. 'Nothing new about box balls,' you may say, but these do not merely edge borders.

They also run into them, while other plants, such as variously-shaded, yellow-and-cream *Anthemis tinctoria*, thread and weave among them. There is one formally-designed area where box, to a height of 1m or more, forms four plinths in a widely-spaced square, in the centre of each of which rises a solid spire of that inestimable, semi-formal holly (so much more satisfactory as accents than any juniper or cypress), *Ilex aquifolium* Hascombensis. Other shrubs are moulded into large globes by regular clipping, these making a change from box. There is, for instance, the evergreen oak, *Quercus phillyreoides*, whose young foliage is red. The leaves are quite small. It is clipped at the end of April and again in summer, so that successive flushes of young shoots are obtained.

The grey-leaved *Leptospermum lanigerum*, from New Zealand, and one of the hardiest of that genus, is another that is shaped by twice-yearly clipping into a yeasty mound. Its leaves are quite tiny, so it makes a contribution different from anything else. Tim Vaughan is fond of the evergreen *Elaeagnus* × *ebbingei* Gilt Edge. This has largish leaves and is clipped to form fair-sized specimens in a part of the garden where there is much yellow. Anything with a large leaf should always be trimmed with secateurs, as clipped leaves present such horribly massacred and obviously sliced remains. The box, interestingly, is clipped in February–March, and again in summer, but not in autumn. If done then, the remaining leaves brown at the cut surface and remain in this ugly condition all through the winter.

Other shrubs, pruned annually but not otherwise shaped, include grey *Artemisia alba* Canescens, with leaves twisted like wire netting; and Powis Castle, which has the advantage of not flowering. That would spoil the desired foliage effect. There's also two or three kinds of sage, including the yellow-variegated *Salvia officinalis* Icterina and the grey *S. o.* Berggarten.

Then there are the bold, rosette-forming shoots of *Euphorbia*

315

mellifera, which is entirely hardy here and makes big shrubs, self-sowing when and where allowed to. Things seed themselves everywhere, which, says Tim, 'happens in all the best gardens'. There are a few phormiums in key places and ornamental grasses.

There are more agapanthus in this garden than I have seen in any other. In one enclosed area, known as the round garden, they are a central circular feature, but from this centre they seemed to have sparked outwards so as to form smaller flecks of blue or white, always with bold umbels of blossom. These, too, self-sow. In the lowest garden, where there is much yellow, blue agapanthus are planted in a loose ring shared by cream spikes of *Kniphofia* Little Maid.

There are several of what most of us think of as bedding plants in this garden, but they are perennials and, in this climate, often survive winter. Such are the osteospermums, diascias, argyranthemums, bedding verbenas and some gazanias. Also, splendid *Convolvulus sabatius*, which scrambles around and opens a fresh crop of blue flowers every morning. But regular bedding-out is unnecessary.

— December 23/30, 1999 —

THE MILLENNIUM

It is difficult to avoid a sense of occasion when writing my final piece of the century of *Country Life*, even though the occasion is man-manipulated. The message suggested itself in a letter from Anna Pavord, whose magnificent monograph, *The Tulip,* came out earlier this year.

As you can see from historic illustrations, tulips used to be far more exciting than they now are, or, rather, than the law would have them be. Breeder tulips – those that are all of one colour –

have a way of 'breaking'. The colour is redistributed and broken by areas of foundation white or yellow. This gives rise to the most gloriously artistic results, as witness the tulips shown in old Dutch paintings, but also in our own gardens, if we will but hang on to our tulips, from year to year, instead of treating them as annuals.

At Dixter, right at the end of the bulb-planting season, we line out and grow on the small tulip bulbils that do not appear to be large enough to flower in the borders. With a year's recuperation, they make up and will be large enough the year after.

Last year, one of these bulbs threw a most beautiful Bybloemen – a tulip whose colouring has broken into purple and white. Anna happened to be here while it was flowering and she was thrilled. The bulb of such a tulip, in Holland in 1634, would have been worth the price of Dixter itself. At that time, every device imaginable was practiced in the hope of breaking Breeder tulip, but no one knew the secret.

Only in the 1920s was it discovered that this breaking was caused by virus infection, spread by aphids. In the belief that viruses were bad by definition, the marketing of virus-infected tulips was forbidden and the world was made a poorer, although no safer, place. In our own gardens, if we treat tulips as perennials, virus infection and breaking is happening all the time and no law can prevent it.

But it is sad that we can no longer buy those wonderful Rembrandts and other tulips of yesteryear. Constriction on diversity has been strongly evident throughout the century.

In Sutton's catalogue of 1909, there were no fewer than 13 different kinds of mignonette on offer, nine having Sutton's own insignia. It was the same with every genus. These seeds were ordered either by parks departments, which had their own teams of fully employed gardeners and a large propagation section, or by the head gardeners of well-staffed private estates. The staff

317

learned their trade in these places, rising from garden boy to head gardener, if suitably capable. Parks tender for plants and labour and have no training scheme. Most private gardens are now reduced to one or two permanent staff at most, with no one to train them. No wonder our annuals, if grown, are just a mixture.

I have a Hilliers' mail-order catalogue of, I think, 1964 to which I still refer. Its contents represented what that famous nursery had on offer – a huge range of species and amazing cultivars. But the extensive propagation required to furnish the mail-order business was uneconomic and the catalogue was abandoned in the 1980s, although the nursery flourishes. One reason for this is that the skilled propagators, trained in grafting rarities, which is the only way to propagate many of them, are no longer about nor being trained. We have mist propagation, which has certainly worked wonders for many woody plants that were previously thought to be impossible from cuttings, but if a tree or shrub does not lend itself to the system and is difficult in any way, it is simply dropped.

We have, thank heavens, seen many advances during the past century, too. If diversity is the battle cry, look at the scope for the varied planting of borders now compared with those of Miss Jekyll's day. That is what I hate about imitations. 'We're doing our borders exactly according to Miss Jekyll's plans,' it is proudly announced, as though there were intrinsic merit in aping the past, but in fact confessing that they do not have Miss Jekyll's flair and creativity to do something new and different, as she would have been doing herself had she enjoyed the benefit of all the species and cultivars that have come along since her day.

The emphasis in present day gardening, with more limited space and resources, but with more people than ever taking an interest in it, has shifted from trees and shrubs to perennials. The very word perennials has attained a new connotation and

318

status. The world's resources may be limited but they are still yielding a cornucopia of treasure.

What has changed is our observation. Plants in the wild which would have been entirely overlooked as being of no horticultural value, in the days of Wilson and Forrest, are now seen to have an important role in our more artistically conceived gardens of today.

It is hard to garden artistically with a blockbuster scarlet rhododendron, such as once was the acme of the plant breeder's achievement. What do you do with it? What can you plant near it to create a picture? And what's to be done about its dark green, lumbering bulk throughout most of the year? You could grow climbers over it, but even that is quite a modern concept.

So we are moving forwards on many fronts, as witness our preoccupation with combinations of colour and form, also of our uses of plants in other than their traditional roles. But the loss of diversity is what we most need to guard against.

— April 29, 2000 —

SPLICE OF LIFE

Now is an excellent time to take cuttings – so go forth, snip and multiply. Soft cuttings root very easily at this time of the year and may be the best way to increase stock. Dahlias are a classic example. You may say it is late for dahlia cuttings, but we shall be taking quite a lot of them early next month, simply because we don't bring our tubers out of storage until early April, and it takes time for them to start sprouting.

Short, stubby cuttings, severed with a sharp blade where they join the tuber, are ideal. Root them in a freely-draining compost in which there is plenty – at least half – sand. When we speak

319

of sand in horticultural terms, we do not, of course, mean fine builder's sand but grit, which is ground up shingle: it drains freely. The cuttings will need close conditions with plenty of light, but not in sunlight, which will wilt them. The plants made from these late-struck dahlia cuttings will flower in the autumn, looking fresh when much else is tired – always with the hope that early frosts won't strike. Where I am, on a hill, they often hold off till November.

Salvia × *superba* (1m) is one of my most valued perennials, flowering both in July and again in September, but it makes thick roots that do not at all lend themselves to splitting. Take cuttings of its young shoots, but expect slow and uneven results. It is not one of the easiest, unlike the similar but dwarfer (and less long-flowering) *S. nemorosa* Ostfriesland (East Friesland), which always roots easily. Shrubby salvias came through the winter well, so if you missed propagating them in the autumn, you can do so from young shoots now.

One of the perennials that I always seem to need more of is the cultivar of *Campanula lactiflora* called Prichard's Variety. It is convenient, 1m tall (the species straight is often 2m), and the deepest, richest campanula blue of any. Again, it has thick, fleshy roots that dislike interference, which is the reason for cuttings being the best method of increase.

The old – but now defunct – Christchurch (Dorset) firm of Prichard is also celebrated in one of my favourite cranesbills, *Geranium* × *riversleaianum* (try saying that in a hurry) Russell Prichard. A prostrate plant, it has a delightful way of exploring its neighbours by hoisting itself into them; also of surging forwards in a great pool of magenta, over paving or lawn (less popular with the mower). It flowers, non-stop, from late May until October.

There is always a price for such prodigal generosity. Plants do not usually last much above three years; but they can be renewed – from cuttings. Established colonies will have short, woody stems with a tuft of leaves at the crown. These stems can be severed and rooted individually. A number of other geraniums can be increased in exactly the same way, notably, so far as I am concerned, *G. cinereum* var. *subcaulescens*. This again is low mat-forming and is not quite aggressive enough to be up to mixed border life; a rock ledge is more suitable. Its flowers, in early summer, are the most dazzling shade of magenta imaginable, this colour being highlighted by a dark eye. If you hate magenta, try this one; it will kill or cure you.

You must surely have that scintillating comfrey, *Symphytum* × *uplandicum* Variegatum. Its leaves have a broad cream margin. Clump-forming, it certainly stands out in a crowd. Unfortunately, if you damage its roots in any way, the damaged portion will give rise to plain green leaves, which will have greater vigour than the variegated and will overwhelm them in time. On a short-term basis, you can remove green shoots as they appear, but in the end you may need new plants, which you can site somewhere different. Cuttings of young, variegated shoots root well. When this comfrey has flowered, cut everything in sight to the ground and, in a few weeks, the plant will have refurnished itself with a crop of young foliage even more spectacular than the first.

The double white *Arabis alpina* Flore Pleno makes loose, greyish mats that flower in spring with neat rosettes like miniature stock flowers. Between the flowering stems, there are non-flowering shoots, just right at this moment for propagation. All you need to do is to cut them off, say 10cm long, remove the lowest leaves with a sharp blade and dibble them into a light bit of soil outdoors. Some will take, some won't. So the best plan is to bunch three cuttings together into each dibbled hole. Only one needs to root and you'll be well away. Naturally, you must not expose your cuttings to drying wind before inserting them, and you must not only water them in, but remember to water again in dry weather. All this is a part of having green fingers and doesn't need to be said to those who can imagine themselves as plants (or cuttings) and can put themselves in their place.

Sedums are fleshy and the better for not being kept close. Close conditions will tend to rot cuttings made from them. But they don't like hot, wilting conditions either. Best to try for something between, and the lightest of composts to root in. All sand, if you like. When rooted, they can be given a more nourishing compost. The dwarf sedum Ruby Glow is one that I have done by the hundred in this way. It is a charming late flowerer for a border's margin, with dusky reddish flowers, and won't do anything mischievous such as spoiling the lawn in front. But, like other sedums, it is particularly popular with the maggots of vine weevils – those nasty, squishy, white things, curled up into a C-shape.

– August 5, 2000 –

THE LONE HYDRANGEA

Derided as 'Granny' plants, hydrangeas bring vital colour to late-summer borders long after other shrubs have given up the ghost. And that's nothing to sneer at. Few colourful shrubs are at their peak of flowering right now. Most that are, are white-flowered – don't ask me why – so if you want colourful, ebullient shrubs from late June until the first frosts, hydrangeas are the ones for you. They include whites, but also pink, red, purple, mauve and blue.

Last year, mine were pretty miserable, thanks to an April frost that swiped the young growth. This year, however, they are as good as I have ever seen them, and what a show they make. Hydrangeas make rounded bushes, by and large; sometimes very large, but you can control their size by pruning (a subject I like to discuss in March). A point to make here is that rounded hydrangeas, all herded together, cry out for something to break them up. The giant reed grass, *Arundo donax*, is most satisfactory for this purpose, being tall, narrow and bold, with tiers of wide, blue-grey leaves. In a cool summer, when we are shivering as we did through much of this July, hydrangeas are at their best. They love it – if too hot or dry at the root, they tell you so at once. Their reproachful, wilting looks force you to give them a heavy drenching. By the next morning, they will be radiant, once more. They love plenty of nourishment, too. Heavy mulches should be given in winter, when they are dormant – but not of mushroom compost, which has chalk in it and will turn the foliage yellow. You can also give them a boost in March, at the start of their growing season, with a dose of Growmore fertiliser. From early summer on, give them no manuring at all, as they need to enter winter with as well-ripened shoots as possible; nothing soft and sappy that will be vulnerable to frost.

If a hydrangea is non-flowering, the chances are that it is never ripening the growth it made the previous summer. Most, but not all, hydrangeas depend on bringing this intact through winter, so as to flower from it the next year. Hydrangeas are consequently none too satisfactory where winters are unduly cold, though some are tough even then. *Hydrangea serrata* Bluebird (1m), with lacecap-style flowerheads (big pips or florets surround a disc of small, fertile ones), is outstandingly winter-tough, although it can be clobbered by spring frosts.

Most are excellent in maritime areas, which is why our coastal resorts are so full of them – one of the most ebullient is 'Joseph Banks', with huge pale-pink bun-heads on a bush almost as big as the house behind it – or at least that is how it seems from the road in front.

Another don't, or won't, with hydrangeas is chalky or in other ways strongly alkaline soil. Their leaves turn yellow and they

323

look thoroughly unhappy. To an extent, if the soil is only slightly alkaline, you can correct the situation with iron sequestrine. On neutral or slightly alkaline soils, most colourful hydrangeas have pink or red flowers; red particularly suits some of the more dwarf-like varieties, such as Westfalen (0.7m), whose rich colour takes everyone by surprise. That is a hortensia, which means that it has bun-headed inflorescences. Geoffrey Chadbund (up to 2m) is a red lacecap.

On acid soils, the same hydrangeas will be purple, mauve or blue. I find the deeper blues too electric. Light blue is more charming, as in the early and long-flowering Générale Vicomtesse de Vibraye (1.5m and generally shortened to Vibraye), which is bun-headed with small pips. When pink, this looks a trifle cheap, I think – on soils that are not too far removed from neutral, you can alter the colour to blue over two growing seasons by applying regular doses of aluminium sulphate from February to June. If your soil is naturally acid, you won't need to bother.

I find Hamburg (1m) a most satisfactory hortensia, on my fairly neutral soil, where it makes big, blowsy buns of deep-pink pips. Where these receive plenty of light, they turn to bronze as they fade; if shaded, they turn green. If you wish to dry them for winter decorations, pick in early autumn, as the pink is changing to reddish bronze (or green), and dry them like that.

Some hydrangeas have a very long flowering season, thanks to their capacity to keep on producing new flowering shoots. The white hortensia, Mme E Mouillere, gets going in late June and often continues into November, if frost holds off. Mid-season, it is worth sprucing up the bush by removing branches that have faded. Ayesha (1.5m and needing shelter) is a long-flowering hortensia, pink on my soil but blue on acid. It is most distinctive for the in-curving margins of the pips, and is often likened to lilac. The old-fashioned Nigra (1.5m) also has a long season. Of rather lax habit (pruning out of the lowest branches corrects this), it has masses of smallish bun-heads in pink or blue, but also the distinguishing feature of black stems.

LOVE IN A COLD CLIMATE

My friend Frank Ronan is at last living in the country with a garden to get his teeth into, instead of no more than a roof in London. He is crazy about tender plants and succulents (especially aloes), and likes to have them outside during the summer. I asked about winter storage. 'What about the car?' I asked, when he mentioned a garage. 'A car's never been in there. Cars aren't tender, anyway.' I call that getting your priorities right. Succulents, if they are kept dry and unheated, will tolerate very low light levels for months on end. Dahlias and cannas need none, as they are dormant. We don't usually lift them until their tops have been frosted; then box them up in damp, old potting compost.

If a frost refuses to materialise, we cut them down anyway and proceed as usual. But allowing the tubers of dahlias to go on withdrawing nutrients from the foliage until as late as there is some there does encourage them to plump up as much as is possible. Thin, spindly tubers are all too apt to shrivel and disappear in the course of the winter, so it is as well to water them from time to time without ever allowing them to become soaking wet (as can easily happen if the container is lined with plastic).

The fleshy-rooted *Colocasia esculenta* (of the big elephant's ears foliage) and its relatives can be treated like dahlias. Begonias are of varying habits. The fibrous-rooted kinds so widely used for bedding are generally raised afresh from seed each year, sowing under heated glass in February. Tuberous-rooted begonias have their own in-built method of overwintering and are very little

325

trouble. Their tubers can be completely dried off and stored in the dark, somewhere cool. Don't forget about them in the spring, or they'll start to sprout at all sorts of weird angles before you've dealt with their needs. Set them in damp peat in a warm spot, right side up – that is the slightly hollow side where shoots will be produced.

But then there are all the other kinds of begonias that are never dormant; we bed masses of them out, too, although many owners keep them permanently as pot plants in house or conservatory. They may not need much winter heat and light – just enough to keep them ticking over. If they lose much foliage when we're bringing them in, it sets them back rather seriously the next spring, so we handle them gently and any necessary pruning is delayed until they are on the move come the spring. Dead or dying leaves must always be removed, as necessary, to prevent any rots from spreading. Some of them, such as *Begonia fuchsioides* and *B. scharffii*, never present the slightest problem.

One of our favourites, the Egyptian papyrus, *Cyperus papyrus*, is distinctly tricky to overwinter. It is easy enough to raise afresh from seed in the spring, but that year's plants will be small. So we keep some of them in a greenhouse throughout the summer, and they are then no trouble to bring through the winter and can be bedded out in their second spring. The easiest thing with old plants, unless you can give them high winter temperatures, is to discard them.

Some plants make a large proportion of their annual growth in the winter months. *Geranium maderense* and the shrubby *Echium fastuosum* are notable among these. They are just not hardy in our climate, except in warm seaside localities, and must have plenty of light and root room, although generous feeding will, in part, compensate for some of this. To have them flowering really well from March to May, or even June, is quite a triumph.

The beautiful, lacy, grey-leaved *Euryops pectinatus* can make quite a large and spectacular shrub if well treated, and that will be covered with bright yellow daisies through a long spring season (but needs deadheading). It would go well with the blue spikes of the echium.

Tender or near-tender ferns should generally be lifted and potted. They might have survived outside, but the winter will have acted as a severe check to their progress in the following spring. One of my favourites is the gun-metal-blue *Polypodium aureum*, and I have a pot of that on my dining room windowsill for six months.

Impatiens tinctoria is a giant. The plant we left out last winter grew a couple of metres tall by July. Its roots are tuberous and we merely protected them with fern fronds. But you can't trust to luck. We also took cuttings from its young shoots in the spring – just as you would dahlias – and they will overwinter under frost-free glass. The charming mat-forming *I. pseudoviola*, with masses of cheeky little white, violet-like flowers, is utterly tender, so we have rooted plants of that for overwintering in small pots.

The tall, herbaceous lobelias, such as Queen Victoria and the F1 Fan series, die back to basal, leafy rosettes and they cannot be kept in the dark. We box them up and overwinter them in a snug, solid-walled cold frame. Tender shrubs, such as *Grevillea robusta* (initially seed-raised), we lift and pot more or less intact, not cutting them back for shape until there is enough light and warmth from the sun in February, to encourage them to make new growth.

– April 14, 2001 –

HEAVY DUTY TASKS

Jobs in a garden divide themselves into two camps: those that occur routinely and predictably, year after year, and those that are one-offs. Of the latter, no one will be surprised that draining water away looms large. Over the past six months, the climate has been persistently wet. Given our clay soil, we need to do something about this.

One bad area is next to our front path, which is meadow and should be full of bulbs. But many of these – crocuses and wild daffodils, notably – have drowned. It is easier to dig drains if your trenches do not fill with water as you dig them, but we cannot wait. The grass will be lengthening, which makes the job far more difficult. Fergus seems resigned to getting on with it. We shall dig out the top layer of earth to the depth of a spade – otherwise known as a spit. This layer still has many wild orchids in it, including *Orchis morio* (green-winged) and *Dactylorhiza fuchsii* (spotted), so we set it on one side.

There is no point in going deep to lay the perforated draining pipe. Instead we will lay that in the next spit, at a depth of 40cm, and surround it with shingle. The drains will be laid in the usual herringbone pattern. The turf will stand proud of the overall meadow level, but it will sink in due course.

Another big, one-off job, is the cutting back of our yew trees. We have a big cubic buttress of clipped yew which, at one corner, had seriously encroached on a flagstone path where it turns a right-angled bend. The result of this was that the public cut this corner, walking on the grass which, naturally, became worn out with repeated treading. As the four yews that comprise the cube were planted some 90 years ago, we can hardly complain about their bulk (says he, thinking of his own bulk after only 80 years). It is customary to spread a hatchet job of this kind over two or three years, so as to lessen shock to the plants. Well, we have broken with custom and done the whole job in one go. The bushes were healthy enough with signs of growth at the centre, and we shall feed them. I feel pretty confident they'll be okay, especially as they seem unlikely to run into an immediate drought. But we've certainly made them skeletal. It is important in such cases to go right back to the central trunks, from which pretty even regrowth can be expected, and not to leave lateral branches from which regrowth would be uneven at best, with many failing entirely.

Yew is one of your best friends when this kind of reducing becomes necessary. You would kill a Lawson or Leyland cypress hedge entirely (hurrah!). Thuja, on the other hand, 'breaks' well, as do hawthorn and hornbeam. Beech is more hesitant, but also gets there in the end.

Among the routine jobs to be completed will be cleaning up around fairly recently planted trees – where they are in turf – because turf is highly competitive for water and nutrients. Keeping the turf and weeds clear for a metre radius around the tree stem is not overdoing it, and this area is then mulched with garden compost. Likewise, yew hedges that abut on meadow should be cleared at the base. Unless hedge roots are exposed here, we do not automatically mulch, but we do apply a slow-release fertiliser that will give them a feed during their growing season.

All our larger bamboos are grown as specimens, and it makes a great difference to their appearance and presentation if they are annually thinned, which is done by removing all the older, tired canes and accumulated debris within a colony so that you can see right through it and beyond. This makes such a difference. If the bamboo is one of the very flexible kinds, wherein the canes need to support one another, thinning may result in the collapse of remaining ones. That is a nuisance if the bamboo is sited in a mixed border, for instance, but there are many more informal places where splaying outwards will do no harm. A particularly upright and proud-looking bamboo, easily kept within a narrow space, is *Semiarundinaria fastuosa*. I can enjoy it from where I am writing. But even this spreads a little. Most bamboos spread quite a lot more, and this is the best moment for reducing their circumference. We pot up the detached pieces and grow them for sale. With bamboos active again, from now till August is right for messing around with them if you need to – splitting, replanting, potting or whatever. Even so, some grasses such as molinias and miscanthus may sulk for a season after wholesale disturbance.

If it is simply a need to reduce the size of a clump, it's often best to chop it away on one side or at the circumference, so that what remains isn't disturbed. This can be a tough job, requiring a sharp spade, a good aim and a lot of muscle. Fergus loves it.

We have quite a lot of bedding, sown last autumn, to plant out now, notably cornflowers, nigellas and *Dianthus* Rainbow Loveliness, which has a swooning airborne scent, so I like a large area of that and room has been left for it. These bedders, sown in September, were potted individually and have been overwintering in a cold frame. They are rather lusher than I should like. It is always tempting, because it is less trouble, to leave the lights on when they could be off. *Ammi majus* is ready to go out, too. That won't flower till June; the others will start up before May is out.

– October 18, 2001 –

ENJOYING THE RAIN

When it's raining and there's no wind, it is lovely to be out in the garden. Yellow-leaved plants look especially full of vitality with wet foliage. I noticed this in Rubus cockburnianus Goldenvale but more especially in *Populus alba* Richardii (treasured partly because Rosemary Verey gave it to me). It is luminous. After a hot, dry summer, many of its leaves scorch with black patches. Few have this year. These detach easily and a gathered handful solved any problem there was. We keep this stooled, annually, so that it is a mere bush, suitable for borders.

At the front of this border there is a new planting of *Nepeta nervosa*, only now in full flower because the plants were quite young from struck cuttings. You can also raise it from seed. Established plants would naturally flower in June. The flower spikes are about a foot tall, upright, not lolling, and as near to blue as you could expect of any nepeta. I am surprised that you do not see them more often.

Breaking through it are clumps of pinky mauve colchicums, while behind is the dwarf annual *Rudbeckia* Toto, a black-eyed-Susan which gave a splendid account of itself in the Royal Horticultural Society rudbeckia trial at Wisley last year.

Fuchsias are having a great time of it this year. Riccartonii, the most vigorous and popular of them all, is unpredictable in when it looks best. In one part of my garden, a hedge of it reached its peak in early July. But on the other side of the Long Border, its blood red display looks terrific from a long way off at the moment.

The dwarf, hardy Genii is always an autumn flowerer and I like the contrast between its yellowish foliage with red stalks and its flowers, which continue the red theme. We cut that to the ground every winter (there are early bulbs to be revealed among its clumps) and it makes about 18in of growth during the growing season.

Of begonias, the hardy *B. grandis* subsp. *evansiana* (15ins) is perfect just now and a delightful shade of pink. I can see no point in the white version. The display is apt to be short-lived because, well before all the buds have opened, a turn in the weather causes everything to drop off, flowers and all. Of the tender kinds, *B. fuchsioides* (2½ft) is enchanting, with a wealth of small, intense pink blossom. I fancy this must be a short-day plant. It flowers well in spring but spends the summer in a mainly vegetative condition, getting going again as the nights lengthen. Of course, it is an excellent pot plant, which is how you normally see it grown.

Of the begonia seed strains, we have bedded out Illumination

Orange on a rather shady corner, and it is most satisfying like this although more generally grown as a hanging basket subject. (Someone suggested that we should have a row of hanging baskets suspended along the front of our 15th-century, half-timbered house.) As we raise none of our seeds under heated glass, this begonia was sown in a cold frame on May 18 last year. The young tubers, overwintered dormant under a greenhouse bench, were then all ready to perform this year – a slow but sure method and economical.

The autumn-flowering crocuses came on in a great surge. *Crocus nudiflorus*, under meadow conditions, has quite recovered its poise and numbers since badgers stopped eating its corms. In fact, there seems to have been a diminution in badger number this year, which is very welcome. They were becoming a serious nuisance.

I believe I may be able to grow carrots again, without enclosing them in a wire cage to prevent badgers from scoffing the lot. They used to mop up the damsons every night, as they fell from the tree, but have not done so this year. Not that I resented that. They cannot resist sweetcorn, but as I can easily, I was happy to give up growing it.

I have a weakness for the hawthorn tribe. Many years ago, *Crataegus ellwangeriana* was shown to my Committee (Floral 'B') at an RHS show and I bought it on the strength of its outsize and brilliantly bright red haws. When I looked for it in *The Plant Finder* a few years ago no one was offering it, but I am glad to see that three sources are currently quoted. For me, under competitive meadow conditions, it has made a small, round-topped tree, perhaps 12ft by 12ft, and always carries an abundant crop. I have never been able to compare mine with its performance in another garden.

Fruiting well this year is the Turkish species, *C. azarolus*, with greyish leaves and yellow haws.

THE LAST DAY OF WINTER

The last day of winter; what thoughts does that provoke in the gardener? Relief, I should say, but also an awareness that time is short. Once again, everything in the garden is forward, which promotes much head-shaking. I am as aware of the dangers as the next man, but as neither I nor you can do anything about it, I believe in enjoying the sight of all those bulbs pressing forwards. Nothing will stop them.

But one does still have the time for more generalised thoughts. I have been thinking of the way people love to pigeon-hole, to categorise you: 'He (or she) is an expert, a specialist in this, but hates that.' In this view of mankind, there is no room for shades or exceptions. Everything is seen in terms of black and white (or cut and dried).

I am said to dislike camellias. This, on the basis of my some-times publicly pointing out some of their deficiencies. But I have five bushes of them in my garden and they're not there by default. However, *Amateur Gardening* has recently run a piece on camellias quoting the views of a number of us horticulturists on what's wrong with them, myself included. They concurrently had sent to each of us a specimen camellia of their own choice, to 'larn us to be to-ards', I suppose. (I'm not sure what to-ards means, but that's the way it's always said.)

What the basis of their choice was, I have no idea, but it certainly bore no relevance to what the recipient was likely to find tolerable. Guess what they've given to Carol Klein, of the flaming red hair, whose exhibits at Chelsea and elsewhere are a model of restraint: *Camellia* × *williamsii* Donation. She will be able to stand next to it and be photographed with a shrub noted

333

for its ebullience in flaunting sheets of shocking pink.

You will, of course, find gardeners who state categorically that they hate – all rhododendrons, let us say. They are thinking of the coarse-leaved hybrids which make a blinding mass of colour for a fortnight, followed by months of coarsely non-contributing boorishness. But there are rhododendrons for every taste. They are not just one thing; like Cleopatra, they have infinite variety.

Anna Pavord, whose name will now, since her monograph was published, forever be associated in the English-speaking world with the tulip, cannot abide *Aucuba japonica* under any circumstances – not as a healthy, growing specimen, neither plain-leaved nor variegated, not when covered with luscious red berries (which have just ripened and are a picture on my f. *longifolia),* not picked to mix in with a winter bunch straight from the garden; in no way can she think of or look at an aucuba without disgust. ('Well done, Anna.' Did I hear a murmur of approval?)

Well, you may catch me out, but I should like to think that there's no plant genus to which I couldn't find exceptions to an overall disapproval (or approval, for that matter). Often it is not so much the plant that is at fault, but those who adulate it, staking their personal reputations on their doting fondness. 'If you criticise the old roses, you criticise me,' seems to be implied. Must I, then, love them in every circumstance? Those overgrown, unpruned, amorphous lumps that are lurching over your box hedges? Laden with rainwater and rotting blossom, all mixed in with as yet unopened buds. It's the wet June, did you say? Last year, you were blaming the drought. 'I haven't had the time to deadhead them.' Of course you haven't. No one has, except at Sissinghurst.

Why will you insist on growing all your roses together, with nothing at hand to mitigate their deficiencies? There they all are, well placed for giving each other their well-known quota of rose diseases and we have to see them like that. Why cannot you forget them as a monoculture; grow rather fewer, but allow them

334

to take their place in a more varied assortment of plants, among which they will largely escape many of their problems and not assault our vision with all that is worst about them? These are not original comments, of course, and the Rose Garden at Sissinghurst is a shining example of putting my tenets into practice. But, in general, the categorising instinct is strong.

We are now faced with grass mania. Grasses for every season and situation. Current thinking would even have us grow nothing but herbaceous plants with our grasses. Visit the new double borders at Wisley this summer, which should be reaching their peak, and you'll see what I mean. Carefully planned disaster. Well, I suppose that none of us is entirely proof against fashion.

— August 15, 2002 —

IN PRAISE OF ORANGE

Orange is perhaps found, or believed to be, the most difficult colour to handle in a garden, so I will make some suggestions. In a large trough, we have planted a gazania seed strain called Kiss Orange from Moles Seeds. Orange and blue can go well together, but it depends on the blue. We have used a dwarf lobelia of rambling habit, *Lobelia richardsonii*, which we propagate from cutting annually. It is quite a light, gentle shade of blue. If you used one of those rather aggressively dark blue kinds producing dense, dumpy plants, the effect would not be good at all.

All sorts of colours have been brought into nasturtiums, but typically they are brightest orange and I don't want to be without that, whichever else I grow. They seed themselves from year to year. Nasturtiums can behave rather unpredictably, but this year, to date, they have been good and ramble about among their neighbours.

335

What neighbours? Near to the edge of the border, some of mine are looking great behind the magenta *Geranium* Russell Prichard. The nasturtiums' own foliage, when there is not too much of it, so that the flowers are concealed, is the mitigating factor. There are no undiluted wads of orange. Nearby, they annually thread their way through the dwarf pine, *Pinus mugo*, and the contrast between round nasturtium leaves and pine needles is excellent. But the nasturtium must not be allowed to swamp its partner, to the latter's permanent detriment. That is a danger you are always up against when mixing permanent with temporary. And yet that mixing, well done, is the secret of the best tapestry effects. Nasturtiums climbing up a yew hedge can look wonderful, but you must consider the health of the hedge and act as referee.

If the orange flower is small, then the chances are that it will not appear as a problem at all. That is the case with *Cuphea cyanea* (15in), a tender perennial of upright habit which never sprawls over its neighbours. Its small, tubular flowers are orange and yellow, and they will become increasingly prolific as the season advances, provided the plants are not overfed and hence too leafy at the expense of flowers. So if you have an acute-angled corner, where anything with any tendency to sprawl will get trodden on, the cuphea is an alternative to the rosette-forming succulent that you might otherwise have put there (or that you might not).

In an ornamental pot, I often combine the cuphea with the blue, yellow-eyed little bush daisy, *Felicia amelloides* Santa Anita, and the grey, felted foliage of sprawling *Helichrysum petiolare*. I grow one shoot of the helichrysum up a cane, clipping it to the cane as it grows, so that it makes a little branching tree.

Some bedding or hanging basket begonias are orange, although I shall warn that Illumination Orange is, in fact, red. Panorama Apricot is orange, however. The plants start by being a little short and stout, but they become steadily more spreading as the season progresses. Being a seed strain, the colour varies a little. Begonia leaves, if they have the chance to show up at all, are always a wonderful foil to their own flowers. We have these begonias and other low-growing kinds as fillers under taller-growing contents in our Exotic Garden (old Rose Garden). They appreciate the shade provided by their taller partners. Shade tolerance is a great asset in begonias.

In this same garden, we have a group of the single-flowered dahlia, Moonfire, whose flowers are in two shades of orange, the darker towards the centre, the disc being dark, too, and so are the leaves. But everyone takes to this one, so I don't need to plead on its behalf. It provides its own background.

Some lilies are orange, notably the fiery Enchantment. I think the solution in a case like this is to grow it in the dappled shade of a tree. The tall turkscap *Lilium henryi* is orange, of course, but of quite a soft shade and I don't know of anyone who finds that a problem.

Seedsmen are longing to be able to boast of an orange opium poppy, as this is a colour never found in *Papaver somniferum*, although it has a wide range outside that, including red. So, the recent Burnt Orange is not orange at all, but a light shade of red and very good, too. Its flowers are double, and the advantage of brightly coloured double flowers is that the shadows within them, brought about by the petals themselves, provide the depth of light and dark.

— March 27, 2003 —

PEAS

Garden peas are the most delicious of all vegetables, but are always in short supply. The easiest crop of them to grow will be from a mid-spring sowing, to pick in July. At this point you need to be sure of a number of willing slaves for the business of shucking, so that you can freeze your crop. No vegetable deep-freezes more successfully, but it must be done at the right moment.

Of course you can easily buy frozen peas, but the difference in flavour is amazing. And in sweetness, because whereas the frozen product is certainly sweet, you can easily detect that this sweetness is phoney, whereas that from your own peas is ambrosial.

Peas straight from the garden, boiled for 10 minutes and served as part of your savoury course, will be so popular that there'll be the danger of none being left to freeze – not that that matters. It is the delight of tasting fresh vegetables from one's own garden that gives us our great moments.

It is a focus on peas published in *Gardening Which?* for March that started my train of thought. With its very first sentence I disagreed. 'Ask any veg gardener – the best way to eat garden peas is raw straight from the pod, sweet and tasty.' Well, if you pass your row of peas and think that there may already be a foretaste of things to come within them, you'd be inhuman not to pull off a pod, even though its contents had barely started swelling. But the heights are reached later.

The next currently fashionable fad will be to tell you, if you must cook them, to boil for no more than a minute and to eat them al dente. You always gain Brownie points by using a French or Italian (or even, if pushed, a German) phrase, rather than your own language. Probably most of my readers were already shocked when I recommended boiling peas for 10 minutes. This, it seems to me, brings out their best flavour. If I want something crunchy between my teeth, I'd rather it was a well-hearted lettuce.

Mange-tout peas (there we go again) are what we used to call sugar-peas, and they are eaten whole. I don't grow them myself because, like courgettes, they are always breathing down your

338

neck. If you leave them even for a day, without keeping on top of the crop, they'll get ahead of you and you'll have marrows, or peas that are too stringy to be eaten pod and all. We are lucky enough to have, fairly near us, a family-run farm shop where you can buy sugar-peas absolutely fresh and just right for immediate consumption. This is a case where it is better to buy rather than to grow yourself.

Peas take up a lot of space. *Gardening Which?* gives us the results of having trialled a whole range of garden peas, both old and new varieties, tall and dwarf, round-seeded and wrinkled. The tasters being human, you may not agree with their flavour assessments, but that is inevitable. From this trial you can decide what sounds best for you.

I am terribly old-fashioned in my choice. For years I automatically grew Onward (still available), till Pam Schwerdt (who gardened at Sissinghurst and is still very active on the gardening front) suggested that I might do better with Hurst Greenshaft. So I moved on to that, found it good (I especially like the way its pods are borne in pairs, so that you can pick two at a time) and have stuck with it. But it grows some 4ft tall.

A pea crop can be picked at a couple of days' interval over a period of 10 days or so, which may be convenient in many households. I don't believe in striving for an early crop against the dictates of best weather for sowing. That will vary, each spring. Even our heavy ground can be in excellent condition in late March, in which case we would sow then, but anything up to a month later in a wet spring. After the end of April, you'll probably be in trouble, as late pea sowings are so subject to mildew.

To be able to enjoy peas as early as June, I once visited a pick-your-own farm. On that scale, a dwarf pea without support is the rule. Usually, it will be harvested by machine all at the same time. This was a round, smooth-skinned pea, not the better-flavoured wrinkled kind that we more normally grow ourselves. Even

339

though the crop was young and fresh, it was short on flavour. As so often in the vegetable world, if you want the best you must grow it yourself.

— May 8, 2003 —

MEMORIES ARE MADE OF THESE

In his 83rd year, Christopher Lloyd's passion for plants burns as brightly as ever. For this 40th anniversary celebration of his weekly In My Garden *column, he describes some of the plants which have been at Great Dixter for all or many of those years.*

The few of us who still, when in their eighties, live in the same home that they were born in, inevitably accumulate many chattels, each of them with a particular association. So it is with the plants in my garden, at Great Dixter in East Sussex, which for half my lifetime I have been writing about in *Country Life*.

My love of and interest in plants goes back as far as I can remember, and my garden is stuffed with heirlooms (I have a long list of them by my side) – none of which, I hasten to add, deter me from trying out new plants and ways in which to use them.

There is, for instance, a dear but derelict mulberry tree. It was planted in about 1911 as one of a pair, framing a principal vista created by Lutyens, with his famed circular steps as the centrepiece. These two trees grew far too large for their position, but then one of them when laden with fruit, suddenly and irremediably fell apart.

Not wanting the same fate to befall the other, I got a tree surgeon to fix a triangle of wire in its upper branches. This probably saved it from being utterly destroyed by the great storm of October 1987. Nevertheless, the tree was largely shattered. All that was left was its trunk and one large branch, going obliquely upwards. The following summer that maimed tree put on a forest of new shoots, each of them up to 5ft long. It was amazing – its growth has continued and it was soon fruiting as well as ever. Mulberries, contrary to their spurious reputation, are not long-lived.

Prospects for the apricot that was planted on a south-west aspect of the house itself, quite near the mulberries, are pretty good, although it has frequently had to be detached from the wall, which needed treatment of one kind and another, chiefly in order to prevent rainwater, borne on south-westerly gales, from flooding into the house. In its good years, this apricot is a prodigious fruiter, and has been for as long as I can remember. It seems not to know about old age. Once you have tasted your own-ripened apricots, it will spoil you for any you can buy in this country.

There is the large service tree, *Sorbus domestica*, which Miles Hadfield gave me in 1962 as a seedling of his own raising. He was a garden historian whom I revered for the depth and breadth of his learning. His *Gardening in Britain* was published in 1960 and I devoured it, making masses of notes, which I then sent to the poor fellow, who wrote me a long letter (which, of course, I still have) in reply. I told him that I had never until then heard of *S. domestica*.

Before he moved to Ledbury, he lived with his mother at Handsworth, on the edge of Birmingham. I visited him there with my dachshund pup. His mother did not appear but demanded to have the puppy brought to her, which was duly done. I know my place in the scheme of things.

As readers of my writings will know, I am not a rosarian, but I'm not stupid enough to dismiss the lot, despite the excess adulation they receive in this country. And although I try not to be so sentimental about my gardening that I keep many ugly or overgrown plants just because of their associations, I do have a few roses that maybe I should be strong-minded enough to dismiss. And I can truthfully claim that there are two or three days in the year when they are looking really attractive. Such is Irish Elegance, planted against a (Lutyens) pillar by my parents before the First World War. It has single salmon flowers but is prettiest in bud, just before opening. Next to it and of the same age is a large old rambler, Albiric Barbier, which was the latest thing at the time it was planted. Almost evergreen, with glossy foliage, and double, creamy yellow flowers. Like Albertine, it is really beautiful for a few days at the start of its long season, but with the vicious habit of many roses of holding onto its dead, brown petals.

Very much of an heirloom is a bush of the single, apricot-coloured Mrs Oakley Fisher, which has coppery young foliage. That was given me as a cutting by Vita Sackville-West, who was always very kind to me.

Of course, like any true gardener, I love to raise plants by my own propagating efforts. There is the double red Paul's Scarlet hawthorn, now quite a large tree. It grew in the garden of a friend living along Stone Street, near Canterbury. I took a young shoot and budded it onto a bird-sown wild hawthorn seedling, that was growing in my Rose Garden. When the bud had taken and I had a nice maiden tree, I moved it, not many yards, to a position just outside the yew hedge enclosing the roses.

I have a weakness for hawthorns, and my favourite small tree at Dixter is a *Crosargus oicesalis*, which I budded from wood off a specimen at Wye College, Kent, where once I was a student and then on the staff. It has grey-green foliage and large orange hips in September. It is on your right as you walk down the front path and just before the bay tree. That is truly an heirloom, since it was established at Dixter before the Lloyds arrived in 1910. The hardest winters have severely cut it back at one time or another, but it always comes back enthusiastically. This is *Laurus nobilis*, and it is a male, flowering abundantly in early May. Its cheerful bay green leaves (sufficiently handy for the kitchen for me to dash out for one, if needed in a stew) are most welcome through the winter, when their warmth is heightened by low sunlight.

On the other side of the path is a large wild pear, bang in the middle of a yew hedge. The pear was also there when we came and the hedge was planted round it. Why a wild pear rather than an edible one? I think the answer almost certainly is that it was the stock for a cultivated variety, but that the graft failed and the stock took over. It flowers beautifully for five days at the turn of April–May.

My father used to treat this tree like a topiary specimen, trimming it annually into an oval. At the end of each growing season, it looked rather like a shaving brush, and never flowered. When my father died, in 1933, my mother and I allowed the tree its freedom and it flowered abundantly. It also fruits abundantly, round golf-ball-sized fruits that rain down right into December. Although tasteless, they are sweet and my dogs adore them.

A little farther off we have a Williams pear which we also inherited, and it still fruits and is worth gathering, in August, in alternate years. It is very susceptible to scab, which can hopelessly disfigure the fruits, but if the weather is dry at the time, in June, when they are swelling, they remain in decent condition and you'd never want to buy the marketed version once you had tasted what the fruits can be like if not grown 'properly', with fertiliser and the other adjuncts to commercial crop production. It is the same story with our Comice pears, planted as espaliers in the early 1930s, never sprayed, covered with decorative lichens, and what a flavour. Late October for them, but if, when picking, we put each fruit separately into a plastic lettuce bag, they not only don't shrivel but ripen over a long period, even into December.

Let me conclude with our old myrtle, *Myrtus communis*, currently a huge bush, growing on the terrace and against the house where it receives the maximum of south-westerly gales, but also lots of sunshine. That is getting on for a century old and it came from a cutting that was taken from a myrtle sprig that had been, as was thought lucky, in a wedding bouquet. In hard winters such as 1939, 1963 and three in a row in the early 1980s, it gets killed to the ground, but always comes back smiling. Currently, it has had 20 years' respite. It blooms abundantly every August, with a spicy airborne scent, and a showy crop of purple-black fruit is ripened in November, in good years. A blackbird eventually eats them. That is a very favourite shrub.

— July 3, 2003 —

TOOLS

It is important, when acquiring tools for your own use, to go for the best, which are often the most expensive because well made. But it is frustrating, and just a waste of time, to buy cheap sets of tools at a supermarket: trowels and forks that bend on pressure; brightly coloured, plastic watering cans that blow about the garden when empty. They go brittle when left in the sun, and split. Get a galvanised iron Haws can with a long spout, easily directed exactly where you want to water, and you'll never regret it.

Sneeboer tools are excellent and come in a good range. Made by a trio of Dutch brothers, they are sold in this country by Link-Stakes, by ourselves at Great Dixter Nurseries and by a few other upmarket enterprises. I always carry two of their trowels into the garden: a narrow one and a broad. Both come to sharp points. They will not fall apart and they are not too deeply dished, laterally, which makes for handy use. Sneeboer has an excellent little hand-hoe, widely known as an onion hoe, its head set at just the correct angle to the shaft.

Your spade must have a boot protector across the top of the blade. The angle that the blade is set to the shaft is most important and must suit its owner. Often it is set at too sharp an angle – suitable for a shovel but not for a digging spade. Make sure the shaft is comfortable for you to use. For tall people, it will need to be longer.

On heavy soils, a fork may be better for digging than a spade. For work between plant groups in our borders, where there is not much space, Fergus likes a narrow, three-pronged fork with a long handle. We've had that made for us and are selling it at Dixter; likewise, a long-shafted bulb-planter for taking out plugs in meadows. This doesn't want to be too heavy. You need to be able to take out a plug (at random spacing) every five seconds. Our bulb planters are replicated from the one, still used, that we had in 1910. Don't ever be gulled into getting one of those silly short, hand-held things that are a tremendous effort to manipulate. You can get no purchase on them.

A folding knife is useful, the French Opinel, which you can sharpen on a paving slab. Cutting down grasses, chives and other soft, thin-stemmed plants can be done, at a low level, in seconds.

A broad, wooden rake is excellent for gathering together heaps of long grass. You'll lose its teeth from time to time, but you can buy lengths of wooden dowelling rods from a DIY supplier and cut them to the required length for your purpose. A dowel is a headless nail, usually wooden.

A garden line, enabling you to sow a straight row, is essential and it wants to be on a spinning reel. This is not always easily found, however. You can get it in plastic, but iron is much better and will last indefinitely.

Of secateurs, the Swiss make Felcro is still unbeatable, as it has been for many years. We have wasted so much money on 'cheap' secateur offers. We once, on a personal recommendation, bought 20 at a go, but they turned out to be useless. 'Never go into the

345

garden without secateurs', was Lord Carrington's pithy advice to gardeners, and he was right.

I like to take my bushel-sized trug basket, too. Trugs are something of a speciality for a few Sussex manufacturers. It's no good messing about with a small one on feet, in my opinion, as one of the feet is sure to drop off. Unless you make a practice of leaving your trug standing on wet ground, it doesn't need feet at all, but it does need a strong handle that you can lean on (when you're advancing in years) to help you stand up after weeding on your knees. A capacious trug may be expensive, but it is worth the money.

The May issue of *Gardening Which?* had a piece assessing a range of hedging shears, separating men's reactions from those of women. I have to admit that at Dixter we don't use hand-held shears very much, having become mechanised in about 1947 when we bought our first Tarpen hedge trimmers. We are keen, however, on hand-held loppers.

Waterproof clothing is an important item, given our climate. Fergus gets Gortex breathable waterproof clothes and shoes for our staff. I stay indoors.

— September 11, 2003 —

THE BENEFITS OF POTS

In key positions where they will make a particular impact, we love to make pot-plant displays between spring and autumn. Some plants will last the season through, others will be brought on the scenes from a back-up area when reaching their peak, but removed when they have taken their bow.

You must be highly critical of what you are doing, which is a work of art, albeit ephemeral. Of course, the more material you have to draw on, the more critical you can afford to be. There must be bold plants, the bones of your set piece, but softer in-fillers are needed too. Often you can pick up just what you need from a good plant-selling centre. Foliage is often more significant than are flowers.

For instance, Fergus has grown a banana, *Ensete ventricosum*, from commercial seed (it may have been Thompson & Morgan's). It is about four years old now, but was large enough for display from its second year. Soon it will be too tall and bulky to be useful and we must start again.

Looking pretty in front of it is the annual *Coreopsis tinctoria*, yellow with a maroon eye. That is about 3ft tall, but heights can be adjusted by the use of props such as bricks or boxes to stand the pots. By the banana's side is a purple-leaved canna, Mystique, grown as a foliage plant. *Canna indica* Purpurea would serve as well.

Senecio macrospermus was a great find, purely as a foliage plant: lowish rosettes of silky, pale grey, elliptical leaves. We have only one plant so far, but must be courageous and try to split it, next spring.

With narrow, more grass-like leaves but arranged in loose ro-settes is a sedge, *Carex phyllocephala* Sparkler, variegated with white margins. *Pseudopanax lessonii* Gold Splash, now many years old and a great stalwart throughout the season, has pal-mate leaves in green and gold. Ours is now more than 6ft tall but Fergus's growing in the ground of his tiny seaside garden in Hastings, is twice that height and hardy under these special maritime conditions.

We include many begonias, some as foliage plants, others more for flowers, such as the brilliant Illumination Scarlet, of a rather drooping habit. You may want to highlight a particular position with startling touches of red.

Round our sunk garden, I have four terracotta pots at a slightly higher level whose margins are softened with drooping *Helichrysum petiolare*, having grey-felted heart leaves, and with a spread light blue lobelia grown annually from cuttings, *Lobelia richardsonii*. But in the middle, a really loud red geranium. Don't ask me its name. I got it at a farm shop and keep it going from cutting taken now.

On our sitting-out terrace, I have a square of four large pots, whose planting I vary from year to year, but invariably, in the middle of each, I have a bushy geranium (pelargonium) Happy Thought, given to me years ago by Brian Halliwell from Kew. The leaves are green with a yellow centre and the flowers a light shade of red.

I should like to use and still struggle with the double red nasturium (*Tropaeolum majus*) Hermine Grashoff, to hang over the pot margins, but am often defeated by cabbage white caterpillars.

This year's experiment included *Plectranthus argentatus* Hill House, which has quite large leaves with marginal pale yellow variegation; but it looks too aggressive and needs submerging in a large border of bitty plants. The well-known *P. coleoides* Variegatus with quite small, white-margined leaves and a spreading habit, is more easily managed.

One of the best pot edge-breakers is a deep blue form of *Convolvulus sabatius* (*mauritanicus*), at its best in the morning. Another good and prolific morning flower is the yellow *Oxalis vulcanicola*. I grow this by itself in a large, low pot.

Many succulents make excellent pot arrangement ingredients, either one kind to a pot or – an effective change – a wide, low potful of several contrasting succulents side by side. The large, formal rosettes of aeoniums are great eye-catchers, whether green or purple (*A. arboreum* Zwartkop), or something in between.

I must have a fleshy agave or two somewhere, and the most obvious choice is *Agave americana* Variegata, which has bold yellow margins on either side of a green centre.

348

Bedding verbenas are among my favourite fillers. They not only weave among their neighbours but hand downwards. La France is a winner, mauve and sweetly scented. In this year, when hummingbird hawkmoths have abounded, it has been visited by these fascinating, hovering insects many times a day, as has *Verbena bonariensis*, seeding itself between paving cracks.

— December 18, 2003 —

EVERGREEN

At this time of the year, I am grateful to evergreen plants that have glossy leaves. They reflect from the sky whatever light there is and are especially cheering in places that are normally shady.

One has to place camellias – all the cultivars of *Camellia japonica* that are so popular on acid soils – at the top of the list, because they prefer to be in part-shade, where they happen to be most useful anyway. Try photographing a camellia and you will be maddened by all those insistent points of reflected light that assault your lens. But the eye won't mind them. Although I don't dote on camellias, because their bushes are far from elegant and the flowers are blobbily arranged, like a hybrid tea rose's, they have exceptions, and I grow half a dozen kinds. *C. j.* Lady Vansittart is a favourite because of the seductive way in which its narrow leaves are twisted, which again complicates the reflected light it sheds.

Another great favourite is × *Fatshedera lizei*, the cross between ivy and *Fatsia japonica*; with its fresh green, glossy leaves, pristine at this season, it brings cheer into the darkest corner of my garden. It is not out and out hardy, but gets plenty of shelter from walls on two sides of it. The natural habit of this shrub is lolling, so that, given a chance, it leans on its elbow, but I prune

349

mine annually in spring by shortening last year's growth quite hard back, which results in its being a compact shrub, up to 6ft tall. With ivies and huge old fatsia near it, it has good company.

There is also a quite tiny, semi-ground-covering, glossy-leaved evergreen, *Asarum europaeum*, on a flagstone-paved corner, here. It has almost circular leaves, and I remember it growing wild in open woodland in the Carpathians, clumps of it, never continuous cover, but there again it picked up all the light there was above and between the trees.

The Japanese one-off tree/shrub *Trochodendron aralioides* came to me through Tony Schilling from Wakehurst Place and, although perfectly healthy, it is still, after quite a number of years, a polite-sized shrub. It has no relations and, with its amazingly thick leaves, is a strange-looking plant. It can easily be grown from seed, less easily from cuttings, although we have succeeded with a few. The leaves of my strain are glossy, and I like them that way, but seedlings as generally sold tend to be matt-surfaced.

Sarcococcas have smallish but shiny leaves and they prefer a good bit of shade, so they are allies, especially as their sweetly, albeit sickly, scented flowers come in January. Actually, my favourite, *Sarcococca ruscifolia*, has little scent. It does not sucker, as many do, and it makes quite a bulky shrub; mine is 6ft tall, at present, and more than twice as wide. The berries are dull red. Not a show stopper, perhaps, but satisfying. Possibly my description hasn't quite done it justice.

Laurels can be dowdy and covered in urban grime, but given a chance they scintillate, or so it seems to me. We have here two quite different genera, not counting the bay laurel. *Laurus nobilis*, which is a winner, but its leaves are only semi-glossy. The cherry laurel is *Prunus laurocerasus* and it is a great survivor. One of the most popular clones is the one I like best, Otto Luyken, of neat habit, not big and having a wonderful gloss on its leaves. It flowers twice, white, scented, and I grow it next to *Thuja oc-*

cidentalis Rheingold. They make a pretty pair. I also have the large-growing but handsome *P. l.* Latifolia (syn. Magnoliifolia). Fergus and I both admire it greatly, but in this respect I seem to have few friends. Somehow they think it demeaning to praise such a common thing as a laurel. Perhaps I'm making the wrong sort of friends.

The Portugal laurel is *P. lusitanica* and I have its variegated form Variegata, which grew far larger than I expected. Never mind; I'm fond of it, although many are not. The type plant flowers freely, which is nice, although the flowers are a slightly grubby white. But Variegata doesn't flower properly at all, except on branches that have reverted to plain green.

The other so-called laurel is *Aucuba japonica*, again widely and undeservedly reviled. Why can't people really look at a plant, keeping an open mind about it, instead of always judging it by the worst examples they have seen? Of course it looks tired, dirty and drab when surrounding a public lavatory, but that's not its fault. It is a shrub of infinite variety, both male and female, the females berrying heavily in February if there's a male nearby. The plain-leaved female, *longifolia*, is a winner in every way. Clear your mind and look again.

— October 14, 2004 —

PAINTING WITH PLANTS

I touched lightly last month on a bedding-out combination that we have planned to go in front of the house for spring flowering: two kinds of wallflower, Fire King and Primrose Monarch, combined in some way with the lily-flowered tulip, Queen of Sheba, deep orange with a pale margin.

The time has come to decide on how actually to do the

planting. We have grown our own wallflowers, ensuring that they will be good plants. Mixtures are a hopeless jumble of colours, but seeds in separate colours are available. In this case, both are of comparable valency, so we can use equal numbers without either outshining the other. Had it been the deep Blood Red, for instance, with Primrose Monarch, we should have needed more plants of the darker colour, perhaps in the proportion of three to one.

How to plant our two varieties is the next question. Do we want them scattered evenly, or in neighbouring blocks or in interlocking swirls? Fergus and I prefer the last, but whatever your choice, the plants should go in close to and touching one another. In this way, they give each other support and won't lean or get loosened by wind and rain.

Then, how to fit in the tulips? We have 200 new bulbs, and there are some left in the ground from previous years among perennials behind the bedding-out area, but this variety doesn't keep up its numbers well from year to year, so we shall add some there. We might use the rest in blocks behind or in the middle of the wallflowers, or we could make meandering bands of them. That worked well elsewhere in the garden last spring. What we shall not make is an even scattering, because then the wallflowers would not support each other in a dense planting. Bamboo canes placed flat on the ground to mark out the individual groups helps us to visualise the combination.

I wish it were easier to get carnation seed in separate colours. At present, from a spring sowing, I have Florestan Mixed lined out. Some of them have produced a few premature, early flowers. These are carnations treated principally as biennials, and we shall bed them out soon, interplanted with red tulips, Red Shine, which greatly benefit from the silver grey colour of the carnation foliage. If the tulip were planted in a block behind the carnations the effect would not be the same. I also like a row of annual carnations from a spring sowing, to pick from. I shall have seed ready to sow in February, as they will germinate at quite low temperatures and an early sowing gives a longer season of flowering.

The batch of June-flowering *Campanula persicifolia* var. *alba* seed-raised plants that we have both in pots and lined out, is huge. So easily done, too. One way we should like to use them is interplanted with ladybird poppies, *Papaver commutatum* – red with a large black blotch at the base of each petal. Fergus finds that there is no advantage in this case in autumn sowing, and that it is best to wait until early spring. Although poppies have notoriously fragile roots, he manages to prick them out into plugs, and it is then easy to obtain strong plants by moving them on into larger containers before bedding out. An even mixture of campanulas and poppies should work well in this case. Not one of the poppy followed by one of the campanula – that would be too spotty – but groups of four or five plants of the one, next to a similar-sized group of the other. The campanulas will grow the taller, but it would be impossible to subdue the poppies' colour impact. They can make amazingly large plants, and the larger they are, the longer they will flower.

In a semi-shaded bed against the north-west side of an old cowhouse, known as the hovel, we plan to have four ingredients: tall, yellow, long-spurred *Aquilegia chrysantha*, dazzling orange *Anthemis sancti-johannis*, tall purple *Allium hollandicum* and, at the front, pure white *Viola cornuta* Alba. How do we place these?

The viola in groups at the front, obviously; it has no height to speak of, but the others? The aquilegia and allium go well together, but the anthemis is difficult. A solid block of it worked well last year, but then we had the strong verticals of foxgloves behind. The alliums and aquilegias are far less powerful, so this year we shall have interrupted trickles of anthemis running through them.

NO MIDGES BUT PLENTY OF RAIN

It is a good thing to get away from home from time to time, even if you feel at the end of it that returning was the main point of it all. I always enjoy my annual visit to Scotland, and October, as a choice of when, has a number of advantages, not least the fact of midges having gone into hibernation.

I breakfasted in one home on a fungus that was new to me, the hedgehog mushroom, *Hydnum repandum*, brought in by an adventurous fellow-guest. It was good but no exception to the general rule that common mushrooms are the best.

Attadale, by Loch Carron on the north-west coast, has a new Japanese garden. My hostess realises that I am not an admirer of Japanese gardens outside Japan. Our own style is much too loose and sloppy to make a success of them. Nothing wrong in that, but we should learn to recognise a different culture when we meet it, which was my main reason for going to Japan myself.

At Attadale we had some very heavy rains; how the stalkers coped with it I hardly know, but they did. The morning for viewing the Japanese garden had left such a huge pool in front of its entrance that, improperly shod as I was (no waders), we couldn't enter it. Imagine my disappointment.

At home, in Sussex, the Mexican orange, *Choisya ternata*, whose main flowering is in May, often has a small second flush in October, when individual blooms are considerably larger than in May and just as well scented. I had thought that the growing season was too short in the North for this to be possible. Not so; at Dundonnell, just inland from Little Loch Broom, the choisya was performing.

Will Soos is now gardening there, having transferred from Inverewe, where he made a brilliant success of a wide and

354

interesting range of vegetables in the walled garden. He is an adventurous young gardener, who loves to experiment. There are some amazing park trees round Dundonnell, and Will, last autumn, gathered some sweet chestnuts, *Castanea sativa*, from a specimen there and sowed them. Result: a nice batch of seedling. I thought this something of a triumph, seeing that these chestnuts are just about at the northern limit of where they can be grown at all, let alone fruited.

The climate suits ferns, as you would expect, but Will pointed out to me that the western sword fern, *Polystichum munitum*, one of the commonest wildings in the Pacific north-west of the USA, here too is so much at home as to self-sow freely. Why hadn't I noticed that before? I've been visiting Dundonnell since 1963.

I have observed before that the foliage of the water saxifrage, *Darmera peltata*, changes in the North to vivid carmine in the autumn, before dying – just to brown down here – and it looked most handsome at Gruinard (in its sheltered coastal bay) behind colonies of broad-leaved hostas. Even in my garden, these turn translucent yellow before collapsing, but only for a couple of days. The span is longer there and the contrast striking.

On a smaller scale at Gruinard, another delightful effect was at the edge of a small pool, carved into a slope, where there was a large mat of *Gunnera magellanica*. This is one of the mini-gunneras. It was covered with rich red, upright flower spikes, each about 4in high. The mat intermingled at one side with another mat, this one of the near-black, strap-leaved *Ophiopogon planiscapus* Nigrescens. It is always hard to find a matching partner for this popular plant (the New Zealand fern, *Blechnum penna-marina*, with its creeping habit, is another idea), but here it was.

At Kerrachar, in west Sutherland, the owners spent their working lives in Sheffield but for the past nine years or so, in retirement, have taken on a piece of moorland, whose size they increase as their needs require. Their ambition is to grow as many different garden plants as they can. All obstacles are met and dealt with if humanly possible. I was rather astonished that they find badgers a problem, as I do at home.

I particularly noted and was pleasantly reminded of a shrub that I've not seen for quite a while: the neat little mini-elm, *Ulmus* Jacqueline Hillier, only 2½ft high and holding its leaves well into autumn.

One of the shrubs defending Kerrachar against wind is *Olearia solandri*. With its dusky colouring and airborne aroma of heliotrope, it is a great favourite with Fergus and me (although not with the public). At Dixter, it covers itself with tiny white flowers in August, but here was nearly two months later.

— September 29, 2005 —

A CLIMATE OF CHANGE

The Americans are highly conscious of which climate zone they are in. They run from Zone 1 (freezing) to Zone 10 (tropical). We have just held a seminar for a group of them at Dixter and 'Which zone is it?' is the repeated question. But we can't tell them. Our microclimates are so varied that zones would vary widely in different parts of the same garden.

Verbena bonariensis is an interesting case. It has a reputation for being on the tender side. I have been in correspondence with a few other gardeners about this. Two points are at issue. Will it survive our winters? Will it not only survive, but perpetuate itself by self-sowing? The point is that it is a short-lived perennial (if that isn't a contradiction in terms) and usually gives us only two years. In the first, it starts flowering quite late and continues until cold weather arrives. In the second, it starts in early summer, sets seed in abundance and then packs it in, its duties done. Seedlings will appear in huge quantities early the next spring.

So far as the gardener is concerned, the upshot is that the verbena will be flowering on old plants and young, continuously from June to October. I have a correspondent as far north as Tyneside (near the coast) for whom it self-sows just as willingly as though it were down here in Sussex.

We have to touch on global warming, as it affects us. We can't say for how long this will last, but for as long as it does, we should make best use of it.

The verbena is interesting in a number of ways. It secrets nectar and is extremely popular with insects. Hummingbird hawkmoths fly over from the Continent in suitable years (we have had them this year) and the *Verbena bonariensis* is one of their favourite nectar plants. With its long proboscis, it hovers at a considerable distance from its food flower, darting with great speed and accuracy from bloom to bloom. A joyful sight, which we enjoy on our sitting-out terrace, where verbenas self-sow in the paving cracks. Other kinds of verbena, such as La France, are not visited at all.

Although there were plenty of outbursts of rain earlier on, late summer and autumn gave us long spells of quiet, sunny weather. I've never known such a prolonged crop of mulberries (*Morus nigra*). Visitors from France are especially keen on hovering round them. The fruit turns as near to black as a plant can get. Of course, it stains, but there has to be a price. This mulberry is very rewarding as it starts fruiting at an early age. But do buy your young tree from a reputable firm otherwise you may get a seedling and any sort of rubbish.

We've been picking raspberries daily since mid-June, moving from one variety to the next. The red Autumn Bliss, as I have written before, has the best flavour. It is followed by Fallgold, a yellow raspberry, very welcome and sweet, but rather short on flavour.

In our Exotic Garden, this year, you seem to enter another world, hushed and full of warm vapours. It is ironic that the

357

warmest area in daytime or, indeed in summer, is likely to be the coldest at night, as also in frosty winter spells.

We call it the Exotic Garden because it is, indeed, full of exotica. In warm weather, the bananas, *Musa basjoo*, will put out a new leaf every 10 days, even one a week if the weather is really hot. Papyrus, *Cyperus papyrus*, have done particularly well this year, and are a good 8ft tall, associating well as a contrast to the bananas. We grow the cyperus from seed, which germinates easily. The problem comes the following autumn, bringing the plants through during the winter. Established plants hate disturbance at this time of year and need the immediate comfort of a hothouse in warm water. We split them at the end of April and pot them up, but keep them in our warmest house to get them out of the shock of having been moved. They will gradually be hardened off before planting in mid-June.

Our favourites are the begonias. Most of them relish a bit of shade. The most successful species this year is *Begonia luxurians*, of which we have second-year plants that are 4ft tall and extremely handsome with their long, fingered leaves. Very un-begonia-like you may think, until you notice the characteristic lop-sidedness.

Dahlias are excellent to give us colour. At last, there need be no shortage of red, as is notable in the early summer garden. Hillcrest Royal is a great favourite with everyone, as it manages a subtle combination of red and purple.

‒ October 13, 2005 ‒

HAVE A HAPPY NEW YEAR

You may be surprised to discover that our gardening year starts now. Autumn is not the end of the year, as so many people seem to imagine, but its beginning.

Pruning figs is a task that delights the tidy-minded. The naked wood is pale grey in winter and you can make a perfect fan with it. But what is it you're thinking about, the fan or the fruit? If the fruit, you are destroying the whole of next year's crop. But the tidy-minded won't give that a thought. He (it's always a he) is only interested in his symmetrical work of art.

Speaking for myself, it's the fruit that sends me into ecstasies. The less you prune the more fruit you get, but your beautiful fan will have gone with the wind. Why are the figs there at all? The answer is that the Brunswick fig, which is the variety we grow, has the most indentations to its leaf, and makes the best pattern against the wall in summer. The Brunswick fig has five lobes to its leaf instead of the usual three. Lutyens knew this very well and used it in several gardens with which he was involved.

How did the expression 'I don't give a fig for . . !' ever arise? Obviously, I do care for ever so many figs. Out with that heathen, who is only interested in patterns.

This is also the time for propagating a range of plants. Hardwood cuttings root best if made just as growth is winding down to its slowest. It should be understood that a dormant season is only relative. It is a slowing down, not a complete cessation of all growth.

Stem cuttings made now are thicker, longer and firmer than those made from soft material in spring and summer. They should be sited outside but where they will not dry out. Another way to prevent this drying out is to get a high proportion of the stem underground, where it will remain cool at all times, even in March, when the ground is warming up.

Root cutting will work on plants whose roots are naturally inclined to make new stem growth from the root itself. The dandelion is a classic example here. You try to dig the root but merely succeed in breaking it, because the root is too long for you to extract it *in toto*. In many cases, this works to our advantage. Oriental poppies,

Papaver orientiale, for instance. The much sought after *Eryngium* ×
oliverianun, generically known as sea holly, has a handsome prick-
ly inflorescence wherein, in this case, the flowering stem itself is
an extraordinary metallic blue. 'Can it be real?' you wonder.

You should take, say, 6in lengths of root and line them out
in a gritty compost suitable for cuttings in a cold frame, not
trying to force growth at all. Damp and cool is the recipe, and
slow. You might well be better employed cleaning the glass on
the greenhouse so that it lets in the maximum amount of winter
light. The glass gets terribly dirty in the course of the summer.
The plants that will be housed there through the winter need as
much light as we can give them. At Dixter, we use a vast array of
tender plants to bed out in summer. Winter survival, at a not too
outrageous cost, is a principal concern.

Think of your dahlias, now. How will you store them? If they
have nice chunky tubers, box them up (old wine crates are ideal),
water them thoroughly and then store them somewhere cool
where they won't dry out. If they're green and still growing, but
with thin tubers or no tubers at all, keep them going through the
winter so that they are just ticking over, not actually growing.
You'll need enough heat to keep them frost-free.

Cannas can be left in the borders until they are as black as
scarecrows. Their rhizomes will be in fine fettle and will be
ready for boxing up in old potting soil. Give them a good drenching, followed by the minimum amount of watering, once in 10
days perhaps, in the coolest frost-free place that you can find.
By spring, they will already be growing strongly in their winter
quarters, from which we will transfer them to a deep cold-frame
with plenty of headroom.